The Ghost Reader

T0283365

The Ghost Reader

Recovering Women's Contributions to Media Studies

Edited by

Elena D. Hristova, Aimee-Marie Dorsten, and Carol A. Stabile

Editorial Assistants: Malia Mulligan, Morning Glory Ritchie, Laura Strait, and Lauren Tokos

Cover by Jack Blake

Goldsmiths
Press

Contents

Archival Sources

Amistad Research Center, Tulane University, New Orleans, LA (Fredi Washington Papers)

Booth Family Center for Special Collections, Georgetown University, Washington, D.C. (Lisa Sergio Papers)

Churchill Family Collection, Los Angeles, CA (Mae D. Huettig)

Franklin D. Roosevelt Presidential Library, Hyde Park, NY, Isador Lubin Papers (Mae D. Huettig)

Kent State University Special Collections and Archives, Kent, OH, Staughton and Alice Lynd Collection (Helen Merrell Lynd)

Lissance Family Collection, Seattle, WA (Marjorie Fiske)

National Records and Archives Administration, College Park, MD, Records of the Federal Bureau of Investigation

New York Public Library, New York, Manuscripts and Archives Division, (Romana Javitz Papers); Picture Collection Records (Romana Javitz)

New York Public Library, New York, Schomburg Center for Research in Black Culture: Arthur A. Schomburg Papers (Romana Javitz); Photographs and Prints Division (Claudia Jones)

New York University, Tamiment Archive and Library, Jay Leyda and Si-Lan Chen Papers (Romana Javitz)

Rare Book and Manuscript Library, Columbia University, New York: Bureau of Applied Social Research records (Patricia Kendall; Marjorie Fiske)

Rockefeller Archive Center, Sleepy Hollow, NY: Rockefeller Foundation Archives (Patricia Kendall and Dorothy B. Jones), Rockefeller Foundation Records (Patricia Kendall)

Sarah Lawrence College Archives, Bronxville, NY (Helen Merrell Lynd Papers)

Schlesinger Library, Harvard Radcliffe Institute, Cambridge, MA (Shirley Graham Du Bois Papers)

Smith Family Collection, Reston, VA (Jeanette Sayre Smith)

The University of California at San Francisco Archives and Special Collections, San Francisco, CA (Marjorie Fiske Papers)

University of Pennsylvania, Philadelphia, PA, University Archives and Records Center, Wharton School, Industrial Research Unit Records (Mae D. Huettig)

US Census Bureau, Washington, D.C., Census Records (Gene Weltfish)

Chapter 1

Introduction

By Elena D. Hristova, Aimee-Marie Dorsten, and Carol A. Stabile

The earth is seven-tenths water, but the ratio of silence to voice is far greater. Libraries hold all the stories that have been told, there are ghost libraries of all the stories that have not. The ghosts outnumber the books by some unimaginably vast sum. Even those who have been audible have often earned the privilege through strategic silences or the inability to hear certain voices, including their own.[1]

All canons have their ghosts. We catch glimpses of them in footnotes and bibliographies, but more often than not they are buried altogether, casualties of dense citational and intellectual kinship networks, editorial decisions, shifting ideas about relevance and value, and the structural inequalities that have shaped academe, libraries, and other institutions that create, curate, and preserve knowledge. Those who create canons work to make them appear natural and spontaneous, generational wellsprings of creativity and innovation, rather than the result of careful and painstaking processes of selection and legacy-building.

While we tend to think about canons in terms of aesthetic and creative production—literary, visual, auditory—disciplines and fields of intellectual inquiry create canons of their own, telling stories about the genesis of ideas, analyses, and methods that shape and legitimize scholarship in the present. Dynamics of recognition and privilege, as Rebecca Solnit observes in the opening epigram, have determined the survival and salience of narratives about how fields of intellectual inquiry emerge and thus how we think about who made those fields, as well as those who belong in them. Mainly, the intellectual histories we tell rarely include perspectives other than those of White men, reflecting the commonsense belief that only White men participated in the intellectual debates and research activities of the past.

The Ghost Reader: Recovering Women's Contributions to Media Studies offers a fresh perspective on the intellectual history of the field of media/cultural/communication studies (hereafter referred to as media studies), a broad scholarly field that encompasses these and other interdisciplinary and overlapping fields. By researching and recovering the work of the diverse group of women who labored at the center, the margins, and adjacent to media studies as it took shape in Europe and North America during the formative years of communication research between the 1930s and the 1950s, *The Ghost Reader* goes beyond what Carolyn Birdsall and Elinor Carmi describe as an "enriched historical canon that offers a richer and more nuanced understanding of the broader field and its subfields," to questioning the need for a canon altogether.[2] Providing context for, and access to, the intellectual work of the women included in this volume, this approach shows that intersectional considerations were key modes of engagement for intellectuals, academics, and activists who happened to be women, decades before feminist perspectives were reintegrated into histories of the field. Focusing on the research interests of these and other progressive women marks an alternate historiography of media studies, in which struggles to understand and address inequalities and imbalances of power were central to intellectual work.

The exclusion of these women from intellectual histories of media studies reflects both structural inequalities owing to race, gender, and class, as well as the deleterious impact of anti-communism on academe. The women included in *The Ghost Reader* did not enjoy the many advantages of their male counterparts. They often could not find jobs in their fields, but worked as researchers—as Elena D. Hristova points out in Chapter 12 on Patricia Kendall—in the laboratories, offices, and homes of better-known men. Many—especially women of color, who were even more marginalized within academe or excluded from it altogether—wrote for newspapers and other non-academic venues. Women's intellectual work was both appropriated and strategically ignored by established male scholars, like Robert Merton, Robert S. Lynd, Paul Lazarsfeld, and, quite possibly, Theodor Adorno, as Gretchen Soderlund observes in her chapter on Greta Karplus Adorno.

Several of these women joined organizations like the Communist Party in the interest of advancing civil rights (see Shirley Graham, Chapter 5 and Claudia Jones, Chapter 10), others created networks amongst themselves— for example, between Marjorie Fiske (Chapter 4), Herta Herzog (Chapter 6), Patricia Kendall (Chapter 12), and Jeanette Sayre (Chapter 16), or between Violet Edwards (Chapter 3) and Gene Weltfish (Chapter 19). But those alliances did not necessarily help them produce long-term reputational capital. Nor were women served by networking as "faculty wives" whose labor fashioned the reputations of the men to whom they were married (see the section on Helen MacGill Hughes in the digital companion to this volume and Helen Merrell Lynd, Chapter 14).[3] Their work was not regularly archived. And they did not benefit from the labor of generations of graduate students, who cited their work, invited them to give talks, and helped curate legacies and create genealogies of influence.

Anti-communism and its legacies across university departments eliminated many of these women. Whether they were members of the Communist Party or not, their research on and criticism of racism and sexism rendered them political targets, as was the case with Jahoda, Leacock, Washington, and Weltfish. Across industries and institutions, women were the first casualties of blacklists in the witch-hunting climate of the Cold War.[4] Many were reviled and blacklisted for their political beliefs and activist careers: deported, like Claudia Jones; exiled, like Shirley Graham and Marie Jahoda; harassed like Dorothy B. Jones (Chapter 11); or surveilled like Graham, Mae Huettig (Chapter 7), news commentator and author Lisa Sergio (Chapter 17), and writer and performer Fredi Washington (Chapter 18). They were exiled from memory as well, dismissed like Graham as Stalinists or suppressed like Weltfish, all embarrassing footnotes to a period that censured and rejected the work of anti-racist progressive women.

This volume offers a corrective. The women whose work appears in the following pages were active participants and forward-looking thinkers in the intellectual debates occurring between the 1930s and the 1960s. For example, Shirley Graham and Claudia Jones theorized oppression as relational, rather than hierarchical, more than a half-century before intersectionality entered media studies' vocabulary. Leacock and Weltfish's work with Native American and First Nations' peoples similarly marks research trajectories still marginalized within the field of media studies, with important exceptions by Native and Indigenous scholars.[5] Chapter 9 highlights image librarian Romana Javitz's advocacy for a free, user-centered national pictorial service in the 1930s, which as Diana Kamin notes, presages current debates about an "historical juncture in which the flow of images (their production, classification, and indexing) are increasingly black-boxed and privatized." Herzog and Jahoda's attention to, and respect for, audiences sharply contrasted with media industries' and media studies' condescension toward feminized audiences. This is not to say that the work of these women was free of the problems and contradictions that continue to plague global cultures, but rather that their work marked the beginning of conversations that might have shifted the course of intellectual history decades before such conversations became possible again.

For the most part, the legacies of many of these women remained unrecorded, unacknowledged, uncurated, and thus inaccessible to subsequent generations of scholars. Because of this, many later scholars have unknowingly followed in the invisible footprints of the women who introduced ideas, methods, and theories in the turbulent years before and following World

War II. *The Ghost Reader* invites us to contemplate the intellectual legacies that might have been and to engage in the continuing work of reclaiming the intellectual efforts of these and other women, so that we may map their intellectual legacies and build new scholarship on these foundations.

The Ghost Reader provides a blueprint for this undertaking, inspired by the work of feminists who previously recovered, reviewed, and restored the work of women writers. In her 1975 *Black-Eyed Susans and Midnight Birds: Stories by and about Black Women*, literary scholar Mary Helen Washington reprinted the stories of Black women writers in an effort to remedy the fact that in over twenty years of formal education, she had never "read a book written by a black woman."[6] Beverly Guy-Sheftall's paradigm-changing publication, *Words of Fire: An Anthology of African-American Feminist Thought* (1995) includes biographical introductions and primary sources from authors excluded from literary canons. Farah Jasmine Griffin has accounted for the "terms and successes" by which Black feminist criticism "gave birth to a rich and varied body of literature that seeks to uncover, explore, analyze, and theorize the lives and works of (primarily North American) black women."[7] These efforts were supported by the work of feminist publishers, like the Feminist Press and Kitchen Table: Women of Color Press.

The Ghost Reader asks us to look before the feminist publishing and recovery efforts of the 1970s, to the first half of the twentieth century, when in North America and Europe women had been making inroads into universities. Some of them completed undergraduate degrees, and some received PhDs from research universities. These women conducted groundbreaking research and scholarship in anthropology, communication, history, literary studies, psychology, sociology, and other fields of inquiry, in disciplines that overlapped with media studies. Other women, excluded from institutions of higher education because of race and class, analyzed and criticized media industries as intellectuals, journalists, and activists, emphasizing that the work of recovery must look beyond the usual canonical pathways to fully recognize diverse women's contributions to intellectual history.

The body of work women produced in the 1930s, 1940s, and 1950s reflected the unique methodological perspectives they brought to the study of media and culture, perspectives that would re-emerge in the late 1960s and 1970s. As media scholar Shelley Stamp shows in Chapter 15, anthropologist Hortense Powdermaker conducted extensive ethnographic research on race and gender in her study of the American South, as well as in her innovative and better-known ethnography of the film industry. Aimee-Marie Dorsten emphasizes in the digital companion that feminist sociologist Helen

MacGill Hughes wrote a dissertation on the role of the human interest story in mobilizing audiences to challenge the status quo, reflecting progressive women's engagement with areas of media production that were devalued or marginalized within mainstream communication research. Media sociologist Jeanette Sayre (Chapter 16) developed a methodology for policy analysis of the US broadcast industry, advocating for a federally funded model that included protections for non-commercial foreign language, union, agricultural, and educational programming. Social psychologist Marie Jahoda, the subject of Chapter 8, conducted immersive ethnological research on the everyday lives and culture of unemployed people and their families in the early 1930s, revealing not only the psychological devastation of chronic poverty, but its uniquely gendered dimensions. Jahoda wrote extensively about racial and religious intolerance and investigated the impact of the broadcast blacklist on employment practices and the climate in the entertainment industry, before being blacklisted herself. In Chapter 18, Mulligan, Ritchie, and Dreiling explore activist, actor, and journalist Fredi Washington's media criticism published in the pages of the Harlem newspaper *People's Voice*, criticism that analyzed and challenged stereotypes of African Americans. Other Black women, including Claudia Jones and Shirley Graham, developed theoretical and aesthetic approaches that explored relationships among race, class, gender, and national identity. They also wrote media criticism for the Black press (*People's Voice, Chicago Defender, Pittsburgh Courier*) and either founded or wrote for scholarly or literary journals such as the *Negro Digest* and *Freedomways*. Mentored by Gene Weltfish, anthropologist Eleanor Leacock "studied capitalism's impact on indigenous groups, especially analyzing how once egalitarian societies were transformed into ones marked by social inequalities," as Tiffany Kinney points out in Chapter 13.

The Ghost Reader also restores a radiant tradition of activist-scholarship among progressive women intellectuals and cultural producers. Many of these women studied power and its terrifying manifestations in the 1930s and 1940s: economic and political injustice, state violence, racism, xenophobia, anti-Semitism, sexism, and capitalism. They joined with others, including the Communist Party, to fight against these forces. Jahoda was imprisoned in Austria for her socialist activism, fleeing to England with her young daughter before the Nazis took control. Jahoda, Weltfish, and Leacock lost jobs because of their unflinching opposition to White supremacy. Black women experienced more targeted attacks by the Cold War security state: Claudia Jones was deported, Shirley Graham left the US for Ghana after a decade of CIA and FBI harassment, and Fredi Washington was blacklisted because of her anti-racist activism.

Many of these women carried their political commitments into the Cold War and beyond. Because of their politics—which in most cases included a refusal to renounce communist principles of anti-racism and criticism of capitalism and its expanding military industrial complex—they were further excluded from subsequent accounts by the powerful backlash known as McCarthyism. Some were driven from academe and industry; others left to pursue work in places where they could be more anonymous and perhaps more effective. Huettig left academe, for instance, but her study of the motion picture industry led to activism around another powerful California institution and its abuses of power: the Los Angeles Police Department's Intelligence Division. Washington turned her back on Hollywood early in her career, but for years she sought to produce films about Nat Turner and Denmark Vesey's uprisings against slavery.

"Traditions," Hortense Spillers reminds us, "are not born. They are made [...] they are not, like objects of nature, here to stay, but survive as created social events only to the extent that an audience cares to intersect them."[8] This volume offers a modest step toward restoring the contributions of women and people of color to the intellectual history of this interdisciplinary field and reshaping our understanding of it. Nearly fifty years after literary scholars first began including the work of women in the anthologies used to teach students about the history of literature, it is time to document women's contributions to theory and method—the intellectual building-blocks of fields. By encouraging students and scholars to encounter the spectral presence of this small sampling of the women elided or erased from the intellectual histories that comprise the field, we hope to engage these ghosts, to encourage them not to move on, but to stay, and by remaining, reveal the absences in canons shaped by the politics of gender, race, and class.

As this volume demonstrates, the work of these eighteen women has continued resonance for contemporary scholarship. Shirley Graham's plays, novels, and critical writings give new depth to histories of anti-racist cultural production. Our understanding of activist scholarship is enriched when it includes anthropologist Gene Weltfish's commitment, as contributor Marianne Kinkel puts it in Chapter 19, to "a scholarly practice aimed at defeating prejudice and social injustice," and the realization of this commitment in transmedia versions of the anti-racist classic *The Races of Mankind*. Eleanor Leacock, Weltfish's student, studied gender relations among First Nations people, exploring how Jesuits provided instruction in European patriarchy.

A single volume like this can only hint at the wealth of source material that exists. Our project is not to explore the impossibility of archives (an important companion project, undertaken by scholars elsewhere), but to participate in the collaborative and iterative work of reintroducing intellectual work that has been overlooked or forgotten.[9] In so doing, we also intervene in the reproduction of an intellectual genealogy based on the perspectives and experiences of White men, as if they alone were researching and analyzing the massive communications cross-currents of the first half of the twentieth century. By re-inserting the work of women who had researched the rise of mass media like radio and television, public opinion, audiences, prejudice and hate, and much more, *The Ghost Reader* insists on the need for a long overdue historiographic adjustment. This adjustment recognizes and reasserts the intellectual and scholarly contributions of a now apparitional generation of women that worked in and around the field, providing raw materials for the development of critical perspectives on their works, a grounded theory of communication based on their research and scholarship, and a template and inspiration for generations of ghost-hunting to come.

Recovering, re-publishing, reading, reviewing, teaching, and citing these suppressed works is part of a historiographic sea change. All traditions are constructed with intention. We need to create traditions that track different possibilities of knowledge and understanding. Reanimating literary and cultural traditions that map alternate historical trajectories and genealogies of possibility is a political strategy, aimed at making visible the straitjacket of the canon's narrow range of perspectives and its influences on the present. Imagine a social media tradition whose arc begins with the hundreds of daguerreotypes taken of Frederick Douglass and his strategic use of media to further the cause of abolitionism and ends with contemporary social media activism. Or a history of investigative journalism that starts with Ida B. Wells' *Southern Horrors: Lynch Law in All Its Phases*. Or a survey of audience research in the first half of the twentieth century that includes radical, anti-racist thinkers like Eleanor Leacock, Hortense Powdermaker, Gene Weltfish, and many others.

These alternatives force us to consider the consequences of the suppression of the intellectual contributions of the women whose work appears in this volume. What if Weltfish had not been fired from Columbia University in 1953, but had continued to mentor graduate students and to produce work that criticized scientific racism and worked to popularize those critiques and modes of thinking? What if Claudia Jones had not been deported because of her membership in the Communist Party, but had—along with other Black Marxist thinkers like W.E.B. Du Bois, Shirley Graham, and C.L.R. James (not all of whom agreed with one another)—remained in New York City, as an interlocutor of US capitalism and imperialism? These are not only—or merely—speculative questions. Rather, as Imani Perry put it in writing about Lorraine Hansberry, these questions belie the need for "a rigorous contemplation of what we have at our disposal, what is missing, and what we must imagine or re-imagine over and over again."[10]

In addition to contemplating what is missing and what must be imagined or reimagined, *The Ghost Reader* asks us also to rethink traditional historiographic sources. To account for the contributions of women and people of color requires time and effort. Researchers need to look beyond their reflections in the mirror—books published in prestigious presses and peer-reviewed academic journals—to see the contributions made by those marginalized from academic institutions. Official sources are ghost hunters' *bêtes noires*. Sometimes we only know about women's intellectual work because we find it in denigrated sources like memoirs and personal letters (peer-reviewed sources are presumably free of feminized bias); sometimes we glimpse its potential in surveys or grant proposals or memos tucked into folders of the dusty boxes that contain our ghosts' intellectual remains. We most often see the intellectual contributions of these hidden contributors in grant proposals, correspondence, speech transcripts, newspaper columns, unpublished archival sources, and other materials. Of course, many ghosts never made it into official publications or archives at all, although their words and work persist, often in the pages of still undigitized newspapers and other sources.

Rethinking these sources also means speculating on the basis of what we can find about all those sources and documents that remain concealed, phantasmal reminders of what might have been in a field that denied possibilities for many. As Gretchen Soderlund observes of Gretel Karplus Adorno, she "parlayed her many skills into helping to conceptualize, create, and preserve the works of a far-flung group of German leftist intellectuals" who became known as the Frankfurt School. Although her name appears only in acknowledgments, and she destroyed her personal papers after Theodor Adorno's death in 1969, Soderlund shows how "traces of her scholarly production exist everywhere."

To counter the ways in which official sources conspire to make women's contributions less visible, *The Ghost Reader* showcases previously unpublished, out-of-print, or under-reviewed materials and provides contextual introductions for the published pieces. By including introductory information about these women, as well as newly published or republished primary sources by them, we hope to encourage readers to understand the works included in *The Ghost Reader* in their biographical, historical, and political contexts, and in conversation with one another's ideas. Like Birdsall and Carmi, in *The Ghost Reader* we engage in storytelling that de-centers "a single protagonist who is framed as the hero," in favor of an approach that includes a broader sense of an emerging field of intellectual production in media studies.[11] Thus we understand women's efforts to participate not as individuals, but as groups of thinkers who had been marginalized in trying to gain entry to official sites of research and intellectual discourse.

Throughout our work on this volume and our interactions with contributors, we have tried to remain mindful of the limitations of this volume and the perils of creating a canon of our own, agreeing with Birdsall and Carmi that "we have responsibility to keep critiquing and evaluating—not only our research objects and subjects but also our own practices and their consequences."[12] The collective research in this volume is just a single step toward recovering those who have been overlooked or suppressed from this field, one part of broader global histories of this field that have yet to be written. We hope this text will help us (re)encounter the work of just a few of those who were pushed out of media, communication, and cultural studies, as researchers, critics, and producers of culture. Or, as Elana Levine illuminates in Chapter 6 on Herta Herzog, those who were conveniently tracked out of academic research through existing university and research center structures that valued men's academic publications, while devaluing and pushing women into commercial studies.[13]

The Ghost Reader is part of a broader field of recovery efforts aimed not at creating new canons, but in addressing and undoing the very idea of canonicity. *The Recovery Hub for American Women Writers* provides digital access to forgotten or neglected works by women.[14] Arte Publico Press has long published contemporary and recovered works by Hispanic authors and is currently engaged in a project to recover the US Hispanic literary heritage.[15] Blackfeminisms.com's *Black Women Archives* provides a list of archival holdings.[16] For the past forty years, the Yiddish Book Center has engaged in "book rescue, digitization, [and] translation" efforts aimed at sharing the rich history of materials—many of them progressive—originally published in Yiddish. Roopika Risam and Carol Stabile collaborate on the *Reanimate* project, with a volume of the collected works of Fredi Washington (see Chapter 18) published online in 2022. The list of organizations and individuals working on such recovery efforts is vast, and growing every year.

Our contribution to these efforts features research, scholarship, and criticism produced by only eighteen women. The selection resulted from three interrelated processes. In the first, the co-editors proposed contributions by women whose work had been influential during their time, based on our own research. We reached out to scholars we knew were researching some of these women. The second involved an open call for papers that we publicized beginning in 2018 on communication, media studies, cultural studies, and humanities listservs and sites. In that call, we included the names of fifty women we knew to have been influential contributors to foundational knowledge in media, communication, and cultural studies. Some contributors agreed to write about those figures. Other scholars made passionate appeals for including people like Romana Javitz, Dorothy B. Jones, and Gene Weltfish. Still others proposed entries on women who, because of the constraints of the published volume, could not be included. Each contributor selected the excerpts to be included for each profile, and where possible they chose from works they believed to be representative of their subject's contributions to media studies. In some cases, however, the choice of excerpt had to be reconsidered when copyright permissions could not be acquired or were financially prohibitive.

In compiling *The Ghost Reader*, we were confronted with a series of financial constraints that limited our ability to publish original work by the eighteen women we have included in this volume. In the first place, many commercial (and some academic) publishers demanded fees to republish excerpts. In a number of cases, the longer the excerpt, the steeper the cost. Because of the financial pressures on academic publishers, *The Ghost Reader* also had to work within a word count that would make the print book affordable for both publisher and readers. To circumvent these constraints, Reanimate Publishing is simultaneously publishing *The Ghost Reader: A Digital Companion*, an online reader that includes longer excerpts and additional materials, as well as essays by media studies scholars on how to incorporate the work of these women into media studies curricula. The digital companion appears on Reanimate's instance of the Manifold platform, developed by the University of Minnesota Press and CUNY Graduate Center. Manifold facilitates the publication of e-books (in web-based and e-pub formats), inclusion of multimedia resources, and collaborative reading with texts through annotation and comment features. Thus, the digital companion will promote ongoing engagement with material in *The Ghost Reader* and complement its use in classrooms.

We hope that *The Ghost Reader* and its digital companion will inspire further research on these scholars, critics, and activists, as well as on those ghosts whose traces we overlooked in this volume, either by necessity (the book form can only hold so many stories) or unintentional oversight. *The Ghost Reader*'s primary purpose is a pedagogical one. Teachers can use *The Ghost Reader* to re-educate students on the development of the discipline and key knowledge formations within it. While it is important to understand the work of academics like Theodor Adorno, Harold Lasswell, Paul Lazarsfeld, and others, *The Ghost Reader* can help understand how women's often unacknowledged contributions fed into texts we have been taught to consider the work of a single author. Courses on audience and fan studies, for example, could use chapters on Herzog, Jahoda, Sayre, Fiske, Kendall, and Powdermaker to show how women scholars from a range of disciplinary backgrounds were listening to women and everyday people as a corrective to the generalizations often drawn from quantitative survey approaches to listening and viewing publics. Courses on media production could highlight Shirley Graham and Gene Weltfish's efforts to make anti-racist media, as well as Violet Edwards, Marie Jahoda, and Dorothy B. Jones' efforts to understand racist and anti-Semitic propaganda. And courses on gender and race in media could use the work of Graham, Leacock, Washington, and Weltfish, among others, to map a tradition that begins not in the 1970s, but much earlier in the twentieth century.

From the very beginning of this project, we have also grappled with another key limitation of *The Ghost Reader*: its US-centric approach, a limitation imposed by our own admittedly narrow areas of expertise and linguistic abilities. We encourage scholars to use *The Ghost Reader* as a template for ghost readers in other regional and national contexts. Indeed, we welcome conversations with those wishing to work on the myriad ghost readers that need to be written, and who might find our experiences working on this volume useful in crafting their own. By creating volumes that explore women's contributions outside North America and Europe, as well as in other historical periods, a series of ghost readers not only can help us gain a more comprehensive sense of women's contributions to media studies in an international context, and their conversations across national boundaries, but to ensure that the very concept of a ghost reader is understood to be fragile and evolving.

The Ghost Reader's co-editors and contributors undertook most of our work on this project during the global COVID-19 pandemic. Research for historical recovery projects, such as this one, have been significantly impacted due to lack of access to archival materials. Work on this volume was upended by the pandemic. With varying access to resources, we juggled pregnancies, illness, childcare, care for sick family members, domestic labor, wage labor, the contingencies of academe, and the economic and social exigencies and anxieties attendant on the pandemic.[17] The barriers we experienced echo those faced by the women who are the subject of this volume, while at the same time reminding us of the privileges we enjoy that remain inaccessible to those who have been described as "essential" workers. The women whose work appears within these pages would understand not only the historicity of these struggles, but the importance of acknowledging and appreciating the privileges that we enjoy as academics.

The women that haunt media studies are more than just "ghosts" or the absence of physical presence. They are perhaps more substantive than that which is corporeal because they are the essence of a powerful subjectivity: they embody experience, memory, infinite potential, and they have the power to challenge the narratives constructed by the living. Like ghosts themselves, ghost readers represent the palpable absence of those whose stories remain to be told. They haunt historiographic gatekeepers by threatening to reveal the false constructs and ellipses inherent in canons and canonicity, rehabilitating lost narratives in the process. In developing a new feminist historiography, the restorative nature of *The Ghost Reader* is similarly powerful. By foregrounding women's work on media and culture during the twentieth century, *The Ghost Reader* exposes the structural relations that rendered these women invisible to reveal the potential of their work for new theoretical contributions and methods. We hope the stories of these women will inspire students and scholars to engage in transformative projects that combine scholarship and activist approaches to social change.

Notes

1 Rebecca Solnit, *The Mother of All Questions* (Chicago: Haymarket Books, 2017), 21.

2 Carolyn Birdsall and Elinor Carmi, "Feminist Avenues for Listening in: Amplifying Silenced Histories of Media and Communication," *Women's History Review* 31, no. 4, 2002: 544.

3 Donica Belisle and Kiera Mitchell, "Mary Quayle Innis: Faculty Wives' Contributions and the Making of Academic Celebrity," *The Canadian Historical Review* 99, no. 3 (September 2018): 456–486; Alison Prentice, "Historical Identities: The Professoriate in Canada," in *Boosting Husbands and Building Community: The Work of Twentieth-Century Faculty Wives*, ed. E. Lisa Panayotidis and Paul Stortz (Toronto: University of Toronto Press, 2006), 271–296.

4 Carol A. Stabile, *The Broadcast 41: Women and the Anti-Communist Blacklist* (London: Goldsmiths Press, 2018); Mary Helen Washington, ed., *The Other Blacklist: The African American Literary and Cultural Left of the 1950s* (New York: Columbia University Press, 2014).

5 See Glen Sean Coulthard, *Red Skin, White Masks: Rejecting the Colonial Politics of Recognition* (Minneapolis: University of Minnesota Press, 2014); Dustin Tahmahkera, *Tribal Television: Viewing Native People in Sitcoms* (Durham, NC: The University of North Carolina Press, 2014).

6 Mary Helen Washington, ed., *Black-Eyed Susans and Midnight Birds: Stories by and about Black Women*, Reprint ed. (New York: Anchor, 1990), 3.

7 Farah Jasmine Griffin, "That the Mothers May Soar and the Daughters May Know Their Names: A Retrospective of Black Feminist Literary Criticism," *Signs* 32, no. 2 (Winter 2007): 483.

8 Spillers, "Afterword," 250.

9 Saidiya Hartman, "Venus in Two Acts," *Small Axe: A Caribbean Journal of Criticism* 12, no. 2 (June 1, 2008): 1–14; Julietta Singh, *No Archive Will Restore You* (New York: Punctum Books, 2018.

10 Imani Perry, "Dredging up the Ever-Living Past," *The New York Review*, July 17, 2021 www.nybooks.com/daily/2021/07/17/dredging-up-the-ever-living-past/, accessed April 9, 2023.

11 Birdsall and Carmi, "Feminist Avenues for Listening in," 543.

12 Ibid., 555.

13 Aimee-Marie Dorsten, "'Thinking Dirty': Digging Up Three Founding 'Matriarchs' of Communication Studies," *Communication Theory* 22, no. 1 (February 2012): 25–47; Elena D. Hristova, "The Speculative in Communication Research: Data, Identity, and the Pursuit of Professionalism, 1940–1960" (PhD diss., University of Minnesota, 2020); Stabile, *The Broadcast 41*; Elena D. Hristova, "Research and Publishing at the Bureau of Applied Social Research: The Gendering of Commercial and Academic Work," *International Journal of Communication* 16 (2022): 655–663.

14 Recovery Hub for American Women Writers, https://recoveryhub.siue.edu/, accessed March 30, 2022.

15 Arte Publico Press, https://artepublicopress.com/recovery-program/, accessed March 30, 2022.

16 Black Women Archives, https://blackfeminisms.com/resources/archives/, accessed March 30, 2022.

17 Brooke Peterson Gabster et al., "Challenges for the Female Academic During the COVID-19 Pandemic," *The Lancet* 395, no. 10242 (June 27, 2020): 1968–1970; Colleen Flaherty, "Something's Got to Give," *Inside Higher Ed*, August 20, 2020, www.insidehighered.com/news/2020/08/20/womens-journal-submission-rates-continue-fall, accessed April 24, 2023; Colleen Flaherty, "Large-Scale Study Backs up Other Research Showing Relative Declines in Women's Research Productivity during COVID-19," *Inside Higher Ed*, October 20, 2020, www.insidehighered.com/news/2020/10/20/large-scale-study-backs-other-research-showing-relative-declines-womens-research, accessed April 24, 2023.

Bibliography

Belisle, Donica and Kiera Mitchell. "Mary Quayle Innis: Faculty Wives' Contributions and the Making of Academic Celebrity." *The Canadian Historical Review* 99, no. 3 (September 2018): 456–486.

Birdsall, Carolyn and Elinor Carmi. "Feminist Avenues for Listening in: Amplifying Silenced Histories of Media and Communication." *Women's History Review* 31, no. 4, 2002: 542–560.

Coulthard, Glen Sean. *Red Skin, White Masks: Rejecting the Colonial Politics of Recognition*. Minneapolis: University of Minnesota Press, 2014.

Dorsten, Aimee-Marie. "'Thinking Dirty': Digging Up Three Founding 'Matriarchs' of Communication Studies." *Communication Theory* 22, no. 1 (February 2012): 25–47.

Flaherty, Colleen. "Large-Scale Study Backs up Other Research Showing Relative Declines in Women's Research Productivity during COVID-19." *Inside Higher Ed*, October 20, 2020. www.insidehighered.com/news/2020/10/20/large-scale-study-backs-other-research-showing-relative-declines-womens-research, accessed April 9, 2023.

_____. "Something's Got to Give." *Inside Higher Ed*, August 20, 2020. www.insidehighered.com/news/2020/08/20/womens-journal-submission-rates-continue-fall, accessed April 9, 2023.

Gabster, Brooke Peterson, Kim Van Daalen, Roopa Dhatt, and Michele Barry. "Challenges for the Female Academic During the COVID-19 Pandemic." *The Lancet* 395, no. 10242 (June 27, 2020): 1968–1970.

Griffin, Farah Jasmine. "That the Mothers May Soar and the Daughters May Know Their Names: A Retrospective of Black Feminist Literary Criticism." *Signs* 32, no. 2 (Winter 2007): 483–507.

Guy-Sheftall, Beverly. *Words of Fire: An Anthology of African-American Feminist Thought.* New York: The New Press, 1995.

Hartman, Saidiya. "Venus in Two Acts." *Small Axe: A Caribbean Journal of Criticism* 12, no. 2 (June 1, 2008): 1–14.

Hristova, Elena D. "Research and Publishing at the Bureau of Applied Social Research: The Gendering of Commercial and Academic Work." *International Journal of Communication* 16 (2022): 655–663.

_____. "The Speculative in Communication Research: Data, Identity, and the Pursuit of Professionalism, 1940–1960." PhD diss., University of Minnesota, 2020.

MacNicol, Glynnis. "50 Years On, the Feminist Press Is Radical and Relevant." *New York Times*, December 4, 2020. www.nytimes.com/2020/12/04/us/50-years-the-feminist-press-gloria-steinem-florence-howe.html, accessed April 9, 2023.

Perry, Imani. "Dredging up the Ever-Living Past." *The New York Review*, July 17, 2021. www.nybooks.com/daily/2021/07/17/dredging-up-the-ever-living-past/, accessed April 9, 2023.

Prentice, Alison. "Historical Identities: The Professoriate in Canada." In *Boosting Husbands and Building Community: The Work of Twentieth-Century Faculty Wives*, ed. E. Lisa Panayotidis and Paul Stortz, 271–296. Toronto: University of Toronto Press, 2006.

Singh, Julietta. *No Archive Will Restore You.* New York: Punctum Books, 2018.

Solnit, Rebecca. *The Mother of All Questions.* Chicago, IL: Haymarket Books, 2017.

Spillers, Hortense J. "Afterword: Cross-Currents, Discontinuities: Black Women's Fiction." In *Conjuring: Black Women, Fiction, and Literary Tradition*, ed. Marjorie Lee Pryse and Hortense J. Spillers, 249–261. Bloomington, IN: Indiana University Press, 1985.

Stabile, Carol A. *The Broadcast 41: Women and the Anti-Communist Blacklist.* London: Goldsmiths Press, 2018.

Tahmahkera, Dustin. *Tribal Television: Viewing Native People in Sitcoms.* Durham, NC: The University of North Carolina Press, 2014.

Washington, Mary Helen, ed. *Black-Eyed Susans and Midnight Birds: Stories by and about Black Women.* Reprint ed. New York: Anchor, 1990.

_____. *The Other Blacklist: The African American Literary and Cultural Left of the 1950s.* New York: Columbia University Press, 2014.

Chapter 2

Gretel Karplus Adorno (1902–1993)

By Gretchen Soderlund

When she is remembered, Gretel Karplus Adorno is best known for her correspondence with Walter Benjamin and her contributions to preparing the manuscripts of her husband, Theodor Adorno. We may never know whether Karplus wrote essays of her own; when her famous husband died suddenly in 1969, she was so grief-stricken that she destroyed most of her personal papers before attempting suicide.[1] The notes, journals, and correspondences she expunged, and others that vanished later, might have provided insight into her own thought processes and helped determine the provenance of key Frankfurt School ideas. Without them, feminist historians can only speculate on the intellectual contributions Karplus made to a body of work that shaped twentieth-century philosophy, critical theory, and communications research. Because of a historical tradition of sidelining women's roles in the production of knowledge and burying their efforts in acknowledgment sections, Karplus tends to be remembered as a wife, secretary, assistant, and facilitator, but not as a scholar in her own right.

The Ghost Reader has reprinted two letters she wrote to Benjamin in 1935 that provide a glimpse, however insufficient, of the role she played in advancing critical theory and media/cultural/communication studies. The rest must be inferred. Like *The Ghost Reader* more generally, this entry calls for a broad understanding of intellectual labor that encompasses a recognition of the undervalued yet essential work we do know Karplus performed in bringing Frankfurt School works to fruition.

The story of Benjamin and Karplus' friendship begins in 1928, at the end of Germany's Golden Twenties, a period of intellectual and artistic ferment, particularly in Berlin, where the two met, but also in smaller cities like Frankfurt, where Max Horkheimer founded the Institute for Social Research in 1923. Karplus had earned a doctorate in chemistry five years earlier and was working in her family's leather factory at the time. She was a scientist and businesswoman who felt most at home among Marxist philosophers and literary critics, though it is unclear how she became part of this close-knit group of intellectuals. Despite rampant anti-Semitism in the Weimar Republic, Hitler's rise to power and the horrors of the Holocaust would have been unimaginable to German Jewish intellectuals before the Great Crash of 1929 upended German politics.

When Benjamin fled Germany in 1933, he and Karplus established a correspondence that would last until he committed suicide on the French-Spanish border in 1940.[2] He wrote to her from Paris and Ibiza, keeping her abreast of the progress of what would become *The Arcades Project*, his vast study of nineteenth-century Parisian life that traces the rise of consumer capitalism. Karplus wrote to him from Berlin and from her exile in New York City.[3] Their letters reveal a deep friendship: he called her "Felicitas," the name of a character in a play he had written, and she called him "Detlef," one of his pseudonyms.[4] But they also suggest that Benjamin looked to Karplus for advice, advocacy, and patronage (she sent him regular money transfers from Berlin that he referred to as "rosy parcels").[5] When the Adornos joined Horkheimer in the United States, she acted as an intermediary between Benjamin and the Institute of Social Research and actively sought out funding and publishing opportunities for him.

When France declared war on Germany, Karplus entreated Benjamin to join them in the United States; he understood the danger involved but postponed his departure from Paris to make progress on *The Arcades Project*. When the situation in Paris worsened, he was forced to cross the Spanish border on foot with a group of German refugees. The authorities in Spain denied their transit visas, and rather than being sent back to France and into Nazi hands, Benjamin tragically committed suicide.

In his final letter, written from an undisclosed location in the Pyrenees, he tells Karplus that he fled Paris with only his "gas mask and toilet bag," and feared for the worst. "If none of the things that I cling to are at my disposal now," he writes, "I can at least entertain a modest hope regarding my manuscripts for my extensive study on the nineteenth century." He was worried about the fate of his manuscripts and left them to Karplus to ensure they outlived him: "I hope with all my heart that both [Horkheimer's] efforts and yours are proving successful [...]. I want you to know how much confidence I have in your combined efforts, and that I am well aware of the difficulties posed by their resolution and the tenacity it demands of you."[6] When the Adornos returned to Frankfurt after the war, the couple edited Benjamin's manuscripts and published them posthumously through Surhkamp. Despite Karplus' extensive correspondence with Benjamin and her efforts to ensure his work was published, most scholarship on Benjamin focuses on his connection to the men at the center of the Institute, eliding the critical role Karplus played in advancing his work.

Not only was Karplus a careful preserver of Benjamin's writings, she was also typist and first editor of Adorno's *Dialectic of Enlightenment*, among other Frankfurt School works. Karplus and Adorno had what Tamlyn Avery calls "a division of textual labor," in which the first drafts of Adorno's manuscripts were produced through a process of dictation and transcription.[7] But Karplus was more than a passive scribe, as has sometimes been assumed. She was an editor, drafting and commenting on works at the moment of transcription. Adorno's own letters suggest that the pair worked as a team. According to Avery, "Adorno often refers to the collaborative 'writing' completed in the home office and the Institute in collective pronouns, collaboration for which Adorno alone is remembered; statements that refer to 'our' work, or 'we are working on', become pronounced admissions of Karplus' involvement."[8] Adorno scholars and biographers have commented on the speed at which his manuscripts were produced, an "almost super-human pace" that was directly attributable to Karplus' role in the process.[9]

After Karplus escaped Germany in 1938, she parlayed her many skills into helping to conceptualize, create, and preserve the works of this far-flung group of German leftist intellectuals. She devoted her life to editing and accelerating the progress of their manuscripts and gaining recognition for their work. While there are no passages in the publications of Benjamin, Adorno, or Horkheimer that can definitively be traced to Karplus, traces of her scholarly production exist everywhere. Perhaps more than any other figure in *The Ghost Reader*, Karplus' role was the most spectral and difficult to trace.

Excerpts, from Gretel Adorno and Walter Benjamin, *Correspondence, 1930–1940* (Cambridge, UK; Malden, MA: Polity, 2008) (permission of Polity Press Ltd.)

Contributor's note: Footnotes from the original. I have preserved the style of the original notes.

Gretel Karplus to Walter Benjamin
Berlin

28 May 1935.

Dear Detlef,
Your letter just arrived, and I am afraid I must confess that I found your news about E. extremely troubling. Not only was it from you—not him—that I learned he has finally been granted the visa;[1] there is airmail for such cases, after all. But you also do not seem so sure that Frank has not seduced him into turning to his previous consolation once again. Nothing could be worse for

---

1 Egon Wissing had applied for a visa for the Soviet Union in order to work there as a doctor.

the friendship between myself and E., I not only asked him to be extremely careful, but also trusted him, and for him to disappoint me now would cause irreparable damage. Please do not be cross if I write you at somewhat greater length about these things today, for I have the feeling that it concerns you too. But I ask you to tear up today's letter, i.e. this piece of paper, immediately. I am sure you have a fair idea of the situation from our conversations and my letters. Although E. often complains of my inexperience in practical matters and probably also life's pleasures, I am overall more mature than he is, in so far as one can still say that at our age. I think the most important thing is for E. to come to himself again, which would involve finding a steady employment that satisfied him; he finally has to achieve something again, and in his profession there is ample opportunity to do so. He must also support himself financially, and banish his abandon and licentiousness to the intellectual realm instead of retaining them in daily life as bad Bohemian manners. I am expressing myself very badly, but perhaps you can nonetheless deduce what I mean, intellectual particularity combined with an orderly life. Please do not consider it presumptuous, but following the results I have often had my doubts about the stability of his marriage, and wonder whether it would not have worked without M in the end. Oh Detlef, cross your fingers for me that these days in Berlin will turn out well.—

Thank you also for your information.—Bloch no longer considers it necessary to write to me, which makes me both sad and angry about the loss of another friend. All I know is that he wanted to meet his friends the Hirschlers[2] in Italy.—Have you met Krac[3] in the meantime, what is he working on? Have you read his novel?—Have you meanwhile told Teddie about your negotiations with Fritz?[4] I consider that absolutely necessary and advisable. Is he coming to Paris after the end of the term?—I will see what I can do about the Kafka fragments tomorrow.

And now I shall come to the thing that is most important to me: the arcades study. I recall the conversation we had in Denmark last September, and I find it highly troubling that I have no idea which of your plans you will now be carrying out. It amazes me that Fritz is trying to find a possibility for the notes, are you thinking of writing something for the journal? I would

---

2 The doctor Maximilian Hirschler (1886-1963) had been a friend of Bloch since their schooldays; Hirschler's wife, Helene (1888-1977), was likewise a doctor.

3 This is Siegfried Kracauer.

4 Fritz Pollock had offered to meet Benjamin to discuss the financing of the arcades project, but was forced to end his stay in Europe prematurely. Benjamin wrote the exposé on Pollock's suggestion.

actually consider that very dangerous, as you would have relatively little space and would never be able to write what your true friends have been awaiting for years, the great philosophical study that exists purely for its own sake and makes no compromises, and whose significance would help to compensate for a great deal of what has happened these last few years. Detlef, it is not simply a matter of rescuing you, but also this work. One should anxiously guard you from everything that could jeopardize it, and devote the greatest possible energy to supporting everything that might further it. I think you have rarely known me to be so enthusiastic about something, which shows you most clearly what high hopes I place in the arcades study.—I hope you will not resent my ecstasy. I await your news with longing and fear, please write to me about the exposé.—I have so much time; if only I could keep you company a little in your hours of solitude and have you read to me from your notes. Fare thee well and kindly let me remain in good favour with you

your Felicitas

Gretel Karplus to Walter Benjamin
Berlin

28 August 1935

My dear Detlef,

   you have had to wait to terribly long for a letter from me, but I think you sensed my absence from time to time nonetheless. Quite a number of things have happened in the meantime. It was very pleasant in the Black Forest, though in the low mountain range we certainly mourned for our beloved Dolomites, but I did have quite a good rest, and feel quite passable at the moment; I hardly dare say any more about my condition for fear of invoking a sudden change for the worse.—You asked me kindly about my business; so far I cannot say anything at all; as I am mainly producing winter gloves, I am very much hoping that we will have a severe, early winter. Let us hope for the best.—As my father constantly has to mind his health, our apartment, with its two floors and the spiral staircase, has proved somewhat impractical, so we will be moving at the start of October to Westphalischestr. 27, by the Hochmesiterplatz. To avoid any resulting interruptions to our correspond-ence, you should then write to me care of Tengler at Dresdenerstr. 50. If you need any of your books and journals, I would gladly send them now, to avoid any unnecessary damage resulting from the move.—My sister just spent a few weeks visiting America, has incredibly interesting stories to relate and hopes she will soon be able to move there for good.—Teddie is in Frankfurt at the moment, will then be coming to Berlin for 2 weeks, and then return to Oxford around 10 October, though he will be in Frankfurt again and in London for a few days before he does.

I was so very happy to be able to discuss the response to your exposé with Teddie, and your reply is just as I would have wished—no, in its nuance of being directed at me it even surpassed my boldest expectations, and I am especially grateful for it. It is very reassuring to me that you yourself mention that first sketch and the other, thus preventing the assumption that you gave up after the first. Thus you share our opinion that the second is on no account final; one would never suspect the hand of WB in it. I already eagerly await your second letter to Teddie.

Have you meanwhile received the essay by Haselpeter?—Unfortunately I only spoke to him on the telephone in Frankfurt, and he told me of his plan for a new study on the Alps.[1] He is a great alpinist, you see, and knows quite a lot of the literature on the subject. He thinks that the Alps were only really discovered as a landscape in the 19th century, and then people recognized the models for the great cities and their buildings in them.—Regarding 'Berliner Kindheit', I would consider it most advantageous if you wrote to Krenek first, to see if he can find an opening for the manuscript. How are things in this respect with Ernst Bloch? He has always been superb at it with his own writings.

You made me extremely happy by sending Baba. And I am always up for a good detective novel. That reminds me: what do you think of the new Kafka edition with the different readings?—Do you think it would be possible to send me the book Machines es Asie[2] by Frédérix?—I know you cannot read English, but perhaps you have heard of T. S. Eliot, who has amazingly also written some very interesting surrealist poems in French?[3]—

How is your sister? I hope for your sake that she will not turn up very soon. Are you in contact with Fränkel, incidentally? Going on what I have heard about him, I could almost suppose it.—I would truly love to have a conversation with Helen Grund, and not only about the fashion products of the major companies, but also about the laws according to which fashions ultimately move socially downwards in the provinces and the middle classes. I am encountering this problem almost daily in my work, but I am not interested in it purely for professional reasons; this cycle has always interested me, and I would almost go so far as to say that the closer I am to it, the more

---

1 Unknown.

2 See Pierre Frédérix, *Machines en Asie: Oural et Sibirie Soviétiques* (Paris, 1934).

3 Gretel Adorno may be thinking of the four French poems "Le Directeur," "Mélange adultére de tout," "Lune de miel" and "Dans le restaurant" from Eliot's collection *Poems* (New York, 1920), which also included "The Hippopotamus" and "Mr. Eliot's Sunday Morning Service."

difficult it seems to find the solution, and the more questionable I find the notion of taste.—

I hope this mammoth letter is not too boring to read, but I did want to compensate for the dearth of recent weeks. Fond regards

ever
your
Felicitas

Notes

1 Staci Lynn Von Boeckmann, "The Life and Work of Gretel Karplus/Adorno: Her Contributions to Frankfurt School Theory" (PhD diss., University of Oklahoma, 2004), 2.
2 Gretel Adorno and Walter Benjamin, *Correspondence, 1930-1940* (Malden, MA: Polity, 2008).
3 See Von Boeckmann, "The Life and Work of Gretel Karplus/Adorno," 124.
4 Ibid., 85.
5 Ibid., 92.
6 Adorno and Benjamin, *Correspondence*, 287-289.
7 Tamlyn Avery, "Gretel Adorno, the Typewriter: Sacrificial Lambs and Critical Theory's 'Risk of Formulation,'" *Australian Feminist Studies* 34, no. 101 (2019): 309-324.
8 Ibid., 312.
9 See Von Boeckmann, "The Life and Work of Gretel Karplus/Adorno," 139.

Bibliography

Adorno, Gretel and Walter Benjamin. *Correspondence 1930-1940*. Malden, MA: Polity Press, 2008.

Avery, Tamlyn. "Gretel Adorno, the Typewriter: Sacrificial Lambs and Critical Theory's 'Risk of Formulation.'" *Australian Feminist Media Studies* 34, no. 101 (2019): 309-324.

Frédérix, Pierre. *Machines en Asie: Oural et Sibirie Soviétiques*. Paris, 1934.

Godde, Christophe and Henri Lonitz, eds. *Theodore Adorno: Letters to His Parents 1939-1951*. Malden, MA: Polity Press, 2006.

Von Boeckmann, Staci Lynn. "The Life and Works of Gretel Karplus Adorno: Her Contributions to Frankfurt School Theory." PhD diss., University of Oklahoma, 2004.

Chapter 3

Violet Edwards Lavine (1906–1983)

By Marianne Kinkel

Interest in studying propaganda has resurfaced as a response to the current collapse of public discourse and crisis in democracy. Looking for potential guidance, scholars have turned to the analysis of propaganda, studies of persuasion and public opinion conducted in the 1930s and 1940s, another moment of great turmoil. The Institute for Propaganda Analysis (IPA) figures into such histories and is largely known for the seven propaganda devices developed by the Institute's director, Clyde Miller, and case studies such as Alfred McClung Lee and Elizabeth Briant Lee's analysis of the anti-Semitic radio broadcasts of Father Charles Coughlin.[1] Scholarship on the IPA, however, has largely ignored the organization's Experimental Study Program and has overlooked the activities of its educational director Violet Edwards and her contributions to communication studies.

Prior to working at the IPA, Violet Edwards earned her BA in Education in 1929 from the University of Arizona, and taught high school English and journalism in Yuma, Arizona.[2] She then enrolled as a doctoral student in the Educational Sociology program at Teachers College, Columbia University. During her graduate studies, she worked on the staff at Teachers College's Bureau of Educational Service, taught journalism courses at the Horace Mann School, and assisted Clyde Miller in the publicity relations office of the College.[3] In October 1936, Edwards co-authored an article with Miller which contained the kernel ideas for his seven propaganda devices.[4] Later that same year she married the journalist Harold Lavine, who would become the editorial director of the IPA.[5] As the educational director of the Experimental Study Program, Edwards helped to coordinate workshops, review teachers' reports, and provide discussion worksheets appearing in the IPA's monthly bulletin, *Propaganda Analysis*. Established in 1937, the Study Program grew into a nationwide program involving over 3000 schools and an estimated one million students in 1941.[6]

To facilitate the Study Program, Edwards wrote *Propaganda, How to Recognize It and Deal with It* (January 1938) and its revised edition, *Group Leader's Guide to Propaganda Analysis* (October 1938). The *Group Leader's Guide* has been viewed as a mere application of the seven devices to detect propaganda.[7] But the *Guide* is much more than that, for Edwards outlined a process of analyzing propaganda consistent with the Deweyan principles of critical thinking promoted by the Progressive Education Association.[8] For Edwards,

education—the development of the ability to make judgments independently—has its
roots in the gathering and classification of pertinent facts bearing upon the problem or
question, in the arranging and organizing of these facts in order that a tentative solution may be suggested, and in the testing and checking of the "solution" before final
action is taken.[9]

Edwards augmented this reasoning process with emotion:

It follows, of course, that in such a study we retain an emotional drive for clarity of
thought, for solving the problem at hand. We also utilize this emotional drive to realize
in beneficial action the acts revealed by clear thinking.[10]

In appraising the IPA's contributions to the field of communication studies, scholars have contrasted Edwards' *Guide* with the writings
of Robert Thouless and Edward Glaser, advocates of "straight thinking."[11]
This pedagogical method, based on formal logic and science, was intended
to help students learn processes of assessing evidence and identifying
fallacies and biases.[12] A close reading of the *Guide* reveals that Edwards
included a unit prepared by Glaser that tethered logical reasoning to the
seven propaganda devices. Edwards also summarized findings of well-
known studies of propaganda, presented a unit on semantics, and provided
an appendix outlining a group discussion method based on the research
of Frank Walser. Participating teachers provided exercises that form the
bulk of the *Guide*, demonstrating how images, words, and sounds from
everyday life provided the materials for analyzing propaganda across the
curriculum.

The *Guide* made a significant contribution to media literacy by emphasizing self-knowledge as a prerequisite for analyzing media. This can be
seen in its advocacy of two interrelated processes: self-reflection and group
discussion, such that "Americans not only learn how to think *independently*,
but that they also learn to *think together*."[13] Edwards recommended beginning the study of propaganda with assessing one's own biases, ideals, and
desires: "One of the chief goals of propaganda analysis is to come to a fuller
understanding of *why we think and act as we do*. We must always remember
that without us and our needs, fears, likes and dislikes there can be no propaganda."[14] The "Looking at Ourselves" unit fostered this process through a
series of reflective exercises such as students writing personal biographies
and determining the origins of their biases.[15] Group discussion, a deliberative
process featured throughout the *Guide*, "encourages continual challenging,

enlargement, and broadening, mutual criticism and correction of each member's point of view."[16] Edwards recommended that a study group formulate their own definition of propaganda after critically evaluating the units in the *Guide*, examining specific examples of media communication, and undergoing a process of reflection on their own learning experience.[17]

While working at the IPA, Edwards also served on the Educational Advisory Committee of the Council Against Intolerance in America and assisted Walser in preparing the publication, *An American Answer to Intolerance* (1939), which developed strategies presented in the "Looking at Ourselves" unit. After leaving the IPA in the spring of 1941, Edwards directed a summer intercultural workshop for the National Conference of Christians and Jews and the Service Bureau of Intercultural Education. In March 1942, she became a Field Consultant for the National Federation of Business and Professional Women's Clubs, where she facilitated the organization's discussion groups and implemented its national war effort program. However, in March 1943, Edwards, along with Marjorie Fiske (see Chapter 4 of this volume) and six other staff members, abruptly resigned in protest after the New York State division of the Federation expelled its Midtown (Manhattan) chapter for admitting African American women.[18]

A few weeks later, Edwards became the Educational and Promotional Director for the Public Affairs Committee (PAC), a nonprofit organization that published inexpensive pamphlets summarizing research about social and economic issues of the time. One of Edwards' first projects was to coordinate the publication of the anti-racist pamphlet, *The Races of Mankind* (1943), co-authored by cultural anthropologists Ruth Benedict and Gene Weltfish (see Chapter 19). Edwards and Weltfish also later collaborated in writing the PAC guidebook for the educational filmstrip, *We Are All Brothers*, adapted from the pamphlet, which inaugurated the organization's production and distribution of educational filmstrips. Edwards' writings at this time promoted the use of pamphlets, films, and filmstrips as a way for individuals to relate research to problems in their everyday lives and to facilitate group discussion of contemporary issues in schools and other organizations.[19]

In 1945, Edwards participated in an experimental project for the *Journal of Social Issues* that examined the emotional underpinnings of prejudice functioning in everyday situations. Her vignette, "A Social Evening at Mrs. Fairchild's," a fictionalized account of conversations expressing white racism, anti-Catholicism, and anti-Semitism, served as a case study for the participating scholars and practitioners to analyze the biases and tensions among the characters. In the summer of 1949, Edwards resigned from PAC after finding it difficult to continue working under the director, Maxwell Stewart. In her letter of resignation, Edwards claimed that Stewart's reputation as a "fellow traveler" was "a definite drawback to the Committee's work," which led to an extensive investigation of the director.[20] According to Stewart, the PAC board of directors found her allegation baseless. Yet, the incident was reported in an anti-communist newsletter and entered into the *Congressional Record* as part of Joseph McCarthy's investigations of the alleged communist activities of Stewart.[21] Edwards later worked for various educational organizations in Connecticut, New Jersey, and New York to foster stronger relations between public schools and their communities.

Violet Edwards made significant contributions to media literacy education: from 1936 to 1949, she equipped educators to teach critical interpretation of media communications bearing on important social issues affecting students' everyday lives. The following two excerpts of Edwards' writing indicate what she envisioned for the Study Program, analysis of propaganda, and fostering democracy during the late 1930s.

Excerpt: Edwards, Violet, *Group Leader's Guide to Propaganda Analysis* (New York: Institute of Propaganda Analysis, 1938) (permission Christine Darby)

Contributor's note: Footnotes from the original. I have preserved the style of the original notes.

Why Propaganda Study?

The cornerstone of democratic society, fundamental to the improvement of democracy as a way of life, is reliance upon the free play of intelligence in solving problems of human concern. This ideal is held in direct contrast with the making of decisions either by a minority or by the majority on the basis of traditional beliefs, uncritical acceptance of authority, or on blind impulse.

In our American democracy social institutions, national and international policies, and social, economic, and political programs are constantly in the process of making. These institutions, policies, and programs are set up by the people themselves, rather than by any external authority or by any small group. They are subject to modification or rejection in accordance with the will of the people as a whole.

It follows then, if in practice as well as in word we cherish the ideal of the free play of intelligence, that we have definite responsibilities as teachers and as citizens of a democracy. It is our special responsibility to see that there are no barriers from any quarter to the free play of criticism and evaluation, to the bringing of "the light of a thousand minds"[1] into focus upon our country's complex problems.

The alternative to reliance upon collective intelligence in solving our common problems is resort either to a philosophy of inertia, in itself fatal to democracy as a way of life, or to authoritarianism in which faith in the people as a whole is scorned, and one set of values is prescribed for all and enforced for all.

Democracy rests upon faith in the common man. Its welfare depends upon him—upon his intelligence, his ability to analyze and to solve the problems of his society, and his willingness to forego personal bias and interest when these are ruled out by the facts concerned, and to act for "the good of the greatest number."

However, amazingly little has been done to encourage and promote intelligent action on the part of the common man. Neither schools nor responsible adult organizations have set out consciously to organize their programs in a way to encourage intelligent action on the part of all the people. We have taken our way of life for granted. We have been, more or less, content to accept the "symbol" of democracy. Certainly we have not undertaken the direct responsibility for its practical functioning, much less its refinement. We speak of teaching "good citizenship" as if it were a lesson to be learned by rote, rather than the everyday practice of intelligent, social thinking and acting.

[...]

Propaganda Analysis Means—

In this publication we use the term "propaganda analysis." It denotes a group learning process of free discussion of problems created by propaganda and by the other forces which shape public opinion. The term refers both to method and to subject matter. It is descriptive of the method used to make possible the emotionally detached consideration and discussion of public affairs.

This generalized conception may be clarified by listing the important aspects of propaganda analysis.

---

1 Morgan, Joy Elmer, *The Ideas and Ideals of Horace Mann*. Lecture on Education. p. 77. National Home Library Foundation. Washington, D.C.: 1936.

A Group Learning Process

1. Propaganda analysis, as an organized process, is the experimental group study—in the classroom, civic organization, adult group—of the following:

    (a) The conflicts or problems of a modern state dedicated to democracy, that is, to the solution of its problems through the application of critical inquiry and intelligent social action.

    (b) The strains or pressures which society creates for the individuals which compose it.

    (c) Why people think and act in certain ways under the stimuli of appeals to their interests, needs, desires, prejudices, fears, and the like.

    (d) The main interests and desires to which organized groups in our society appeal.

    (e) The purposes underlying the appeals of these individuals and groups.

    (f) The methods, or the means, they use to achieve their ends or purposes.

Subject Matter

2. Propaganda analysis is based upon the critical examination and discussion of the following:

    (a) Those public questions and problems which agitate the minds of Americans today.

    (b) The methods and devices, as well as the organization, of groups which attempt to persuade people to act in certain calculated ways.

    (c) The channels of communication, that is, the press, radio, motion picture, through which propagandas are transmitted, and which themselves act as forces in shaping public opinion.

    (d) Other forces, such as the home, the community, the church, the school, language, music, art, and economic, social, and political factors and conditions, which mould public opinion.

    (e) The psychology of individual and group behavior—why people think and act in certain ways.

Cooperation

3. The Institute's experimental study program has its roots in the work of over 350 cooperating high schools; high school, college, and university classes; and in as many adult groups, ranging from professional and adult education organizations to civic, farm, and church groups. The study is further based upon the experimental use and development of methods

and subject matter for group work in critical analysis and free discussion. Efforts along these lines, in cooperating schools and adult groups, as well as with educational organizations and institutions dedicated to similar objectives, are directed towards the building of positive as opposed to negative approaches to the study of present-day social problems. The aim of propaganda analysis is not to produce a kind of skepticism which will destroy belief in everything, but to produce skepticism which will distinguish truth from falsehood.

Participation

4. Central to the process of propaganda analysis are:

   (a) Group participation in free discussion. An experimental guide to group discussion is provided in the appendix of this publication to encourage expression of views, and to arrive at conclusions based upon consideration of relevant facts.

   (b) An understanding and a working knowledge of the scientific method through day-to-day individual and group practice in asking such questions as, "Are our premises supported by evidence?" and "Do our conclusions follow from our premises?"

In schools propaganda analysis is carried on in classes which already exist, such as history, social studies, English, home economics, and mathematics. In adult groups work is centered in practical affairs pertaining to citizenship.

Excerpt: Edwards, Violet, "The School Executive and Propaganda Analysis," *School Management and School Supply and Equipment News* **2 (May 1939) (permission Christine Darby)**

The peoples of the world today are victims of subtle and ceaseless propaganda—suppressing, exaggerating, distorting. Backgrounds are established against which identical facts appear so different as to be almost unrecognizable, and the task of finding solutions for difficulties is made infinitely more complex by the fact that in the modern world we can know only a few things from experience: we must depend upon "authorities," upon what we read and hear for our knowledge. We must depend upon those who supply the news or other material for judgment. The work of educators in a democratic society must be continually to emphasize to young people —and to the general body of citizens—their duty to *search out for themselves* the matters on which it is the function of citizenship to form opinions and to record decisions.

A Vital Necessity

Increasingly, school executives and teachers are coming to see that the corrective which Americans must put to the weakness of their democracy—that is, to the temptation to take too much of their thinking ready-made from others—is practical education in recognizing and evaluating propaganda, which affects their interests and the interests of their community, State, and nation. In a democratic state, purposeful education in propaganda analysis is a vital necessity.

[...]

Acting on this belief, over 500 school executives—[...] public school superintendents and principals—are encouraging, or themselves directing, propaganda study programs in their school systems, at the secondary and junior college levels. These school administrators are actively cooperating in the experimental study program of the Institute for Propaganda Analysis.

[...]

Stated briefly, girls and boys in these cooperating school systems are: (1) Learning how to recognize propaganda when they see and hear it. (2) Studying common devices used by special pleaders, and examining the channels of communication—the press, radio, motion picture—through which propagandas flow. (3) Learning how to appraise persuasion on its own merits—that is, asking the *what*, the *how*, and the *why* of propaganda. (4) Experiencing situations in which they apply the experimental methods of science to specific inquiry into their own daily problems. (5) Learning to withhold judgments until they have had sufficient opportunity to examine and to weigh the facts concerned. And (6) studying controversial propagandas of today, with special attention to the social, economic, political, and psychological conditions which create and sustain these, and all propagandas.

The Institute's experimental study program enters into many phases of the formation of public opinion and the workings of propaganda, but it emphasizes particularly the necessity of "understanding ourselves," of understanding how we as human beings with likes and dislikes, prejudices and ideals, interests and attitudes participate in the process which we have come to call propaganda. It necessarily includes the study of logic (simplified to meet the needs of high school and junior college girls and boys). However, it recognizes that one may know the rules of logic by rote, and still be incapable of applying them, if his prejudices, his biases, his patterns of thought serve as barriers to what has been called "straight thinking." Therefore, basic in the Institute's study program is the belief that we can best prevent this by studying ourselves—by knowing what our prejudices, ideals, biases are; by knowing how they developed, and how they may affect our thinking.

[...]

Teachers need not fear that they are "introducing" young people to propaganda. From infancy they have been influenced by as many kinds of persuasion as there are individuals and groups—as there are special interests and spokesmen for those interests in our modern world. From his embarrassment of experiences with all kinds of propaganda materials, the school executive—perhaps more than most educators—well knows that young people in the public schools will not depend on the teacher or any one textbook for propaganda examples with which to work in the classroom. They will bring into the classroom-laboratory, themselves, such materials as: promotion leaflets left at the door with the early morning milk; editorials clipped from newspapers and a variety of journals of opinion; "safe driving" stickers; scribbled excerpts from a radio broadcast; Pep Club throw-aways; magazine advertisements; cartoons and "funnies"; headlines; and pulp magazine stories. The modern world of entertainment and streamlined communication is their propaganda textbook.

As Young Folks Study

Young people taking part in classroom work in propaganda analysis are concerned with an examination of propaganda as one of the forces which molds public opinion in a democratic state. They do not look upon propaganda as a "problem" which can be "solved" in the manner of solving a problem in mathematics. In the most constructive sense of the word, their work in propaganda analysis is a positive social process: they learn to recognize and to appraise organized persuasion; through basic study they come to realize the importance of socially competent citizens; they see themselves, motivated by many drives and by many appeals to those drives, in relation to the constantly changing institutions, policies, and programs of our democracy. Propaganda analysis, conceived and carried out along these lines, is in fact, as well as theory, education and training *for* intelligent, informed, and competent citizenship.

Notes

1 Alfred McClung Lee and Elizabeth Briant Lee, eds., *The Fine Art of Propaganda: A Study of Father Coughlin's Speeches* (New York: Harcourt, Brace and Company, 1939). The seven devices are: name calling, glittering generalities, transfer, testimonial, plain folks, card stacking, and bandwagon.

2 "Degrees Conferred, June, 1929," University of Arizona Record 23, no. 2, pt. 1 (1930): 304. "Violet E. Lavine; Retired Educator," *Arizona Republic*, February 19, 1983, 23; "Miss Edwards Appointed to Univ. Staff," *Yuma Weekly Sun* and *Yuma Examiner*, May 29, 1936, 3.

3 "Miss Edwards Appointed," 3.

4 J. Michael Sproule, "Authorship and Origins of the Seven Propaganda Devices: A Research Note," *Rhetoric & Public Affairs* 4, no. 1 (2001): 138. Sproule states that Edwards gave Miller full credit for developing the seven devices. Clyde R. Miller, "Preface," *Propaganda Analysis* 1 (1938): v.

5 In the 1940s, Lavine worked as a staff correspondent and later the national news editor and an assistant managing editor of the New York daily newspaper, *PM*.

6 Benjamin Fine, "Propaganda Study Instills Skepticism in 1,000,000 Pupils," *New York Times*, February 21, 1941, 1.

7 Timothy Glander, *Origins of Mass Communications Research during the American Cold War: Educational Effects and Contemporary Implications* (Mahwah, NJ: Lawrence Erlbaum Associates, 2000), 23.

8 For a historical account of critical thinking as a pedagogical concept, see Peter Lamont, "The Construction of 'Critical Thinking': Between How We Think and What We Believe," *History of Psychology* 23, no. 3 (2020): 232–251, and for a discussion of the continuing relevance of John Dewey's ideas in education, see Carol Rodgers, "Defining Reflection: Another Look at John Dewey and Reflective Thinking," *Teachers College Record* 104, no. 4 (2002): 842–866.

9 Violet Edwards, *Group Leader's Guide to Propaganda Analysis* (New York: Institute of Propaganda Analysis, 1938), 3–4.

10 Ibid., 6–7, 29. While Edwards consistently encouraged students to identify how propagandists manipulate people through emotional appeals, she recognized subjective motivations in the processes of critical thinking and taking action and thus did not define propaganda analysis as a solely analytical enterprise.

11 J. Michael Sproule, *Channels of Propaganda* (Bloomington, IN: EDINFO Press, 1994), 34, 48, and J. Michael Sproule, "Propaganda: Five American Schools of Thought," presented at the Biennial Convention of the World Communication Association (1989), 15. Sproule argues that after the IPA disbanded in 1942, the concept of critical thinking was redefined as largely a formalist mode of logical reasoning and became detached from the IPA's social framework of media literacy and education for democracy. Sproule, *Channels of Propaganda*, 34.

12 Lamont, "The Construction of 'Critical Thinking,'" 241. Lamont finds it difficult to pin down one definition of critical thinking. He outlines shifting definitions of the concept of critical thinking in fields of psychology and education from the inter-war period to the present. Like Sproule, he recognizes "straight thinking" as one thread among multiple strands of thought at work during the late 1930s. Lamont, "The Construction of 'Critical Thinking,'" 242.

13 Edwards, *Group Leader's Guide*, appendix 1.

14 Ibid., 98.

15 The "Looking at Ourselves" unit more fully developed suggestive comments presented earlier in "Some ABC's of Propaganda," *Propaganda Analysis* 1, no. 3 (December 1937): 9–12. Sproule locates the origin of Miller's "life history" approach to an internal document and this unauthored essay. J. Michael Sproule, *Propaganda and Democracy*

(Cambridge, UK: Cambridge University Press, 1997), 136 and 291. This approach became important in Miller's later attempts to rebut contemporaneous criticism of the IPA as fostering cynicism in students. Sproule argues that the various critics of the IPA lacked the knowledge of the Study Program, its use of a life history approach, and its group method. Sproule, *Propaganda and Democracy*, 172.

16 Edwards, *Group Leader's Guide*, appendix 17. For a historical overview of the discussion of group educational method that informs the *Guide*'s Appendix, "A Guide to Vital Group Discussion," see William M. Keith, *Democracy as Discussion: Civic Education and the American Forum Movement* (Lanham, MD: Lexington Books, 2007).

17 Edwards, *Group Leader's Guide*, 43, 77, and 78.

18 "Paid Employees Quit B&PW Clubs in Protest," *PM*, March 21, 1943, 12.

19 Violet Edwards, "Let's Help You Find It: Pamphlets for Classroom Use," *Progressive Education* 20 (1943): 308–309, 346; Violet Edwards, "Filmstrips Promote Discussion," *Film Forum Review* 1 (1946): 9–11.

20 U.S. Congress, *Congressional Record*, 82nd Cong., 1st sess., 1951, Vol. 97, pt. 13: A3366.

21 Ibid.; Maxwell Slutz Stewart, *Twentieth-Century Pamphleteering: The History of the Public Affairs Committee* (New York: Public Affairs Committee, 1976), 23.

Bibliography

Cocking, Walter and Violet Edwards. "On the Same Team." *New York State Education* 41 (June 1954): 681–684.

"Degrees Conferred, June, 1929." *University of Arizona Record* 23, no. 2, pt. 1 (1930): 304.

Edwards, Violet. "The Centennial of Free Public Schools." In *Centennial Horizons: The Years Ahead*, by University of the State of New York, Curriculum Development Center, 47–48. Albany: University of the State of New York, 1967.

_____. "Children Find City Giant Laboratory." *New York Times*, August 3, 1937, 4.

_____. "The Citizen and His Schools: New York State Citizens Committee Helps the Layman Work for His Schools." *New York State Education* 46 (May 1959): 581.

_____. "Developing Critical Thinking through Motion Pictures and Newspapers," *The English Journal* 29, no. 4 (April 1940): 301–307.

_____. "Episode 7: A Social Evening at Mrs. Fairchild's—Prejudice and Emotion in the Living Room." *Journal of Social Issues* 1, no. 2 (May 1945): 38–42.

_____. "Filmstrips Promote Discussion." *Film Forum Review* 1 (1946): 9–11.

_____. *Group Leader's Guide to Propaganda Analysis*. New York: Institute of Propaganda Analysis, 1938.

_____. "How Amy Might Have Created Two Different Situations." *Journal of Social Issues* 1, no. 2 (May 1945): 46–48.

_____. "Let's Help You Find It: Pamphlets for Classroom Use." *Progressive Education* 20 (November 1943): 308–309, 346.

_____. "Notes on Political Education: At a Political Clubhouse, in Brooklyn." *Journal of Educational Sociology* 19, no. 1 (1945): 55.

_____. "Note on *The Races of Mankind.*" In *Race: Science and Politics*, by Ruth Benedict, 167–168. New York: Viking Press, 1945.

_____. "Our Schools Need a Partner—The Whole Community." *Educational Leadership* 9, no. 5 (February 1952): 286–291.

_____. "Propaganda Analysis: Today's Challenge." *Bulletin of the American Library Association* 34 (1940): 8–10.

_____. "Representative Citizens Committee at Work." *The School Executive* 72, pt. 2 (April 1953): 19–20.

_____. "The School Executive and Propaganda Analysis." *School Management* 2 (May 1939): 204, 222.

_____. "The World's Greatest Educator: The US Army Is Teaching as Well as Training." *Saturday Review*, September 18, 1943, 7–9, 27.

Edwards, Violet and Bernard Joslin. "When Citizens See the Schools in Action." *The School Executive* 76, pt. 2 (February 1957): 78–81.

Edwards, Violet and Gene Weltfish. *We Are All Brothers.* New York: Public Affairs Committee. Script for a filmstrip based on the Races of Mankind pamphlet, 1944.

Fine, Benjamin. "Propaganda Study Instills Skepticism in 1,000,000 Pupils." *New York Times*, February 21, 1941, 1, 14.

Glander, Timothy. *Origins of Mass Communications Research during the American Cold War: Educational Effects and Contemporary Implications.* Mahwah, NJ: Lawrence Erlbaum Associates, 2000.

Hobbs, Renee and Sandra McGee. "Teaching About Propaganda: An Examination of the Historical Roots of Media Literacy." *Journal of Media Literacy Education* 6, no. 2 (2014): 56–67.

Institute for Propaganda Analysis, prepared by Violet Edwards. 1938. *Propaganda, How to Recognize It and Deal with It.* New York: Institute for Propaganda Analysis.

Keith, William M. *Democracy as Discussion: Civic Education and the American Forum Movement.* Lanham, MD: Lexington Books, 2007.

Lamont, Peter. "The Construction of 'Critical Thinking': Between How We Think and What We Believe." *History of Psychology* 23, no. 3 (2020): 232–251.

Lee, Alfred McClung and Elizabeth Briant Lee, eds. *The Fine Art of Propaganda: A Study of Father Coughlin's Speeches.* New York: Harcourt, Brace and Company, 1939.

Miller, Clyde R. "Preface." *Propaganda Analysis* 1 (1938): iii–v. https://archive.org/details/IPAVol1, accessed April 9, 2023.

_____. "Some Comments on Propaganda Analysis and the Science of Democracy." *Public Opinion Quarterly* 5, no. 4 (1941): 657–665.

Miller, Clyde R. and Violet Edwards. "The Intelligent Teacher's Guide through Campaign Propaganda." *The Clearing House* 11, no. 2 (October 1936): 69–77.

"Miss Edwards Appointed to Univ. Staff." *Yuma Weekly Sun* and *Yuma Examiner*, May 29, 1936, 1, 3.

"Paid Employees Quit B&PW Clubs in Protest." *PM*, March 21, 1943, 12.

Rodgers, Carol. "Defining Reflection: Another Look at John Dewey and Reflective Thinking." *Teachers College Record* 104, no. 4 (2002): 842–866.

"Some ABC's of Propaganda." *Propaganda Analysis* 1, no. 3 (December 1937): 9–12.

Sproule, J. Michael. "Authorship and Origins of the Seven Propaganda Devices: A Research Note." *Rhetoric & Public Affairs* 4, no. 1 (2001): 135–143.

_____. *Channels of Propaganda*. Bloomington, IN: EDINFO Press, 1994. https://files.eric.ed.gov/fulltext/ED372461.pdf, accessed March 10, 2023.

_____. *Propaganda and Democracy*. Cambridge, UK: Cambridge University Press, 1997.

_____. "Propaganda: Five American Schools of Thought." Paper presented at the Biennial Convention of the World Communication Association, 1989. https://files.eric.ed.gov/fulltext/ED312689.pdf, accessed March 10, 2023.

Stewart, Maxwell Slutz. *Twentieth-Century Pamphleteering: The History of the Public Affairs Committee*. New York: Public Affairs Committee.

US Congress. *Congressional Record*. 82nd Cong., 1st sess., 97, pt. 13 (1951).

"Violet E. Lavine; Retired Educator." *Arizona Republic*, February 19, 1983, 23.

Walser, Frank, with the assistance of Annette Smith and Violet Edwards. *An American Answer to Intolerance, Teacher's Manual no. 1, Junior and Senior High Schools*. New York: Council Against Intolerance in America, 1939.

Chapter 4

Marjorie Ella Fiske Lissance Löwenthal (1914–1992)

By Aimee-Marie Dorsten

Marjorie Ella Fiske Lissance Löwenthal's highly productive career cut across radio and audience research, advertising, library studies, and psychology. Early in her career, Fiske was a mainstay at Columbia University's Bureau of Applied Social Research (BASR) where her innovations in audience studies were largely uncredited. Fiske was among several women (see also Patricia Kendall, Chapter 12) who contributed significantly to the research BASR is famous for, but hit a glass ceiling in rank and power at the Bureau. Fiske was lauded for her scholarship in library studies and psychology, as she refashioned her career several times over.[1] Her media research is cited in critical brand theory, mass communication, media effects, media studies, qualitative and quantitative research methods, and social psychology.

Born in 1914 in Attleboro, Massachusetts, Fiske graduated early from Mt. Holyoke with a bachelor's in sociology in 1935. She earned an assistant psychologist fellowship at the New York Institute for the Education of the Blind and at Columbia University from 1935–36 while working toward her master's in psychology. Although a PhD candidate at Columbia and the New School for Social Research, her doctoral degree was never completed; but she was awarded an honorary doctorate from Mt. Holyoke in 1976. Fiske became a research assistant at the Rockefeller Foundation's Princeton Office of Radio Research (ORR) directly out of graduate school. Here, she was a key author, researcher, and administrator, and when the ORR became BASR under Paul Lazarsfeld at Columbia, Fiske was promoted from assistant to senior associate over the course of seventeen years there.

Although Lazarsfeld was the public face of the BASR, archival documents show Fiske administered numerous projects on all forms of mass media: she proposed, organized, executed, analyzed, and authored surveys, studies, and reports for over twenty publications.[2] Many articles Fiske wrote on behalf of the BASR are administrative in tone.[3] However, as a first or singular author, she often employed the uses and gratifications methodology in critique of early effects research.

One of Fiske's BASR studies, *Bonds on the Air: A Report of the Public's Choice as to Who is Best Qualified to Sell Bonds by Radio* (1946), constituted the foundation of *Mass Persuasion: The Social Psychology of a War Bond*

Drive (1946). *Bonds* established a core finding that age, education, and income of the audience, but also perceptions of *other* audience members' interest in a celebrity (like Kate Smith or Frank Sinatra), influenced key decision-making patterns for mass media audiences more than exposure to the celebrity themselves.[4] Despite her findings, Robert Merton took main authorship of *Mass Persuasion* while Fiske is credited simply with "assisting." Merton's book is based on Fiske's raw data set of 978 New Yorkers interviewed about the Kate Smith bond drive. Fiske's finding that personal connections determine the "symbolic fitness" of the persuader forms *Mass Persuasion's* premises.[5]

Further, Fiske's contributions to *The Focused Interview* (1952) were more significant than Merton's first authorship suggests. Not only did Fiske's war bond drive and the Hartford radio studies provide the data, but in an undated 1943 memo from Fiske to Merton and Lazarsfeld during the book's development, Fiske lays out a table of contents plan nearly identical to the published version.[6] The memo clarifies the fact that Fiske and Patricia Kendall developed and wrote the plan for the book, with Fiske informing Lazarsfeld and Merton, "At this writing, topical outlines have been prepared for all sections, except 'Depth,' 'Additional Problems,' and the 'Introduction.' " Fiske also discusses other sections of the book that she and Kendall ultimately developed and revised, including the chapter on "Depth" and the Glossary.[7]

Despite her contributions, further promotion at BASR did not materialize. Fiske joined Herta Herzog (see Chapter 6) at McCann Erikson as a research psychologist in 1946. Then, as the post-World War II Marshall Plan era took shape, Fiske parlayed her experience to become chief of the International Radio Evaluation of the Voice of America in 1948. She also served as the executive director of the Planning Committee on Media Research from 1953 to 1955.[8]

Following her divorce from Austrian Arnold Lissance in 1953, Fiske married cultural Marxist scholar Leo Löwenthal. When the Center for Advanced Study in the Behavioral Sciences at Stanford invited Löwenthal to join in 1955, Fiske and her daughter also relocated to California. She became a professor in the Department of Sociology and the School of Librarianship at the University of California, Berkeley. Her report on censorship in public and high school libraries earned her the annual Library Literature Award of the American and International Library Associations, an award still recognized for its excellence and rigor.[9]

In 1958, Fiske became a full professor at the Department of Psychiatry at UC San Francisco as its Director of the Human Development and Aging Training Research Program, where she remained until 1981.[10] Her social psychology research was robust, including: *Lives in Distress: The Paths of the Elderly to the Psychiatric Ward* (1964), *Four Stages of Life* (with Majda Thurnher and David A. Chiriboga, 1975), *The Middle Age: The Prime of Life?* (1980), and *Change and Continuity in Adult Life* (with David A. Chiriboga, 1990).

Yet, Fiske chafed mightily at the University of California's nepotism rule requiring female faculty to use the same last name as their husbands.[11] Consequently, she published as Marjorie Löwenthal, erasing connections between her media and psychology scholarship. She used Marjorie Fiske Löwenthal by 1975, then reclaimed Marjorie Fiske in 1980 following her divorce.

Often, Fiske's media research represented some of the first and most comprehensive uses and gratifications studies of the time. Fiske's "The Children Talk About Comics" (with Katherine M. Wolf, 1949)—in Lazarsfeld and Stanton's *Communications Research: 1948-1949*—is a bulwark against the effects accusations so frequently lodged at the mass media "straw man" as the source of society's ills.[12] "Children" presages later sociological dismissals of the hierarchy between elite and popular interests as either "art" or "trash."[13] "Children" uses qualitative social psychology and focused interview methods: children speak for themselves, underscoring that home environment and psychological predisposition account for greater influence in children's relationships than mass media. "Children" is cited in the fields of psychology, media studies, cultural studies, and communication research, among others.

A critical element infused Fiske's media research: the tendencies, attitudes, and needs of less powerful groups of consumers and listeners—particularly women, children, and students—were of particular interest.[14] Had Fiske been male, her prototypical cultural and media studies approaches would have been acknowledged. But, like so many other female academics of the era, Fiske found that the same circulating network of men who appropriated research and authorship in communication also headed the bastions of scholarly privilege on the east coast. A testament to her sagacity, she ultimately developed resources to be able to recreate her career (whether she wanted to or not) and find recognition in other fields. Indeed, Marjorie Fiske's career stresses the need to revise received communication history.

Excerpt from Fiske, Marjorie, *Bonds on the Air: A Report of the Public's Choice as to Who is Best Qualified to Sell Bonds by Radio in which Kate Smith Gets her Due Share of Attention,* 1944 (permission, Columbia University Libraries, University Archives, Rare Book & Manuscript Library)

Contributor's note: Footnotes from the original. I have preserved the style of the original notes. Underlining has been changed to italics throughout.

This study was conducted as a means of testing statistically certain conclusions developing from an analysis of detailed interviews with listeners to a day-long Kate Smith bondselling marathon. The findings reported herein are based on interviews with 976 people who represent, approximately, a cross-section of the population of greater New York.*

Respondents were asked which of five public figures they would select as the best person to sell bonds by radio and which one would be their last choice.** This question was asked first so those who were interviewed were not aware of any special interest in Kate Smith on the part of the investigator. They were then asked to state reasons for their selection, and this question was followed by a series of questions about bond-buying habits in general and familiarity with and attitudes toward Kate Smith.

What happens when such a group is asked to decide whether Betty Grable, Frank Sinatra, Wendell Willkie, Kate Smith or Martin Block is the best person to sell bonds?***

[...]

I.   *Kate Smith—First Choice—62%*
     A. *A considerable majority selected Kate Smith.*
        Martin Block, the radio salesman, came next (13%), with Wendell Willkie a rather close third, while movie star and bandleader tied for last place with 7% of the votes apiece.
     B. *Men and Women*
        Men and women alike choose her first. The men give way to Betty Grable and Wendell Willkie to some extent, but nevertheless 57% give laurels to Kate Smith as their chosen bondseller.

---

*   See Appendix 1 for background data.
** Questionnaire attached.
*** The order of presentation was rotated with different respondents in order to prevent any possible bias due to the position of names on the list.

C. *Young and Old*

She won out too with young and old, but as the men sometimes disregarded her for Willkie and Grable, so the "young" were more inclined to vote for their champion record-player, Martin Block. Frank Sinatra too came in for a greater share of "under 40" votes (most of the those were under 50), but there is little evidence here of the "bobby sock" hypnosis: Kate Smith ranked first in the "under 20" group too.

D. *Rich or Poor*

Kate Smith's appeal is no respecter of income. Wendell Willkie, on the other hand, has a marked increase in popularity as income increases, while the reverse is true of Martin Block. Betty Grable and Frank Sinatra show less marked differences through the appeal of the former does increase somewhat as income level decreases.

E. *Educated and Uneducated*

People who have been to college are less inclined to vote for her than others, and her greatest appeal is among those with less than high school education, but even in the college group, more than half put her first. The appeals of Martin Block and Betty Grable seem to be relatively impervious to education, while Wendell Willkie goes steeply down and Frank Sinatra goes sharply up as education decreases.

[...]

III. *Why Kate Smith?*

A. Her Moral Appropriateness

The reasons for selecting the various candidates fell into four rough categories shown in the adjacent table (this was a free answer question and the frame of reference from which his candidate was to be judged was left entirely to the respondent). The first category contains such "objectives" or "technical" reasons as "large following", "good salesman", "has already been successful in bondselling", etc. The second category includes such moral judgments as "sincere", "patriotic", and "sympathetic". The third consists of a kind of intellectual appropriateness: "He knows what it's all about." The fourth is made up of simple "I like him" responses and the miscellaneous group consists of non-committal remarks such as "he is good" or "better than the others", remarks which could not reasonably be placed in any of the other three categories.

It is probably entirely natural that the largest group of reasons consists of those in the "technical" category. This is what one would anticipate as a justification for selecting a person for any kind of selling: "he is a good salesman", "he has a large following", etc. The two remarkable features of these answers are (1) the relative preponderance of "moral" reasons for selecting Kate Smith and (2) the fact that a comprehension of the issues, an awareness of what bonds are for, seemed important only to those selecting Willkie, and even then only to 27 people (25% of those voting for him).

Reasons for choosing Betty Grable and Martin Block are preponderantly in the "technical" class with personal reasons showing as a poor second, while personal reasons rank relatively higher for Frank Sinatra. The almost complete lack of reasons which would fall into the "moral" appropriateness group for Betty Grable and Frank Sinatra, plus the fact that very few people selected them for first choice, would lead to the conclusion that by and large more popularity is not enough to qualify a person as a bondseller—there is also demand for the more special attributes of patriotism, sincerity, etc., which Wendell Willkie and Martin Block have to some extent, Kate Smith to a considerable extent.
[...]

VI. *Practical Implications of Kate Smith's Bondselling Superiority*

A–D The Record

Obviously, Kate Smith can sell no bonds by radio except to those who hear her make a radio appeal. But, judging from past listenership, the chances of her being heard are very great: 68% of all respondents listen to her daily programs—regularly or occasionally, and 55% have heard her make an all-day bond appeal. Of those who never listen to her regular programs, one-third have heard her make an all-day appeal, leaving only about 20% of the total sample who will probably not be exposed to her. (Of this group, 36% nevertheless voted for Kate Smith, with the obvious implications that she is the best person to sell bonds to someone else.)

The chances of her being heard, then, by those who have indicated that they are favorably disposed toward a bond appeal from her are undoubtedly very great—considerably greater, probably, than would be the chances of the other candidates who have neither regular radio programs nor all-day marathons. Had she never made any bond appeals, one would hazard the guess that she would make many sales: people listen to her, they think she is eminently suited to sell bonds—ergo, she should sell bonds. But of the 542 people (54%) who have heard her make an all-day bond appeal, only 9, or 1.6% have actually bought from her. Were this group larger, it would be enlightening to determine who they were in terms of personal background and feelings toward Kate Smith. Since it is small, we can only generalize from radio bond buying habits in general to determine why it is small.

Excerpt from Fiske, Marjorie and Katherine M. Wolf, "The Children Talk about the Comics: A Report on Comic Book Reading, Based on Detailed Case Studies of 100 Children from Various Family Backgrounds," *Communications Research: 1948–1949*, edited by Paul Felix Lazarsfeld and Frank Stanton. New York: Harper & Brothers, 1949, renewed (c) 1977 by Frank Stanton and Patricia Kendall (used by permission of HarperCollins Publishers).

Contributor's note: Footnotes from the original. I have preserved the style of the original notes. Underlining has been changed to italics throughout.

THE CHILDREN TALK ABOUT THE COMICS

Table of Contents

Introduction

Appendices

A. Procedure Followed in Coding Comic Book Stage
B. Procedure Followed in Coding Intensity of Comic Book Reading Experience
C. Procedure Followed in Coding Social Adjustment
D. Observations and Interruptions While Reading
E. Interview Guide and Instructions to Interviewers
F. Sample Interviews

INTRODUCTION

Mother's [sic] clubs, parent teacher meetings and bridge table discussions usually include at least one parent who likes to boast that "*my* children don't like comic books." The remark is likely to be followed by an embarrassed silence while the rest of the group wonders whether to envy or commiserate with her. If the discussion develops true to form, authorities will then be cited to prove that comic reading is good or bad.

Over one hundred articles and pamphlets* have been written by psychologists and educators on this controversial, and to many adults, mysterious subject. The result has been that the parent or teacher concerned with comic reading can find equally impressive arguments for and against them. None of these arguments, however, stem from the person most concerned in the matter: the child himself. They have revolved around him, but he has been left out.

The adult, if he has ever looked at comics, has looked at them as an adult. This study endeavors to avoid this approach. Adults, of course, interviewed and observed the children and analyzed their reports, but the description of comic books presented here is the child's description. The satisfactions of comic reading are described by the children themselves, not inferred by adults. Even the attitudes of adults toward comic reading are seen through the eyes of the children themselves.

Another way in which this study differs from most discussions of comics is that the investigators are not trying to prove that comic book reading is either "good" or "bad". We begin with the premise that comic book reading is a pastime which is well documented both by the facts of this study** and by the tremendous circulation figures of the of the comics themselves. From here we

---

* See "Bibliography on Comics," *Journal of Educational Sociology*, 18, no. 4 (December 1944).

** Only two of the 104 children interviewed for this study reported that they do not read comics, and even they had read them at some period of their lives.

proceed to find out why comic book reading is such an important factor in the lives of our children, and finally we endeavour to search out its effects.

This report is written for those adults who would like to know why comic books have such an appeal to children, how it fits into their general development, and how it affects them. We do not pretend to have the final answers even to these questions, for this was an exploratory rather than definitive study. We shall see that some children prefer one kind of comic book, others another. We shall see that some read comics for relaxation and others seem to be driven by an irresistible compulsion to read as many as possible. Since we have studied and observed children of many ages and backgrounds, it is not unlikely that many parents and teachers will find similarities between the children quoted here and their own children. Seeing them at various stages of their comic reading development, however, may give adults a more objective picture, and a more ready understanding of the role of comics in their children's lives. The authors, hope, too, that this preliminary investigation will serve to stimulate the interest of other investigators in this significant field which has until now been almost completely neglected by empirical research.

As with most studies of the Bureau of Applied Social Research, this one was a cooperative venture. The authors would like, at this point, to make public their appreciation for the cooperation of the staff and others of their colleagues. We wish especially to thank Dr. Herta Herzog whose interest and constructive suggestions accompanied us through the various drafts of the manuscript.

Mrs. Jeannette Green and Mrs. Eva Hofberg were indispensable in their administrative interviewing and analytical contributions. To Josette Frank, Mr. Harry Childs, Mr. William Miller and Mr. Arnold Lissance our thanks for reading the manuscript and making helpful suggestions, and we wish to thank Dr. Goodwin Watson for his contributions to the early phases of this study.

Notes

1 Christie W. Keifer, "Marjorie E. Fiske, Psychiatry: San Francisco," University of California: Calisphere, 2019, http://texts.cdlib.org/view?docId=hb7c6007sj;NAAN= 13030&doc.view=frames&chunk.id=div00017&toc.depth=1&toc.id=&brand=calisphere, accessed May 15, 2019; Gertrude J. Robinson, "The Katz/Löwenthal Encounter: An Episode in the Creation of Personal Influence," *The Annals of the American Academy*, AAPSS 608 (November 2006): 76-96.

2 Series I: Project Index, Contents of Folders, Box 4, Folders B-0153 & B-0185, Bureau of Applied Social Research Records, Rare Book and Manuscript Library, Columbia University, New York.

3 Marjorie Fiske and Leo Handel, "Motion Picture Research: Content and Audience Analysis," *Journal of Marketing* 11, no. 2 (1946): 129-134; Marjorie Fiske and Leo

Handel, "Motion Picture Research: Response Analysis," *Journal of Marketing* 11, no. 3 (1947): 273–280; Marjorie Fiske and Leo Handel, "New Techniques for Studying the Effectiveness of Films," *Journal of Marketing* 11, no. 4 (1947): 390–393.

4 Marjorie Fiske, *Bonds on the Air: A Report of the Public's Choice as to Who is Best Qualified to Sell Bonds by Radio in which Kate Smith Gets her Due Share of Attention* (New York: Columbia University, Bureau of Applied Social Research, 1944), 2a, 2b, 3a.

5 Fiske, *Bonds*, 2.

6 Marjorie Fiske, "Memorandum," 1943, Bureau of Applied Social Research Records, Rare Book and Manuscript Library, Columbia University, New York; Robert K. Merton and Patricia Kendall, *The Focused Interview*, 1, Series I: Project Index, Box 6, Folder B-0202: Bureau of Applied Social Research Records, Rare Book and Manuscript Library, Columbia University, New York.

7 Fiske, "Memorandum," 2.

8 See Adam Arvidsson, *Brands: Meaning and Value in Media Culture* (London: Routledge, 2006); Jacques Ellul, *Propaganda: The Formation of Men's Attitudes* (New York: Vintage Books, 1965); Elihu Katz, Jay G. Blumler, and Michael Gurevitch, "Uses and Gratifications Research," *Public Opinion Quarterly* 37, no. 4 (Winter 1973-1974): 509–523; David Morley, *Television Audiences & Cultural Studies* (London: Routledge, 2003); Herbert J. Rubin and Irene S. Rubin, *Qualitative Interviewing: The Art of Hearing Data* (Los Angeles: Sage Publications, 2012); Roy F. Baumeister and Mark R. Leary, "The Need to Belong: Desire for Interpersonal Attachments as a Fundamental Human Motivation," *Psychological Bulletin* 117, no. 3 (1995): 497–529.

9 Keifer, "Marjorie E. Fiske."

10 Marjorie Fiske, "Curriculum Vitae," August 1987, Lissance Family Private Collection.

11 Carol Lissance, email to the author, May 8, 2020.

12 Katherine M. Wolf and Marjorie Fiske, "The Children Talk about Comics," in *Communications Research: 1948-1949*, ed. Paul F. Lazarsfeld and Frank N. Stanton (New York: Harper Brothers, 1949), 37.

13 Wolf and Fiske, "The Children," 5.

14 Lissance, email to author, May 8, 2020.

Bibliography

Arvidsson, Adam. *Brands: Meaning and Value in Media Culture*. London: Routledge, 2006.

Baumeister, Roy F. and Mark R. Leary. "The Need to Belong: Desire for Interpersonal Attachments as a Fundamental Human Motivation." *Psychological Bulletin* 117, no. 3 (1995): 497–529.

"Bibliography on Comics," *Journal of Educational Sociology*, 18, no. 4 (December 1944).

Ellul, Jacques. *Propaganda: The Formation of Men's Attitudes*. New York: Vintage Books, 1965.

Fiske, Marjorie. *Bonds on the Air: A Report of the Public's Choice as to Who is Best Qualified to Sell Bonds by Radio in Which Kate Smith Gets Her Due Share of Attention*. New York: Columbia University, Bureau of Applied Social Research, 1944.

_____. "The Columbia Office of Radio Research." *Hollywood Quarterly* 1, no. 1 (1945): 51–59.

_____. "Curriculum Vitae." August 1987, Lissance Family Private Collection.

_____. "Germany's Gunpowder Children." *Cosmopolitan Magazine* 125, no. 2 (August 1948): 56–57, 128.

_____. "How Consumers React to Radio Advertising by Retailers." *Sales Management* v, no. xxxv (April 1944): 92–98.

_____. "Implementation Committee on Television." Collection number: MSS 84–87, Box 3, Folder 26. Marjorie Fiske Papers, 1937–1949, University of California at San Francisco Library Archives and Special Collections, San Francisco, CA.

_____. "Memorandum," 1943, Bureau of Applied Social Research Records, Rare Book and Manuscript Library, Columbia University, New York; Robert K. Merton and Patricia Kendall, *The Focused Interview*, 1, Series I: Project Index, Box 6, Folder B-0202: Bureau of Applied Social Research Records, Rare Book and Manuscript Library, Columbia University, New York.

_____. *The Middle Age: The Prime of Life?* London: Harper and Row, 1979.

_____. "The Office of Radio Research: A Division of the Bureau of Applied Social Research, Columbia University." *Educational and Psychological Measurement* 5, no. 4 (1945): 351–370.

_____. "Program Analyzer." *Film News* 5, no. 6 (June 1944): 3.

_____. *Sampling of Public Attitudes Toward the Proposed Subscription Radio Plan.* New York: Office of Radio Research, 1944.

_____. Series I: Project Index. Contents of Folders, Box 4, Folders B-0153 & B-0185, Bureau of Applied Social Research Records, Rare Book and Manuscript Library, Columbia University, New York.

_____. *A Study of School and Libraries in California: Book Selection and Censorship.* Berkeley, CA: University of California Press, 1959.

_____. *Survey of Materials on the Psychology of Radio Listening.* New York: Columbia University, Bureau of Applied Social Research, 1943.

Fiske, Marjorie and David A. Chiriboga. *Change and Continuity in Adult Life.* San Francisco, CA: Jossey-Bass, Inc., 1990.

Fiske, Marjorie and Leo Handel. "Motion Picture Research: Content and Audience Analysis." *Journal of Marketing* 11, no. 2 (1946): 129–134.

_____. "Motion Picture Research: Response Analysis." *Journal of Marketing* 11, no. 3 (1947): 273–280.

_____. "New Techniques for Studying the Effectiveness of Films." *Journal of Marketing* 11, no. 4 (1947) 390–393.

Fiske, Marjorie and Arthur W. Kornhauser. *Morale of Industrial Workers: A Summary and Point of View.* New York: Columbia University, Bureau of Applied Social Research, 1943.

Fiske, Marjorie and Leo Löwenthal. "Some Problems in the Administration of International Communications Research." *Public Opinion Quarterly* 16, no. 2 (1952): 149–159.

Fiske Lissance, Marjorie and Edrita G. Fried. "The Dilemmas of German Youth." *The Journal of Abnormal Psychology* 44, no. 1 (1949): 50–60.

Fiske Löwenthal, Marjorie. *Book Selection and Censorship: A Study of School and Public Libraries in California*. Berkeley, CA: University of California Press, 1959.

_____. *Lives in Distress: The Paths of the Elderly to the Psychiatric Ward*. New York: Basic Books, 1964.

Fiske Löwenthal, Marjorie and Ario Zilli, eds. *Interdisciplinary Topics in Gerontology, Vol. 3: Colloquium on Health and Aging of the Population*. New York, NY: S. Karger, 1969.

Fiske Löwenthal, Marjorie and Paul L. Berkman. *Aging and Mental Disorder in San Francisco: A Social Psychiatric Study*. San Francisco, CA: Jossey-Bass, Inc., 1967.

Fiske Löwenthal, Marjorie and Jeannette Green. *The Detailed Focused Interview as a Technique for the Testing of Institutional Advertising*. New York, NY: Columbia University, Bureau of Applied Social Research, 1944.

Fiske Löwenthal, Marjorie and Paul F. Lazarsfeld. *Retailers' Use of Radio as Judged by the Consumer in Hartford Connecticut*. New York, NY: Columbia University, Bureau of Applied Social Research, 1943.

Fiske Löwenthal, Marjorie and Majda Thurnher, David A. Chiriboga & Associates. *Four Stages of Life: A Comparative Study of Women and Men Facing Transitions*. San Francisco, CA: Jossey-Bass, Inc., 1975.

Katz, Elihu, Jay G. Blumler, and Michael Gurevitch. "Uses and Gratifications Research." *Public Opinion Quarterly* 37, no. 4 (Winter 1973–1974): 509–523.

Keifer, Christie W. "Marjorie E. Fiske, Psychiatry: San Francisco." University of California: Calisphere. http://texts.cdlib.org/view?docId=hb7c6007sj;NAAN=13030&doc.view=frames&chunk.id=div00017&toc.depth=1&toc.id=&brand=calisphere, accessed April 9, 2023.

Lazarsfeld, Paul and Marjorie Fiske. "The 'Panel' as a New Tool for Measuring Opinion." *Public Opinion Quarterly* 2, no. 4 (1938): 596–612.

Lowenthal, Leo. *An Unmastered Past: The Autobiographical Reflections of Leo Lowenthal*, ed. Martin Jay. University of California, California Digital Library, 1987. https://publishing.cdlib.org/ucpressebooks/view?docId=ft8779p24p&chunk.id=d0e3654&toc.id=&brand=ucpress, accessed April 9, 2023.

Löwenthal, Leo and Marjorie Fiske. "The Debate over Art and Popular Culture in Eighteenth-Century England." In *Common Frontiers in the Social Sciences*, ed. Mirra Kamorovsky, 33–112. Glencoe, IL: Free Press, 1957.

Merton, Robert K., Marjorie Fiske, and Alberta Curtis. *Mass Persuasion: The Social Psychology of a War Bond Drive*. New York, NY: Harper & Brothers, 1946.

Merton, Robert K., Marjorie Fiske, and Patricia L. Kendall. *The Focused Interview: A Manual of Problems and Procedures*. New York: Columbia University, Bureau of Applied Social Research, 1952. Revised and reprinted as *The Focused Interview*. Glencoe, IL: Free Press, 1956.

Meyerowitz, Alvin and Marjorie Fiske. "The Relative Preference of Low Income Groups for Small Stations." *Journal of Applied Psychology* 23, no. 1 (1939): 158–162.

Morley, David. *Television Audiences & Cultural Studies*. London: Routledge, 2003.

Robinson, Gertrude J. "The Katz/Löwenthal Encounter: An Episode in the Creation of Personal Influence." *The Annals of the American Academy*, AAPSS 608 (November 2006): 76–96.

Rubin, Herbert J. and Irene S. Rubin, *Qualitative Interviewing: The Art of Hearing Data*. Los Angeles, CA: Sage Publications, 2012.

Simon, Gerard Alexander, Marjorie Fiske Löwenthal, Leon J. Epstein, Betsy Robinson, and Clayton Haven. *Crisis and Intervention: The Fate of the Elderly Mental Patient*. San Francisco, CA: Jossey-Bass, Inc., 1970.

Wolf, Katherine M. and Marjorie Fiske. "The Children Talk about Comics." In *Communications Research: 1948-1949*, ed. Paul F. Lazarsfeld and Frank N. Stanton, 3–45. New York, NY: Harper Brothers, 1949.

Chapter 5

Shirley Graham Du Bois (1896–1977)

By Laura Strait and Carol A. Stabile

Throughout her life, Shirley Graham Du Bois broke new ground across fields of cultural production. She was the first Black woman to write and produce an opera, the only woman to head a Federal Theatre Project Unit, the founder and first editor of the influential journal *Freedomways*, and the only woman to found a national television system. Prior to the publication of Gerald Horne's biography, *Race Woman: The Lives of Shirley Graham Du Bois* (2002), Graham's many contributions to music, literature, media, and politics were suppressed because of her outspoken criticisms of White supremacy and her activism, her criticisms of capitalism, and her membership in the Communist Party.

Lola Shirley Graham was born in Indianapolis, Indiana, in 1896 and grew up throughout the US. Educated in "mixed schools" in segregated cities like Colorado Springs and Seattle (where Black history was suppressed) and "separate schools" in the south (where Black teachers taught Black history in all-Black schools), Graham developed a comprehensive understanding of White supremacy in its regional manifestations, inspiring a lifelong commitment to literacy and education as instruments of liberation and social change.

She met her first husband while living in Seattle and they had two children. Graham traveled to Paris in 1926, where she studied music composition at the Sorbonne and wrote articles for the *Portland Advocate*, a Black newspaper. She divorced her husband in 1927.

Graham was admitted to Oberlin College in 1931, where she completed a BA and an MA. She wrote the opera *Tom-Tom: An Epic of Music and the Negro* while completing her degrees. The first opera known to be written by a Black woman, *Tom-Tom* narrated the history of a community, from its kidnapping by slave holders through a Garveyite revolution set against the backdrop of 1920s Harlem.

Federal Theatre Project national director Hallie Flanagan asked Graham to head the Chicago Negro Unit in 1936. Graham was the first woman to head such a program. When the Federal Theatre Project was closed because of anti-communist pressure in 1939, Graham attended Yale Drama School. She wrote and produced several plays at Yale, including *Coal Dust*, a three-act play that reflected her interest in the intersections of race and class; *It's Morning*, a play that retold the story of Margaret Garner, an enslaved person who cut her daughter's throat rather than have the child sold to a slave holder; a play about the Haitian revolution; and radio plays about poet Phillis Wheatley and inventor George Washington Carver.

In 1941, Graham took a position directing "Negro work" for the YWCA-USO at Fort Huachuca in Arizona, the base of the largest Black division in the US army. Graham created courses on journalism and photography for the men and their wives, starting a literary magazine edited and run by Black soldiers, *Sage and Sand*.[1] In 1943, Graham resigned because of anti-communist pressure, asserting she was forced to leave the YWCA, because "in the final analysis white supremacy has us by [the] throat because the white man has the money."[2]

In New York City, Graham worked for a series of political organizations, campaigning against police misconduct, for fair housing, and for access to jobs. Graham took graduate courses at New York University, writing a paper on "West-African Survivals in the Vocabulary of Gullah" and completing substantial portions of a thesis on Black literature between the two world wars.[3] She also began to write popular biographies of Black historical figures for young adults.

In the late 1940s, Graham began writing a new novel about Anne Newport Royall, a white abolitionist who published a newspaper about political corruption in Washington, D.C. from 1832 to 1854. Finding parallels with her own life, Graham, wrote that Royall

did not go along with the crowd. Not because she was a Negro. She was not; she was White. Not because she was an Indian, but because a Southern White woman said that slavery was a cancer eating into our national life, and that it will in the end destroy us if we do not wipe it out; because she talked about the churches who sent missionaries to Africa and yet held slaves in their own backyard [...] that woman's name has been wiped out of history![4]

Graham joined the Communist Party in the mid-1940s, after the death of her son Robert. According to Graham, Robert had been denied treatment at a segregated military hospital. She fought against the execution of Ethel and Julius Rosenberg, while at the same time co-founding and participating in the civil rights organization Sojourners for Truth and Justice, opposing a criminal justice system that meted out death sentences to Black people, while allowing

White murderers to escape punishment. Graham also mounted a successful campaign to defend W.E.B. Du Bois in 1951, when he was indicted for failing to register as an agent of a foreign state. Graham and Du Bois were married that year.

The growing anti-communist, White supremacist backlash of the 1950s cut short Graham's career, resulting in demands her books be withdrawn from schools and libraries around the country. Publicity appearances for her award-winning novel *Your Most Humble Servant* were cancelled without explanation. Graham's manuscript about Royall was rejected by multiple publishers. Both Graham and Du Bois were surveilled and harassed by the US government. Ultimately, FBI files on the two would number in the tens of thousands of pages.

In 1961, the couple moved to Ghana. President Kwame Nkrumah asked Graham to establish the country's first national television system. Graham began work on a non-commercial television system and an infrastructure for indigenous television production, establishing programs to train writers for the new medium so that "the inhabitants of seldom-visited villages of the interior will know, seeing themselves on the screen, that they are not forgotten."[5] Graham also co-founded the journal *Freedomways: A Quarterly Review of the Negro Freedom Movement*, which provided a forum for discussing racial issues in the US. In 1967, Graham was forced to leave Ghana after a military-led coup d'état. She died on March 27, 1977 in Beijing, China, of breast cancer.

Shirley Graham's operas, plays, and novels about historical figures were part of a broader conversation on the anti-racist left among those who wished to present "the case of the Negro in the making of American history," as Graham described it.[6] Her novels worked against traditions that, as feminist critic Barbara Smith later put it, considered the historical and cultural contributions of black people as "beneath consideration, invisible, unknown" to "white and/or male consciousness."[7] Graham's opera, plays, novels, and work on Ghanaian television foreground her commitment to what a later generation of scholars would describe, following Stuart Hall, as using popular culture for anti-racist aims. Her recovery of Black—and female, White, and Native American—historical figures who were committed to projects of Black emancipation and anti-racist liberation emphasizes how the work of the Black feminist Left set the stage for projects of recovery that resurge in the 1970s and after.

Excerpt: Du Bois, Shirley Graham, "Minority Peoples in China,"
Freedomways **(Spring 1961)**

The first overwhelming impression of the Peoples Republic of China is of its many people. They are all along the way as one drives in from the airport—on foot carrying loads on their backs, driving carts, pulling carts, driving oil tanks, in pedicarts and motor trucks, on bicycles. They are in the nearby fields, working the ground or constructing buildings beside the road. When one drives through the gap in Peking's ancient wall, the throng multiplies. And one is struck by the many different kinds of people, different colors of skin, varying sizes and contour of face. The westerner is prone to exclaim, "But they don't look *Chinese!*"

Density of population in China was cited in the past as excusing the crimes of the exploiters. Cheap labor was "natural" because laborers were so numerous. Floods and famine were explained as dispensations of a "divine Providence" which thinned out overcrowded cities. Today this land is rapidly coming to contain one-fourth of the total world population, but nobody in China deplores the fact. Nobody is worried about it. Where once was fear and dread is now confidence. Of all the rich resources of the land none is so highly valued, none so carefully tended, none promises so bountiful a return as its many people.

About six percent of the 680 million people in China belong to national minorities which, in the past, were driven or fled into the mountains or most distant border regions. Oppressed and exploited by the ruling majority, despised, excluded from development in the regions, hunted down by Japanese invaders and enslaved by Kuomintang despots, many of these people lived in the most primitive conditions. The new Government now names fifty-one different minority nationalities which were separated from each other and from the dominant majority by location, language, customs and rigid laws forbidding marriage, or indeed, any contact outside the community. This classification, however, will be even larger if dialects, differing religion and tribal affiliations be taken into account. The one common denominator between all these minorities was fear and hatred towards other peoples. No matter how primitive was the social system, whether tribal, slave or feudal, each nation had its own small ruling class at the top, with its mass of degraded toilers at the bottom. And each had its fierce religious taboos, superstitions and priesthood.

In some cases the minority people had been the original inhabitants of the land (as were our own Indians), but had been pushed back, though not destroyed, by the Hans who have been the dominant people for near two thousand years. When the Manchus came to power in China they imposed cruel oppression on all non-Manchu nationalities. Even the proud Hans were forced to till the earth. In time, however, Han landlords shared with Mongol princes and Manchu nobles in holding high position and ruling all other peoples. Gradually the Manchurians were absorbed by the Hans until by the beginning of the 20th Century only the Manchu dynasty could be sure of "pure" Manchurian blood and only in the Imperial Court and in a small northwest province was the language of the Manchus spoken or written. The 94 percent of majority Hans now represent the Han people plus vanished nationalities and individuals of nationalities which through hundreds of years they have absorbed.

Not all minority peoples were concentrated in a particular territory. As example, the Huis, numbering about 3,900,000 are scattered throughout China. These people are descendants of Arabs, Turks, and Persians who migrated to China between the 8th and 9th centuries. The first to come were soldiers sent by the Abbasid Caliph al Mansur in 756 to help the reigning Tang Emperor suppress a rebellion in China's northwest regions. After victory these men were granted land and settled down, marrying local women. A little later, Arab and Persian merchants began arriving in China. During the Tang and Sung dynasties many of them made their homes permanently in China. These were Muslims who brought their faith with them. Records show that in the year 878 there were 200,000 foreigners (mainly Muslims, but also Christians and Jews) in Canton alone. But the Huis have suffered long and continued persecution. Right through Kuomintang rule they were mocked as "people with queer ways." As late as 1948 two mosques—one in Peking and one in Tientsin—were destroyed by Chiang Kai-shek's troops. To escape discrimination in education and employment, many Huis, like other minority people, concealed their origin.

Such was the situation with regard to minority peoples when Peoples Republic of China was established in 1949. The years of wars and constant struggle from 1911, when the Manchu dynasty was forced to abdicate, to the victory of the People's Liberation Army in 1949, had brought little change in the regions occupied by national minorities. They had been forced to fight by warlords; boys had been dragged off to the Army and left dying on the road. War had only made their lot harder and brought famine into every home. But now it was the task of the new Government to convince these peoples that the triumph of the Liberation Army was their triumph, that they too had been liberated from the old life of hardships, to show them the path to a better way of life. This was a most difficult task.

Excerpt: Du Bois, Shirley Graham, *This is Ghana Television* (Tema, Ghana: The State Publishing Corporation, 1963)

Editors' note: Although this document is unattributed, we include it as a reflection of Du Bois' leadership of, and thinking about, the role of television designed to serve public interests.

THE IDEA

Ghana Television will be Ghanaian, African and Socialist in content.

Ghanaian, because, as President Nkrumah said in the speech cited on the title page of this booklet: "Television must assist in the Socialist transformation of Ghana." Our aim is to produce programmes based on the needs and interests of our people, which lift the level of understanding and broaden horizons, which spur patriotism and engender pride. Television will revive the art of our people, bring scientific laboratories into the classrooms of our pupils, heighten the feeling of unity among the groups that make up our nation.

African, because Africa is a geographical entity with a common experience of oppression and exploitation.

Our television will be a weapon in the struggle for African unity. It will be a weapon in Africa's fight against imperialism. It will be a weapon in Africa's fight against imperialism, colonialism and neo-colonialism. It will resurrect forgotten glories of African history, of African culture. We shall attempt to organize a quick exchange of films with other African countries, and eventually have travelling news units all over Africa, disseminating news of Ghana and televising what is happening in our sister states.

Socialist, because our societies have been traditionally socialist and egalitarian, and because we have chosen socialism as the most just and efficient economic system. The socialist outlook will determine our judgment of events not only in Africa, but throughout the world. We shall oppose economic, political or military oppression of any peoples, and support the forces of progress against the forces of reaction.

GETTING TELEVISION TO THE PEOPLE

Television sets are relatively expensive. So how shall we get our television programmes to the people?

For one thing, the Government is interesting itself in seeing to it that the prices of sets are kept as low as possible.

But more importantly, Ghana Television will set up free Television Viewing Centres in the urban centres and remote villages of the country.

Everyone will be able to go to these centres and watch the daily programmes. Because television is essentially visual, its appeal will be immediate and universal. Since relatively few words are necessary for television, the language barrier will be less of a problem.

But we are taking steps to overcome this barrier, too. At the Viewing Centres, *monitors* who speak the local languages will be in charge. When necessary, these monitors can assume the roles of the *traditional Story Tellers,* and as the pictures unfold, displaying perhaps some near-forgotten chronicle of West Africa's history, the monitors will recite the story which is being played out by means of dance, music and pantomime.

In such instances, we shall be combining one of the oldest traditions of Ghana with this newest of scientific inventions.

PROGRAMMING

We went to the people to find out what they needed and wanted from Television.

During the last vacation period, students of the Kwame Nkrumah Ideological Institute and the Institute of Scientific Education at Kwame Nkrumah University made surveys in their home villages and rural areas.

With prepared questionnaires in their hands, they gathered information as to:

1. The particular needs of their communities.
2. How television could best serve these needs.
3. Facilities for setting up Television Viewing Centres.
4. Availability of electricity.
5. School and teaching facilities.
6. The basic languages of the communities.

On the basis of their findings and of our own planning, we have decided on the following.

We shall place emphasis on presenting the traditional fine arts—the skills of the wood sculptors, the gold and silver smiths, the potters and the weavers of old.

There will be fashion shows to permit our people to appreciate the beauty of traditional attire and hairstyles.

Established dramatic material is to be placed on TV tape and stored for use when we go into operation. Historical dramas and new plays concerning everyday life are now being rehearsed for presentation—and at the beginning we shall present one of these plays each month, increasing this cadence as the live theatre movement in Ghana grows.

The Cultural Liaison Officer of Ghana Television travels widely, explaining our aims and arousing interest in different groups. In Cape Coast, we discovered an extraordinarily talented family of artists who make puppets. We intend to create a puppet centre in Cape Coast, which will also serve television's needs. We shall use marionettes to interpret certain folkloric tales, such as Ananse (spider) stories of Ghana. Present plans call for three puppet shows per week, particularly for children.

In music, we shall try to extend the work begun by the School of Music of the Institute of African Studies. We intend to present classical Ghanaian and Western music, and traditional contemporary and popular Ghanaian music and dance.

The Ghana Institute of Art and Culture (GIAC) will mount at least one exhibition of arts and crafts in some part of the country each month. In addition, the GIAC and the University of Ghana Institute of Drama and Dancing are expected to provide some of the artists for our programmes.

The Ministries of Education and Social and Community Development have appointed special officers to work closely with TV. With their cooperation, we are organizing programmes to provide visual aids for teachers in polytechnical training and to open the eyes of students to the wonders of nature.

The Ghana Academy of Sciences will play an important role in supplying material for programmes on science, while the Institute of African Studies will help in the production of broadcasts on African history.

THE POWER OF TELEVISION

Television is the newest, the most powerful, the most direct means of communication devised by man. Its potentialities for good or for evil are boundless. In Britain, forty million persons watch TV news bulletins daily. This exceeds the combined circulation of all daily newspapers in London and the provinces.

The eye of the television camera is more penetrating, more accurate and quicker than the human eye. It can magnify the smallest object and bring it close to the viewer for examination. It can scan the skies and peer into the sea. It can enter the human body and search out disorders of any of the functions.

Through television, a transformation may be brought about in living conditions, in health, in agriculture, in all patterns of work. Television in fishing schooners will search through the waters and facilitate the taking on of loads. Television in factories will bring before the workers technological know-how which will speed up production.

Television will assist the schools in preparing Ghanaian children for service in a dynamic, forward-looking socialist state. The News Department will send reporters into every part of Ghana, and the inhabitants of seldom-visited villages of the interior will know, seeing themselves on the screen, that they are not forgotten. The eye of the camera will search for talent, for paintings and sculpturing, for singers. And TV will be political. Every television worker must desire and work for Socialism and for the Union Government of Africa.

Such is the power of television. Ghana Television, with its symbol of Ananse and its talking drums proclaiming "Ghana Calls," will send its beams of light as a unifying force for all Africa.

PROGRAMME DEPARTMENT

Television production has been described as "organized anarchy." This phrase perhaps better than most, describes the clash of artistic impulses and techno-logical disciplines which are the environment of the Programme Department. The ideas which are the life-springs of all television must be compromised within the strictures of a fixed pictorial format and most of all, time. In televi-sion we say, "every night is opening night."

What sets Ghana Television apart from most of its predecessors is at once a release and a challenge. It is not for the Programme Department of Ghana Television to pursue the capricious gods of "popularity." For us the words of the President ring crystal clear; our object is to, "serve," and not to, "sell." Our twenty trained and experienced Producers and equal number of Production Assistants, our Writers, Announcers and Artists can concentrate on a single objective; to educate and to edify.

School Telecasts, beginning in our morning schedule with an hour-and-a-half daily, will stress Science and Technology. Geography and English as well will be given priority and consideration. Our hand-in-glove cooperation with the Ministry of Education assures programmes which fit the need and suit the students.

Mass education, literacy training in particular, have longed for the pos-sibilities of a visual medium. Ghana Television has a regular programme scheduled to fulfil this basic need.

Cultural programmes from the rich legacy of African art and folklore will be given the support and dissemination that our new identity demands and a mass communication medium makes possible.

Notes

1 Alesia McFaddon, "The Artistry and Activism of Shirley Graham Du Bois: A Twentieth Century African Torchbearer" (PhD diss., University of Massachusetts Amherst, 2009), 259.
2 Gerald Horne, *Race Woman: The Lives of Shirley Graham Du Bois* (New York, NY: New York University Press, 2002), 96.
3 Shirley Graham Du Bois, "As a Man Thinketh in His Heart, So Is He," *The Parish News: Church of the Holy Trinity*, February 1954, Volume LVII, Number 4 edition, Box 27, Folder 3, Shirley Graham Du Bois Papers, Schlesinger Library, Cambridge, MA.
4 Ibid., 5.
5 "This is Ghana Television" (Tema, Ghana: The State Publishing Corporation, n.d.), 22, Box 44, Folder 6, Shirley Graham Du Bois Papers, Schlesinger Library, Cambridge, MA.
6 "WMEX Radio Interview: Negro History Month" (Boston, MA, February 18, 1950), Box 27, Folder 3, Shirley Graham Du Bois Papers, Schlesinger Library, Cambridge, MA.
7 Barbara Smith, "Toward a Black Feminist Criticism," *Conditions: Two* 1, no. 2 (1977): 25–44.

Bibliography

Graham Du Bois, Shirley. "5 Days That Made History." *Drum: Africa's Leading Magazine*, no. 149 (September, 1963): 9–14.

_____. "After Addis Ababa." *Freedomways* 3, no. 4 (1963): 471–485.

_____. "As a Man Thinketh in His Heart, So is He." *The Parish News: Church of the Holy Trinity*, February 1954, Volume LVII, Number 4 edition, Box 27, Folder 3, Shirley Graham Du Bois Papers, Schlesinger Library, Cambridge, MA.

_____. "Black Man's Music." *Crisis* 40, no. 8 (1933): 178–179.

_____. *Booker T. Washington, Educator of Hand, Head, and Heart.* New York, NY: Julian Messner, Inc., 1955.

_____. "The Burning of the Asqa Mosque." *Africa and the World* 6, no. 52 (1969): 18–20.

_____. "Cairo—Six Months after the Blitzkrieg." *Africa and the World* 4, no. 39 (1968): 20–24.

_____. "Centenary of Dr. W.E.B. Du Bois." *Africa and the World* 4, no. 44 (1968): 27–30.

_____. *Dr. George Washington Carver, Scientist,.* New York, NY: J. Messner, Inc., 1944.

_____. *Du Bois: A Pictorial Biography.* 1st ed. Chicago, IL: Johnson Pub. Co., 1978.

_____. "Egypt." In *Pan-Africanism*, 20–39. Indianapolis, IN: Bobbs-Merrill, 1974.

_____. "Emergence of the African Personality." *Mainstream* 13, no. 11 (n.d.): 25–31.

_____. *Gamal Abdel Nasser: Son of the Nile a Biography.* New York, NY: The Third Press, 1972.

_____. "A Ghanaian Questions All-India Radio." *Eastern Horizon* 7, no. 3 (1968): 49–52.

_____. "Guinea-Sierra Leone Pact Is a Step to African Unity." *Africa and the World* 3, no. 30 (1967): 10–11.

_____. "Heartwarming Memories." In *Paul Robeson*, ed. Brigitte Boegelsack. Berlin: Academy of Arts of the German Democratic Republic, 1978, 56.

_____. *His Day Is Marching On: A Memoir of W.E.B. Du Bois*. 1st ed. Philadelphia, PA: Lippincott, 1971.

_____. "It's a Journal!" *Freedomways: A Quarterly Review of the Negro Freedom Movement*, 1961.

_____. "It's Morning: A One-Act Play." In *Plays by American Women: 1930-1960*, ed. Judith E. Barlow, 235-262. New York, NY: Applause Books, 2001.

_____. *Jean Baptiste Pointe de Sable, Founder of Chicago*. New York, NY: Julian Messner, Inc., 1953.

_____. *Julius K. Nyerere: Teacher of Africa*. New York, NY: Julian Messner, Inc., 1975.

_____. "Kwame Nkrumah: African Liberator." *Freedomways* 12, no. 3 (1972): 197-206.

_____. "Kwame Nkrumah and Pan-Africa." *Pan-Africanist: A Quarterly Journal of the International Black Movement* 1, no. 1 (1972): 3-7.

_____. "Letter from Tashkent." *Mainstream* 11, no. 12 (1958): 16-21.

_____. "The Liberation of Africa: Power, Peace and Justice." *Black Scholar* 2, no. 6 (1971): 32-37.

_____. "The Little African Summit." *Africa and the World* 3, no. 31 (1967): 9-11.

_____. "Naïveté, The Story of Anne Royale." 1947. Box 38, Folder 1. Cambridge, MA: Schlesinger Library, Shirley Graham Du Bois Papers.

_____. "Nation Building in Ghana." *Freedomways* 2, no. 4 (1962): 371-376.

_____. "Negros Are Fighting for Freedom." *Common Sense* 12, no. 2 (1943): 45-50.

_____. "Negroes in the American Revolution." *Freedomways* 1, no. 2 (1961): 125-135.

_____. "Nkrumah's Record Speaks for Itself." *Africa and the World* 4, no. 42 (1968): 18-20.

_____. *Paul Robeson, Citizen of the World*. New York, NY: Julian Messner, Inc., 1946.

_____. "Return After Ten Years." *Freedomways* 11, no. 2 (1971): 158-169.

_____. "Review of Anna Louise Strong, The Stalin Era (Altadena: Today's Press, 1956)." *New World Review* 25, no. 2 (1957): 36-38.

_____. "Sierra Leone Throws Off Military Dictatorship." *Eastern Horizon* 7, no. 4 (1968): 53-58.

_____. *The Story of Phillis Wheatley*. New York: Julian Messner, Inc., 1969.

_____. *The Story of Pocahontas*. New York: Grosset & Dunlap, 1953.

_____. "Take Heart, My Brother!" *New World Review* 29, no. 4 (1961): 24-28.

_____. "There Can Be No Peace with Zionism." *Africa and the World* 6, no. 62 (1970): 13–15.

_____. "Together We Struggle, Together We Win." *Black Scholar* 6, no. 6 (1975): 36–40.

_____. "What Happened in Ghana?: The Inside Story." *Freedomways* 6, no. 2 (1966): 201–223.

_____. *Your Most Humble Servant.* New York: Simon & Schuster Trade, 1949.

_____. *Zulu Heart: A Novel.* New York: Third Press, 1974.

Horne, Gerald. *Race Woman: The Lives of Shirley Graham Du Bois.* New York: New York University Press, 2002.

McFaddon, Alesia. "The Artistry and Activism of Shirley Graham Du Bois: A Twentieth Century African Torchbearer." PhD diss., University of Massachusetts Amherst, 2009.

Perkins, Kathy A. "The Unknown Career of Shirley Graham." *Freedomways* 25, no. 1 (1985): 6–17.

Smith, Barbara. "Towards a Black Feminist Criticism." *Conditions: Two* 1, no. 2 (1977): 25–44.

"This is Ghana Television." Tema, Ghana: The State Publishing Corporation, n.d. 22, Box 44, Folder 6, Shirley Graham Du Bois Papers, Schlesinger Library, Cambridge, MA.

Van Der Horn-Gibson, Jodi. "Dismantling Americana: Sambo, Shirley Graham, and African Nationalism." *Americana: The Journal of American Popular Culture* 7, no. 1 (2008): n.p.

"WMEX Radio Interview: Negro History Month." February 18, 1950. Box 27, Folder 3, Shirley Graham Du Bois Papers, Schlesinger Library, Cambridge, MA.

Chapter 6
Herta Herzog (1910–2010)

By Elana Levine

Herta Herzog is a crucial figure in the histories of communication and media studies, and foundational to the field of audience research. Born and educated in Austria, Herzog spent most of her life in the United States, moving her career between academia and industry, exemplifying the fluidity of these realms in the mid-twentieth century. Herzog's work was shaped by potentially disparate influences, including critical social theory, empirical social science, and psychological inquiry. As both an academic and a market researcher, Herzog employed a range of methods to better understand the motivations and desires of audiences, but she is best known for her qualitative research on American radio listeners, especially the women who listened to daytime serials in the 1930s and 1940s. While she disavowed an affiliation with feminism, Herzog's willingness to take the perspectives of everyday audiences seriously, and to accord them agency in their engagement with denigrated, popular, and feminized media, set precedents for audience studies and for feminist media research more broadly, carrying into the second half of the twentieth century and the early decades of the twenty-first.

Herzog's contributions to audience research are multiple, not least because she was a scholar of methodological and theoretical diversity. While she drew on quantitative methods such as surveys, she regularly combined such information with qualitative analyses. As such, interviews and focus groups were key to Herzog's research. Indeed, Herzog was a pioneer in focus group methodology, which she employed in her market research work as well as in her academic studies.[1] Her investment in talking *to* audiences, in soliciting their own perspectives on their reactions and experiences, reflected her resistance to "hypodermic needle" theories of direct or universal media effects. As a consequence, present-day scholars associate her research most closely with uses and gratifications studies.[2]

Because Herzog persistently pursued questions of "how" and "why" as she sought to make sense of the people she studied, she allowed audiences to identify their own motivations and responses and analyzed these perspectives in relation to these individuals' life experiences.[3] At the same time, Herzog's analyses often contextualized individual reactions within broader social, cultural, and political forces.[4] These might be structural forces such as hierarchies of class or education, which helped her to explain a given listener's dependence on daytime serials or another's affinity with quiz show contestants. Or they might be historical variables, such as the emergence of World War II in Europe and its impact on American listeners' reactions to *The War of the Worlds*. Such analytical moves anticipate theories of audience advanced through approaches such as cultural studies, which would resist some of the individualist emphases of uses and gratifications work. In her later life, Herzog overtly employed cultural studies approaches, as in her exploration of responses to the American prime time serial, *Dallas*, by audiences in different national contexts.

Even as Herzog always validated the voices and perspectives of actual audiences, she also understood radio—the medium she focused on for much of her academic work—to be a powerful force that influenced behavior and beliefs. Her earlier research in particular demonstrates some engagement with critical theory and perspectives such as that of her fellow émigrés from the Frankfurt School. "On Borrowed Experience," her first study of daytime radio serial listeners, understands the audiences she studies as under the sway of an influential, commercial medium that hid its power through its deceptive appeals to emotion.[5] More typically, however, her work understood the impact of media to be a complex tension between top-down influence and individualized and contextualized reactions not only to media but to a host of social forces shaping media engagement. In these respects, Herzog's work models many of the very debates and theoretical conundrums of communications and media scholarship writ large. These debates were just emerging during Herzog's academic research but have since become more and more significant to these fields.

While Herzog's prescience is evident from the perspective of the present, she did not receive the recognition she deserved during her career. The best-known work in which she participated was the 1940 book, *The Invasion from Mars*. Though Herzog was the first researcher to interview listeners about their reaction to the Orson Welles broadcast, and was an active participant in the full study, its authorship is credited to Hadley Cantril, with Herzog and colleague Hazel Gaudet listed merely as providing "assistance."[6] Diminishing Herzog's and Gaudet's contributions in this way was typical of the lower status of women in research environments of the time and is especially egregious here, given Herzog's initiating role in this project and the project's long-term renown. In addition, scholars have found that Herzog was paid less than her male colleagues at the Princeton Radio Research Project.[7] And, while Robert Merton is largely labeled as the founder of focus group methodology, some have argued that Herzog well preceded him in developing it.[8]

Given the poor recognition she received in the academic sphere, it may not be surprising that Herzog left the Office of Radio Research in 1943 to work in market research at the advertising agency McCann-Erickson. There, she was associated with the rise of "MR," or Motivational Research, the mid-century trend that drew on Freudian psychoanalysis and that was most closely associated with American psychologist and market researcher Ernest Dichter. As had been the case in her academic work, Herzog understood the motivations of consumers in more nuanced terms than did Dichter-style MR. Most significantly, she was not as convinced of consumers' manipulability, a perspective in keeping with her careful attention to audience perspectives as a radio researcher. In her advertising agency career, Herzog made significant inroads in exploring the concept of "brand image," and continued to seek an understanding of *why* audiences behaved as they did, dissatisfied with more facile approaches.[9] Ultimately, and like other women described in *The Ghost Reader*, Herzog was able to achieve more status and recognition in private industry than she had in academia.

Herta Herzog's broad spheres of influence, the longevity of her career, and the generosity of perspective she brought to her analyses of audiences and consumers have made her a foundational figure in media and communication research. Even as scholars increasingly have recognized her contributions, her work bears further study, just as her model of intellectual curiosity and analytical depth bears greater imitation.

Excerpt: Herzog, Herta, "What Do We Really Know about Daytime Serial Listeners?" In *Radio Research 1942–1943*, ed. Paul F. Lazarsfeld and Frank N. Stanton (New York: Duell, Sloan and Pearce, 1944) (permission Robert Lazarsfeld and Simon & Schuster)

Contributor's note: Footnotes from the original. I have preserved the style of the original notes.

A preliminary study based on 100 intensive interviews[1] suggests three major types of gratification experienced by listeners to daytime serials. Some listeners seem to enjoy the serials merely as a means of emotional release. They like "the chance to cry" which the serials provide; they enjoy "the surprises, happy or sad." The opportunity for expressing aggressiveness is also

---

1 Cf. H. Herzog, "On Borrowed Experience," *Studies in Philosophy and Social Science* 9, no. 1 (1941): 65–95.

a source of satisfaction. Burdened with their own problems, listeners claim that it "made them feel better to know that other people have troubles, too."

[...]

The observations in this preliminary case survey were so striking that it was decided to test the matter on a larger scale. Therefore, in the summer of 1942, the respondents in the Iowa survey who listen to daytime serials were asked the following question:

Do these programs help *you* to deal better with the problems in your own everyday life?

[...]

Of some 2,500 listeners, 41 per cent claimed to have been helped and only 28 per cent not to have been helped. The remainder held that they had never thought about it that way or that they did not know, or refused to answer the question.

On the basis of numerous tabulations designed to identify the types of women who consider themselves "helped" by listening to radio serials, two conclusions can be drawn. The less formal education a woman has, the more is she likely to consider these programs helpful. This corroborates a previous observation that less-educated women probably have fewer sources from which to learn "how to win friends and influence people" and are therefore more dependent upon daytime serials for these ends.

[...]

But these overall figures do not yet give us a clear idea of what women mean when they talk about such "help." For the respondents in the Iowa survey, we have no additional information. We can, however, draw upon the results of some 150 case studies of serial listeners in New York and Pittsburgh. Interviewers[2] were instructed to obtain complete examples of advice gleaned from daytime serials. They were cautioned to secure accounts of concrete experiences and not rest content with general assertions of aid derived from serials.

Judging from this information, the spheres of influence exerted by the serials are quite diversified. The listeners feel they have been helped by being told how to get along with other people, how to "handle" their husbands or their boyfriends, how to "bring up" their children.

---

2 For the interviews we are indebted to Mrs. Clare Marks Horowitz of the Pennsylvania College for Women and to Mrs. Jeannette K. Green of Columbia University's Office of Radio Research.

I think Papa David helped me to be more cheerful when Fred, my husband, comes home. I feel tired and instead of being grumpy, I keep on the cheerful side. *The Goldbergs* are another story like that. Mr. Goldberg comes home scolding and he never meant it. I sort of understand Fred better because of it. When he starts to shout, I call him Mr. Goldberg. He comes back and calls me Molly. Husbands do not really understand what a wife goes through. These stories have helped me to understand that husbands are like that. If women are tender, they are better off. I often feel that if my sister had had more tenderness she would not be divorced today. I saw a lot of good in that man.

[...]

The listeners feel they have learned how to express themselves in a particular situation.

When Clifford's wife died in childbirth the advice Paul gave him I used for my nephew when his wife died.

They have learned how to accept old age or a son going off to the war.

I like Helen Trent. She is a woman over 35. You never hear of **her** dyeing her hair! She uses charm and manners to entice men and she **does.** If she can do it, why can't I? I am fighting old age, and having a terrible time. Sometimes I am tempted to go out and fix my hair. These stories give me courage and help me realize I have to accept it.

[...]

They get advice on how to comfort themselves when they are worried.

It helps you to listen to these stories. When Helen Trent has serious trouble she takes it calmly. So you think you'd better be like her and not get upset.

They are in a position to advise others by referring them to the stories.

I always tell the woman upstairs who wants my advice, to listen to the people on the radio because they are smarter than I am. She is worried because she did not have any education and she figures that if her daughter grows up, she would be so much smarter than she was. I told her to listen to *Aunt Jenny* to learn good English. Also, you can learn refinement from *Our Gal Sunday*. I think if I told her to do something and something would happen, I would feel guilty. If it happens from the story, then it is nobody's fault.

The desire to learn from the programs is further confirmed by the fact that one-third of 100 listeners specified problems which they would like to have presented in a serial. A few quotations will serve to illustrate these choices:

> [...]
>
> I should like to know how much a daughter should give her mother from the money she makes. I give everything I earn to my mother. Do I have to?
>
> Whether I should marry if I have to live with my mother-in-law. A story which would teach people not to put things over.
>
> About religious and racial differences.

Unquestionably then, many listeners turn to the stories for advice and feel they get it. Nonetheless, the matter is not quite so simple as it seems.

A question suggested by the quoted comments concerns the adequacy of the aid and comfort. The woman who has learned to deprive her children of something rather than "to slap them" seems to be substituting one procedure for the other without an understanding of the underlying pedagogical doctrine. It is doubtful whether the relationship between a wife and her husband is put on a sounder and more stable basis when she has learned to realize that "men do not understand what their wives have to go through." One might wonder how much the bereaved nephew appreciated, at his wife's death, the speech his aunt had borrowed from her favorite story.

A second question concerns the extent of the influence. Frequently the advice seems confined to good intentions without any substantial influence on basic attitudes. An example of this may be found in the following remarks of a woman who listens to serials because the people in them are so "wonderful":

> They teach you how to be good. I have gone through a lot of suffering but I still can learn from them.

Yet, this same woman, when asked whether she disliked any program, answered:

> I don't listen to *The Goldbergs*. Why waste electricity on the Jews?

Obviously, the "goodness" she was "learning" had not reached the point of materially affecting her attitude towards a minority group. In the same context, we may note that the advice derived from a serial is often doled out to other people, to sisters, or neighbors, thus providing the listener with the status of an adviser without its responsibilities.

Thirdly, the women who claim to have profited from the serials frequently think of quite unrealistic situations. Thus, one listener felt she had learned considerably from a story in which the heroine suddenly came into a great deal of money; the story character was concerned with keeping her children from profligate waste. Although the listener felt there was no prospect of ever having so much money herself, nonetheless she considered that this episode offered valuable advice:

It is a good idea to know and to be prepared for what I would do with so much money. Very likely, the advice obtained from that story served as a substitute for the condition of its applicability. Similarly, the wishful thinking connected with such "potential" advice is brought out in the following account of a young housekeeper:

I learn a lot from these stories. I often figure if anything like that happened to me what I would do. Who knows if I met a crippled man, would I marry him? If he had money I would. In this story *(Life Can Be Beautiful)*, he was a lawyer, so it was really quite nice. These stories teach you how things come out all right.

The overall formula for the help obtained from listening seems to be in terms of "how to take it." This is accomplished in various ways. The *first* of these is outright wishful thinking. The stories "teach" the Panglossian doctrine that "things come out all right." In a less extreme form, a claim on a favorable turn of events is established by the listener's taking a small preliminary step which accords with a pattern established in a serial. This may be illustrated by the following comment of a middle-aged listener:

In *Helen Trent* the girl Jean is in love with this playwright. She used to be fat and he did not pay any attention to her. [...] I am fat and I got to get thin. That story taught me that it is dangerous to reduce all by yourself. Helen Trent took that girl to a doctor. That's just what I did. I went to the doctor last night. I am going to start the diet next week.

This listener actually saw a doctor about her weight. She postponed starting her diet for "next week." By following the serial's "advice" to this extent, she seems to feel assured of having taken sufficient steps to guarantee herself a result as romantic as that in the serial. (By reducing, Jean, the story character, won the love of a man who had not cared for her before.)

A *second* way in which the listeners are helped to accept their fate is by learning to project blame upon others. Thus one of the previously quoted listeners obtains "adjustment" to her marital problems by finding out that husbands never understand their wives. *Thirdly*, the listeners learn to take things by obtaining a ready-made formula of behavior which simply requires application. References such as "Don't slap your children, but deprive them of something" characterize this type of learning. Listeners, worried about problems confronting them, learn to take things "calmly," not to get "excited" about them. As one person said:

[...] Calmness in the face of crises is certainly a useful attitude. However, it is not always sufficient for a solution of the problems.

These data point to the great social responsibility of those engaged in the writing of daytime serials. There can be no doubt that a large proportion of the listeners take these programs seriously and seek to apply what they hear in them to their own personal lives. Much of this application seems somewhat dubious if measured by the yardstick of real mastery of personal problems. No mass communication can fully safeguard itself against abused application. On the other hand, the argument that the primary purpose of daytime serials is entertainment rather than education does not apply here. The writers of daytime serials must live up to the obligations to which the influence of their creations, however unintended, commits them. Both the obligation and the opportunity for its successful execution seem particularly great in these times of war.

Notes

1 Allison L. Rowland and Peter Simonson, "The Founding Mothers of Communication Research: Toward a History of a Gendered Assemblage," *Critical Studies in Media Communication* 31, no. 1 (2014): 11–12.
2 Peter Simonson, "Herta Herzog and the Founding Mothers of Mass Communication Research," in *What Do We Really Know About Herta Herzog?*, ed. Elisabeth Klaus and Josef Seethaler (Frankfurt: Peter Lang, 2016), 70; David L. Swanson, "Understanding Audiences: Continuing Contributions of Gratifications Research," *Poetics* 21, no. 4 (1992): 306–307.
3 We can see similar practices for other researchers in this volume, including Marie Jahoda (Chapter 8) and Eleanor Leacock (Chapter 13).
4 Susan J. Douglas, *Listening In: Radio and the American Imagination* (New York, NY: Times Books, 1999), 144.
5 Tamar Liebes, "Herzog's 'On Borrowed Experience': Its Place in the Debate over the Active Audience," in *Canonic Texts in Media Research*, ed. Elihu Katz, John Durham Peters, Tamar Liebes and Avril Orloff, 39–53 (Cambridge: Polity Press, 2003).
6 Jefferson Pooley and Michael J. Socolow, "War of the Words: The *Invasion from Mars* and Its Legacy for Mass Communication Scholarship," in *War of the Worlds to Social Media: Mediated Communication in Times of Crisis*, ed. Joy Elizabeth Hayes, Kathleen Battles, and Wendy Hilton-Morrow, 35–36 (New York, NY: Peter Lang, 2013).
7 Martina Thiele, "A Female Researcher but not a Feminist," in *What Do We Really Know About Herta Herzog?*, ed. Elisabeth Klaus and Josef Seethaler (Frankfurt: Peter Lang, 2016), 156.
8 Simonson, "Herta Herzog and the Founding Mothers," 70–72.
9 Ibid., 74–75.

Bibliography

Cantril, Hadley, with Hazel Gaudet and Herta Herzog. *The Invasion from Mars: A Study in the Psychology of Panic*. Princeton, NJ: Princeton University Press, 1940.

Douglas, Susan J. *Listening In: Radio and the American Imagination*. New York, NY: Times Books, 1999.

Herzog, Herta. "Behavioral Science Concepts for Analyzing the Consumer." In *Marketing and the Behavioral Sciences: Selected Readings*, ed. Perry Bliss, 76-87. Boston, MA: Allyn and Bacon, 1963.

_____. *Children and Their Leisure Time Listening to the Radio: A Survey of the Literature in the Field*. New York, NY: Bureau of Applied Social Research, 1941.

_____. "The Jews as 'Others': On Communicative Aspects of Antisemitism. A Pilot Study in Austria." *Analysis of Current Trends in Antisemitism*, no. 4 (1994). Jerusalem: Vidal Sassoon International Center for the Study of Antisemitism, Hebrew University. https://sicsa.huji. ac.il/publications/acta-no-4, accessed April 9, 2023.

_____. "Listener Mail to the *Voice of America*." *Public Opinion Quarterly* 16, no. 4 (1952): 607-611.

_____. "On Borrowed Experience: An Analysis of Listening to Daytime Sketches." *Studies in Philosophy and Social Science* 9, no. 1 (1941): 65-95.

_____. "Professor Quiz: A Gratification Study." In *Radio and the Printed Page: An Introduction to the Study of Radio and its Role in the Communication of Ideas*, ed. Paul F. Lazarsfeld, 64-93. New York, NY: Duell, Sloan and Pearce, 1940.

_____. "What Do We Really Know about Daytime Serial Listeners?" In *Radio Research 1942-1943*, ed. Paul F. Lazarsfeld and Frank N. Stanton, 3-33. New York, NY: Duell, Sloan and Pearce, 1944.

_____. "Why did People Believe in the Invasion from Mars? In *The Language of Social Research: A Reader in the Methodology of Social Research*, ed. Paul. F. Lazarsfeld and Morris Rosenberg, 420-428. New York, NY: Free Press, 1955.

Herzog Massing, Herta. "Decoding Dallas." *Society* 24, no. 1 (1986): 74-77.

Liebes, Tamar. "Herzog's 'On Borrowed Experience': Its Place in the Debate over the Active Audience." In *Canonic Texts in Media Research*, ed. Elihu Katz, John Durham Peters, Tamar Liebes and Avril Orloff, 39-53. Cambridge, MA: Polity Press, 2003.

Pooley, Jefferson and Michael J. Socolow. "War of the Words: The *Invasion from Mars* and Its Legacy for Mass Communication Scholarship." In *War of the Worlds to Social Media: Mediated Communication in Times of Crisis*, ed. Joy Elizabeth Hayes, Kathleen Battles, and Wendy Hilton-Morrow, 35-56. New York, NY: Peter Lang, 2013.

Rowland, Allison L. and Peter Simonson. "The Founding Mothers of Communication Research: Toward a History of Gendered Assemblage." *Critical Studies in Media Communication* 31, no. 1 (2014): 3-26.

Simonson, Peter. "Herta Herzog and the Founding Mothers of Mass Communication Research." In *What Do We Really Know About Herta Herzog?*, ed. Elisabeth Klaus and Josef Seethaler, 61–84. Frankfurt: Peter Lang, 2016.

Swanson, David L. "Understanding Audiences: Continuing Contributions of Gratifications Research," *Poetics* 21, no. 4 (1992): 305–328.

Thiele, Martina. "A Female Researcher but not a Feminist." In *What Do We Really Know About Herta Herzog?*, ed. Elisabeth Klaus and Josef Seethaler (Frankfurt: Peter Lang, 2016).

Wyant, Rowena and Herta Herzog. "Voting via the Senate Mailbag: Part II." *Public Opinion Quarterly* 5, no. 4 (1941): 590–624.

Chapter 7

Emma "Mae" Dena Solomon Huettig Churchill (1911–1996)

By Aimee-Marie Dorsten

Mae Dena Huettig Churchill (permission of Robert Churchill)

Mae D. Huettig was the first scholar to analyze the centrality of micro and macroeconomics in the US filmmaking industry; she was also rumored to be one of the ten most subversive people of the McCarthy era. Huettig's formative text, *Economic Control of the Motion Picture Industry: A Study in Industrial Organization* (1944) exemplifies her keen ability to plot points illuminating the nexus of control and power: either in data as a progressive economist and film historian, or between people as a labor organizer, spy, and civil rights activist. Using forensic accounting and critical industrial analysis, *Economic Control* exposed the interdependent relationship between film production, distribution, exhibition, and studio financials (such as real estate) key to corporate Hollywood's survival at a critical juncture: the 1948 Paramount Decree antitrust case. Analyzing the "big eight"[1] movie studios' oligopolistic strangle-hold over film, *Economic Control* is precedential for critical media studies, media economics, labor and organization studies, political economy of communication, media sociology, and communication law scholars.[2] Indeed, Huettig's critique of capitalistic corporate media remains radical.

Born Emma Dena Solomon (but called Mae) in Michigan in 1911 to Russian émigré anarchist parents, Huettig's family settled in the Mexican-American Boyle Heights neighborhood of Los Angeles.[3] A precocious undergraduate, Huettig earned her bachelor's degree in economics on scholarship from UCLA in 1931 at age 19. At 21, she married German emigrant Lester Huettig and began graduate work at the University of Pennsylvania Wharton School Industrial Research Unit (IRU). In the mid-1930s, the IRU was Marxist in orientation; it piqued Huettig's interest in critical industrial organization. Unfortunately, Huettig endured chronic harassment from the FBI for her IRU connections, her relationship with first husband Lester (accused of being a Russian spy), her union labor organizing work, and her Communist Party membership.[4]

Huettig researched *Economic Control* under the aegis of the Motion Picture Research Project (MPRP), directed by Leo C. Rosten, a Yiddish satirist who dabbled briefly in sociological analysis of the film industry with *Hollywood: The Movie Colony, the Movie Makers.*[5] Huettig became the MPRP's economist in 1939. She charted scarcity, efficiency, opportunity costs, and gains of the film industry recovering from the Great Depression. As one of several assistants at the MPRP, Huettig developed sustained relationships with other economists, US policymakers, and studio executives involved in the Hollywood antitrust litigation.

Economic Control is heavily quantitative, laced with critical qualitative interpretation. Studying the data, Huettig observed that Hollywood's productive creativity was limited by "film distributors and exhibitors, rather than filmmakers."[6] While others studied Hollywood's control mechanisms, Huettig alone asserted the studio system impacted the kind and quality of films made and exhibited; she was inspired by its poorer quality products, which she frequently critiqued. *Economic Control* demonstrates how low quality was "baked into" films even in the industry's infancy. Fiscally conservative, vertically integrated trusts and rigid production values were historically characteristic because demand often outstripped supply, and camera and projector equipment remained prohibitively expensive. Thus, "demands for better quality [...] were met by the argument" that consumers, "tasked with absorbing increased admission prices," would reject improved production.[7] The conclusion to *Economic Control* warns that the status quo was the most significant threat to the creative and economic health of the industry.

Economic Control is prescient for thinking of the 1940s Hollywood system industrially, just like coal or automobiles. But Huettig said her initial research demonstrated that film illuminated a fact about *all* industries: that one element could not be examined in a vacuum—say, studio system film production—in order to understand the product. Instead, the industry must be understood as an economic "maze of intricate relationships" that included distribution and exhibition.[8] In hindsight, the legacy of Huettig's work applies beyond film to all media industries.

Huettig worked as the MPRP's economist for just over two years (1939–1941). Both a blessing and a curse, Huettig's MPRP stint provided information for her analysis—such as unpublished data provided by Isador Lubin, commissioner of the Bureau of Labor Statistics, as well as other agencies that gathered data in preparation for the antitrust legislation against the largest studios. Yet Rosten claimed he had "proprietary right to the research data she had collected," and cherry-picked from her data for his own book, *Hollywood: The Movie Colony, The Movie Makers* (1941).[9] While Rosten credited Huettig with "invaluable analysis of the economic and financial structure of the motion picture industry," he also held her research hostage until such time as he decided not to use it, asserting future volumes of *Hollywood* would focus on economics.[10] Rosten was demonstrative of the control those in power can exert; fortunately, Huettig also found others to network with while inhabiting a nucleus of those opposing the dominance of big Hollywood.

Following her departure from the MPRP, Huettig completed her PhD in 1942. Her dissertation ultimately became *Economic Control* in 1944, but it turned out to be Huettig's only foray into film studies (with occasional excerpts published as a book chapter in the edited books of other authors).[11] Yet, as the only integrated economic analysis of Hollywood published prior to the Paramount Decree, *Economic Control* was likely influential in the government's decision to force distribution and exhibition divestiture on the major studios in 1948.

By the time of her PhD graduation in 1942, Huettig had become president of Diamond Productions, Inc. an industrial tool company in Manhattan.[12] She also worked intermittently at The Twentieth Century Fund, a progressive policy think-tank for economic, racial, and gender equity in education, health care, and work, under economist J. Frederic Dewhurst, where she analyzed corporate pay structures and stocks. She also still taught occasionally at the IRU.

Ultimately, Huettig's close relationships with governmental officials were touched with irony: her 1996 *Los Angeles Times* obituary describes her as "often at odds with law enforcement authorities and others with government power."[13] Huettig (and her family) were subject to both FBI and House Un-American Activities Committee surveillance for over a decade, beginning in 1941.[14] Huettig and her first husband, Lester (who was employed at the Remington Arms munition factory in New York), were suspected of sharing information about arms production and management with Russia. But even after Huettig divorced Lester and married filmmaker Robert Churchill (with whom she had two children), surveillance continued and intensified. According to Huettig's daughter, they were forced to relocate to Ojai Valley from Los Angeles.[15]

No longer working for industry or in labor organizing, by 1985 Huettig forged other kinds of alliances against structural injustice: she founded the nonprofit watchdog organization Election Watch, which was critical of the electronic voting industry. As a quasi-media activist, she also trained minority youths to use film as a means to monitor and publicize police misconduct after the 1965 Watts riots. An activist in the fight against malfeasance, in 1996 Huettig successfully litigated to disband the Los Angeles Police Department's Public Disorder and Intelligence Division. She also worked against school segregation, police abuse, and police corruption until her death at the age of 84.[16] In memory of her legacy, the University of Wisconsin at Madison endowed a professorship in her name: The Mae D. Huettig Professor of Communication Arts.

Excerpt: Huettig, Mae D., *Economic Control of the Motion Picture Industry: A Study in Industrial Organization* (Philadelphia: University of Pennsylvania Press, 1944) (permission University of Pennsylvania Press)

Contributor's note: Footnotes from the original. I have preserved the style of the original notes.

II
THE MOTION PICTURE INDUSTRY TODAY
SOME QUESTIONS TO BE ANSWERED

Despite the glamour of Hollywood, the crux of the motion picture industry is the theatre. It is in the brick-and-mortar branch of the industry that most of the money is invested and made. Without understanding this fact, devotees of the film are likely to remain forever baffled by some characteristics of an industry which is in turn exciting, perplexing, and irritating. Emphasis on the economic role of the theatre is not meant to belittle the film itself. Obviously, it is the film which draws people to the theatre. Nevertheless, the structure of the motion picture industry (a large inverted pyramid, top-heavy with real estate and theatres, resting on a narrow base of the intangibles which constitute films) has had far-reaching effects on the film itself.

[...]

But the facts indicate clearly that there is a connection between the form taken by the film and the mechanics of the business, even if the connection is somewhat obscure. It is true, as one student has pointed out, that "the issues involved are not peculiar to the motion picture history."[1] Despite this lack of uniqueness, the problems of organization, intercorporate relationships, and financial policy in the motion picture industry deserve more than passing mention. The attitude of the industry itself toward discussion of these problems has not been completely candid.[2] A great reluctance to disclose faculty information with respect to its operations has unfortunately characterized most of the leaders of the industry.

Among the many questions which lack a reliable answer are: How many people attend movies? How often? How large is the industry in terms of invested capital and volume of business? What is the annual income of all theatres? How many theatres are owned by what group? What type of film is most uniformly successful? What is the relationship between the cost of films and their drawing power? Little is known of the industry's place in the broader pattern of American industry, or its method of solving the specialized problems of commercial entertainment. There are few reliable statistics available (and of these none is compiled by the industry itself) with regard to these questions.

WHAT IS THE ECONOMIC IMPORTANCE OF THE INDUSTRY?

There are various ways of measuring the role of an industry in our economy. The indices most commonly used are: (1) volume of business, (2) invested capital, and (3) number of employees. The value of such criteria is limited, since comparison between all types of industries produces results too general to be significant. However, in the case of the motion picture industry, these

---

1 Howard T. Lewis, *The Motion Picture Industry*, p.13.

2 Lewis points out that the industry has made no real attempt to give the public any thorough-going, unbiased discussion of its organization, operation, or profits and that such information as has been given has been frankly unbiased and intended primarily to promote friendly public relations. *Ibid.*, Introduction, p. x.

indices are valuable as a means of delimiting its economic importance and recording some basic information regarding its size.

[...]

Here, then, let it be noted that in so far as size of industry is measured by dollar volume of business, the motion picture industry is not only not among the first ten, it is not even among the first forty. It is surpassed by such industries, to name only a few, as laundries, hotels, restaurants, loan companies, investment trusts, liquor, tobacco, and musical instruments.

[...]

When motion picture corporations are compared with those in other branches of the entertainment field, another story is presented. The entire field of commercial amusement, including billiard halls, bowling alleys, dance halls, etc., is dominated by the motion picture industry.[3] Motion picture corporations, constituting 44 per cent of the total number of amusement corporations in 1937, accounted for 78 per cent of the gross income and 92 per cent of the total net income of the group. This should prove what has long been suspected and probably needs little proof: that movies are the favorite form of entertainment for most Americans.

PRODUCTION VERSUS EXHIBITION

From the point of view of the movie-going public, one of the most important questions about the industry is: Who decides what films are made; or as it is more commonly put, why are films what they are? From the industry's point of view, too, this question of the kind of product released is ultimately its most important single problem. Quality of product is increasingly vital now that the motion picture business is settling down into a semblance of middle age, devoid of the novelty appeal it formerly had.

The answer to the question posed above is in the relationship between the various branches of the industry. By virtue of the division of labor within the business, film distributors and exhibitors are much more closely in touch with the movie-going public than are the producers, and they trade heavily on their advantageous positions. From their seat in the box office they

---

3 In 1938, amusement corporations constituted roughly 2 per cent of the entire number of active corporations filing income tax returns. The gross income of all amusement corporations was slightly over $1 billion, or less than 1 per cent of the total gross income ($120 billion) of all corporations filing return. Net income (less deficit) of amusement corporations was $52 million. Bureau of Internal Revenue, *Statistics of Income, 1939.*

announce that so-and-so is "poison at the box office," that what the public wants is musicals or blood-and-thunder westerns, that English stars murder business, and that sophisticated farce comedies leave their audiences completely cold.

Broadly speaking, and omitting the relatively unimportant independent producers, the relationship between the three branches of the industry may be described in two ways. First, there is the relationship between a major producer and theatre operators not affiliated with his company. Secondly, there is a relationship within a major company between the various departments of production, distribution, and exhibition. The intra-company relationship is the more important with respect to the kind of films made, since contact within the organization is much closer than contact between the unaffiliated exhibitors and producers. The unaffiliated exhibitors are not generally consulted by producers with respect to the nature of the films to be made. However, they occasionally make their views known through advertisements in the trade press and probably express their opinions quite freely in talking with the sales representatives of the producers. Most of their arguments are ex post facto, however, and affect the future line-up of product negatively, or not at all.

On the other hand, the sales and theatre people within the integrated companies are extremely important in determining the type of picture to be made, the number of pictures in each cost class, the type of story, etc. It is not intended to give here a detailed account of the manner in which these decisions are reached, but in general the procedure is as follows: The person in charge of distribution announces the number of films wanted for the following season. This figure is presumably based on some estimate of what can be profitably sold, but it is also related to the needs of the company's own theatres for product. The chief executive announces the amount of money available for the total product. The amounts vary among the individual companies from $7 or $8 million for the smaller companies to $28 million for Loew's. The next step is the division and allocation of the total amount to groups of pictures. The names given these classes vary, but the grouping is in accordance with the quality to be aimed at as defined by the amount of money to be spent. That is, there are the "specials" and the more ordinary "program" features. There are "A" pictures and "B" pictures. The latter are designed, more or less frankly, to meet the need for the lesser half of the double-feature program. Once the allocation of production funds is made, the next step is that of determining the budgets for the individual picture with each group. The amount spent on a given picture presumably relates in some way to the anticipated drawing power of the particular combination of talent and production values planned for the given picture.[4] After the detailed budget is worked out, a tentative release schedule is prepared for the use of the sales force (distribution). From this point on the problems belong primarily to the production department.

Note what this cursory outline reveals. Company executives, i.e., theatre, sales, and production people, determine the following: the number of pictures to be made, the total amount of money to be spent, the distribution of the funds between the various classes of pictures, the budgets of the individual pictures, and the dates when the pictures are to be finished.

[...]

The objective factors are found in a prosaic listing of the various sources of income to the five principal companies. In approximate order of importance, they are: (1) theatre admissions, (2) film rentals, (3) the sale of film accessories, and (4) dividends from affiliated companies. The relative importance of each source varies for the individual majors, but in almost every instance the chief single source of income is theatre admissions. Although there is an inseparable connection between the quality of films and company earnings from film rentals and theatres, the division of functions within the company structure operates to give the preponderance of power to those nearest the principal source of income, i.e., the theatres. Furthermore, the earning power of a given chain of theatres depends not so much upon the quality of films made by its parent company as on the quality of films in general. If successful films are available, the dominant group of affiliated theatres in a given area generally has preferential access to them, regardless of which major produced them. [...] This interdependence seems a unique characteristic of the motion picture business. In other industries, an exceptionally good product is feared and disliked by other producers or sellers of similar goods. But of the small groups of dominant movie companies, it is really true that the good of one is the good of all.

The production and exhibition phases of the business behave toward each other like a chronically quarrelsome but firmly married couple and not without reason. The exhibitor group controls the purse strings; it accounts for more than nine-tenths of the invested capital and approximately two-thirds of the industry's income. Nevertheless, it requires films. Consequently, the

---

4 It is claimed by the people within the industry that an accurate estimate can be made of what any given picture will gross if the talent is known. This seems doubtful in view of the great number of unknowns affecting public taste for films, but some students of the industry apparently accept this hypothesis. See, for example, Lewis, *op. cit.*, p. 39, where he states that the budget of individual pictures were based on statistical knowledge of the starring artist's value as a box office attraction.

conflict between the two groups more nearly resembles a family quarrel than is ordinarily true of trade disputes, since the essential interdependence between production and exhibition is recognized by all. To a theatre operator there is no substitute for "celluloid." Conversely, the producers of movies have no real alternative to the theatres as outlets for their products. The normal interdependency between supplier and customer is accentuated in the motion picture industry by the combination of functions within the same corporate framework. But difficulty results from the fact that while the selling of entertainment is a commercial process, making films is largely creative and artistic in nature. Movie-makers, like artists in other fields, are generally inclined to experiment with new techniques and are not above wanting to interpret or affect their surroundings. Exhibitors, on the other hand, may not know much about the art of the film, but they know what has been good box office before. Consequently, theirs is the conservative influence; they are the traditionalists of the trade, exerting their influence in the direction of the safe-and-sound in film making.

Notes

1 The "big eight" motion picture studios included Metro-Goldwyn-Mayer, Paramount Picture Corporation, Twentieth Century Fox Film Corporation, Warner Brothers, RKO Pictures, Universal Pictures, United Artists, and Columbia Pictures.
2 For example, see Janet Wasko, "Critiquing Hollywood: The Political Economy of Motion Pictures," in *A Concise Handbook of Movie Industry Economics*, ed. Charles C. Moul (Cambridge: Cambridge University Press, 2005), 5–31; Janet Wasko, "Learning from the History of the Field," *Media Industries* 1, no. 3 (2015): 67–70. See also J.C. Strick, "The Economics of the Motion Picture Industry: A Survey," *Philosophy of the Social Sciences* 8 (1978): 406–417; Stanley I. Ornstein, "Motion Picture Distribution, Film Splitting, and Antitrust Policy," *Hastings Communications and Entertainment Law Journal* 17, no. 2 (1994): 415–444.
3 Joan and Jim Churchill, email to author, March 24, 2021.
4 Ibid.
5 Margalit Fox, "Leo Rosten, a Writer Who Helped Yiddish Make Its Way Into English, is Dead at 88," *New York Times*, February 20, 1997.
6 Aimee-Marie Dorsten, "'Thinking Dirty: Digging up Three Founding 'Matriarchs' of Communication Studies," *Communication Theory* 22 (2012): 25–47.
7 Mae D. Huettig, *Economic Control of the Motion Picture Industry: A Study in Industrial Organization* (Philadelphia: University of Pennsylvania Press, 1944), 18.
8 Ibid., v.
9 Wyatt Phillips, "'A Maze of Intricate Relationships': Mae D. Huettig and Early Forays into Film Industry Studies," *Film History* 27, no. 1 (2015): 150.
10 Leo C. Rosten, *Hollywood: The Movie Colony, the Movie Makers* (New York, NY: Harcourt, Brace, and Company, 1941), vii.
11 See, for example, Tino T. Balio, *The American Film Industry* (Madison, WI: University of Wisconsin Press, 1985).

12 Letter, Mae Huettig to Isador Lubin, March 10, 1942, Series: 2: Personal Correspondence (1935–1971), Box 53, Folder 4: Mae Huettig, Isador Lubin Papers (1896–1978), Franklin D. Roosevelt Presidential Library, Hyde Park, New York.

13 "Mae Churchill; Activist for Privacy and Other Civil Rights," *Los Angeles Times*, February 10, 1996, www.latimes.com/archives/la-xpm-1996-02-10-mn-34342-story.html, accessed April 11, 2022.

14 Daniel Eagan, "Joan Churchill, ASC—An Evolving Eye," *American Cinematographer,* https://ascmag.com/articles/joan-churchill-asc-an-evolving-eye, accessed July 14, 2020.

15 Ibid.

16 "Mae Churchill," *Los Angeles Times.*

Bibliography

Balio, Tino T. *The American Film Industry*. Madison, WI: University of Wisconsin Press, 1985.

Dorsten, Aimee-Marie. "'Thinking Dirty: Digging up Three Founding 'Matriarchs' of Communication Studies." *Communication Theory* 22 (2012): 25–47.

Eagan, Daniel. "Joan Churchill, ASC—An Evolving Eye." *American Cinematographer*, November 9, 2018. https://ascmag.com/articles/joan-churchill-asc-an-evolving-eye, accessed April 11, 2022.

Fox, Margalit. "Leo Rosten, a Writer Who Helped Yiddish Make Its Way into English, is Dead at 88." *New York Times*, February 20, 1997. www.nytimes.com/1997/02/20/books/leo-rosten-a-writer-who-helped-yiddish-make-its-way-into-english-is-dead-at-88.html, accessed April 11, 2022.

Huettig, Mae D. *Economic Control Motion Picture Industry: A Study in Industrial Organization*. Philadelphia, PA: University of Pennsylvania Press, 1944.

_____. *Employment in New England's Industries*. Works Progress Administration. New York, NY: Special Research Section, 1937.

_____. Letter, Mae Huettig to Isador Lubin. March 10, 1942. Series: 2: Personal Correspondence (1935–1971), Box 53, Folder 4: Mae Huettig, Isador Lubin Papers (1896–1978), Franklin D. Roosevelt Presidential Library, Hyde Park, New York.

Lewis, Howard T. *The Motion Picture Industry*. New York: D. Van Nostrand Company, 1933.

"Mae Churchill; Activist for Privacy and Other Civil Rights." *Los Angeles Times*, February 10, 1996. www.latimes.com/archives/la-xpm-1996-02-10-mn-34342-story.html, accessed April 11, 2022.

Ornstein, Stanley I. "Motion Picture Distribution, Film Splitting, and Antitrust Policy." *Hastings Communications and Entertainment Law Journal* 17, no. 2 (1994): 415–444.

Phillips, Wyatt. "'A Maze of Intricate Relationships': Mae D. Huettig and Early Forays into Film Industry Studies," *Film History* 27, no. 1 (2015): 135–163.

Rosten, Leo C. *Hollywood: The Movie Colony, the Movie Makers*. New York, NY: Harcourt, Brace, and Company, 1941.

Strick, J.C. "The Economics of the Motion Picture Industry: A Survey." *Philosophy of the Social Sciences* 8 (1978): 406–417.

Wasko, Janet. "Critiquing Hollywood: The Political Economy of Motion Pictures." In *A Concise Handbook of Movie Industry Economics*, ed. Charles C. Moul, 5–31. Cambridge, MA: Cambridge University Press, 2005.

_____. "Learning from the History of the Field." *Media Industries* 1, no. 3 (2015): 67–70.

Chapter 8
Marie Jahoda (1907-2001)

By Carol A. Stabile

Marie Jahoda (1988) (courtesy Wikimedia Commons)

Marie Jahoda was an activist and social psychologist, who began her career studying the impact of global economic crises on economically precarious communities. Coming of age in an era of political, economic, and social upheaval shaped her intellectual trajectory. Jahoda devoted her career to studying social problems, breaking new ground in interdisciplinary research aimed at understanding and addressing systemic oppression.

Jahoda was born in Vienna on January 5, 1907 to parents who were economically and educationally privileged secular Jews, active in the Austrian Social Democratic party. Jahoda followed in their footsteps at an early age, becoming a leader of the Austrian socialist youth movement as a teenager.[1] In her studies, Jahoda gravitated toward research conducted by social scientists who, as she put it later—"whether they want to be or not—are often the historians of the present."[2] Jahoda studied with Charlotte and Karl Bühler at their Institute of Psychology at the University of Vienna. The Institute was central to "Red Vienna," a hub for Austro-Marxist research, scholarship, and practice. Jahoda's own research and practice were shaped by the intellectual crosswinds of Marxism and psychoanalysis.

Jahoda's dissertation, titled *Life Histories in the Poor House*, hints at her early interest in standpoint and perspective. Her mentor, Charlotte Bühler, developed life-course studies based on published biographies of great men like Goethe and Mozart. As Jahoda put it in a later interview, she felt that Bühler's was a "one-sided approach, that there are other people too, other than the great and famous."[3] To prove this, Jahoda visited elderly people in poor houses, asking them to tell her their life stories and then applying Bühler's schema to their lives as a part of her dissertation.

In 1930–1931, Jahoda led a 15-person research team to study the impact of the closure of a textile factory in the Austrian village of Marienthal. The factory had been Marienthal's primary employer. The goal of the research was to test a central premise of Marxist theory: did economic crisis lead to revolutionary class consciousness? Jahoda was keenly interested in the relationship between work and mental health: she understood employment to be a key dimension of satisfaction and mental wellbeing.

In *Marienthal: The Sociography of an Unemployed Community*, Jahoda developed "an approach that situates lived human experience, not abstract theory, as central to the formulation of research questions and methods."[4] Unlike research in the US, which tautologically focused on poverty as the defining characteristic of the poor, Jahoda reframed the conversation to focus on unemployment and the structural caprices of an economic system over which workers had no control. Jahoda and her co-authors found that unemployment led not to revolution, but to apathy and despair. Co-authored by Paul Lazarsfeld and Hans Zeisel, *Marienthal* was published without attribution in 1933 because the authors were Jewish. The Nazis destroyed the book's first edition for the same reason.[5]

Jahoda met Lazarsfeld while studying at the Institute and the two were married in 1927. Their daughter, Lotte Franziska, was born in 1930. Jahoda received her PhD in social psychology in 1933, the same year she and Lazarsfeld divorced (Lazarsfeld had begun a relationship with his PhD student and research assistant, Herta Herzog—see Chapter 6). Lazarsfeld left Austria for New York City, while Jahoda remained in Austria, taking over directorship of the Institute. Jahoda was arrested for her underground work with her socialist comrades and tried in 1937, when she was found guilty and sentenced to solitary confinement.[6]

Forced as a condition of her release to leave Austria immediately, Jahoda emigrated to England, where she continued to build on her work at Marienthal, conducting a Quaker-sponsored study of unemployed Welsh miners. In 1938, she was awarded a three-year fellowship at Cambridge University. With this support, she began her next project, a "descriptive analysis of the factory situation as experienced by the factory girl."[7]

In 1945, Jahoda was finally reunited with her daughter and family members who had fled Austria for New York City before the beginning of World War II. She began working with Frankfurt School theorist Max Horkheimer in the American Jewish Committee's research department, before a brief stint at Columbia University's Bureau of Applied Research, where she worked as a research assistant for Robert Merton. Jahoda met social psychologist Stuart W. Cook while working at the American Jewish Committee. Cook studied the impact of racism and religious intolerance on children (he was author of a report that was used in support of school desegregation in *Brown v. Board of Education*). When Cook was offered a job at New York University in 1948, he made his acceptance conditional on Jahoda's hire.[8] Jahoda continued her politically informed research during this time, often in collaboration with Cook and other scholars, studying class divisions, mental health and decision-making among women in Levittown and Fairless Hills; the impact of McCarthyism on civil servants, as well as community influences on mental health. In 1958, Jahoda left the US and married Austen Albu, a British Labour member of Parliament. Beginning in 1965, and until her death, she worked as a research assistant and lecturer at the University of Sussex.

Jahoda's research focused on themes and topics that would remain marginal to communication research until the end of the twentieth century: race and ethnicity (especially her research on anti-Semitism and racism), class, gender, and mental health. Jahoda's studies of ethnic and racial prejudice grappled with the role that media played in either reinforcing or challenging bias. She had firsthand experience of this: during World War II, she ran a secret radio station for the resistance, Radio Rotes Wien.[9] From the beginning of her career, and rooted in her commitment to studying "phenomena that actually occur in the world and are not dreamed up for the purpose of a hypothesis," Jahoda's work was interdisciplinary and aimed at understanding embodied experience: the relationship between the physiology of the brain and the social production of meaningful sense, or what she described as the "insoluble problem of psychology."[10]

Like later feminist researchers, Jahoda demanded that ethnographers immerse themselves in the communities they studied by "participating in some activity generally useful to the community," exemplified by her community-focused work at Marienthal. She insisted that without these forms of immersion, research findings were one-sided and unreliable; such immersion required forms of self-reflexivity not compatible with ideologies of scientific objectivity. The introduction to the co-authored volume, *Anti-Semitism and Emotional Disorder*, makes this clear. "A traditional concept of science—which is often uncritically transferred from the physical to the social sciences—maintains that detachment from the issue is the most important qualification for one who desires to study it," Jahoda and her co-author Nathan Ackerman wrote. "We are opposed to this concept," they added, "which we believe is logically and psychologically untenable."[11] The "only safeguard against one's own emotional involvement is awareness of such involvement and its explicit admission," they concluded.[12]

As Rutherford, Unger, and Cherry point out, the dominant historiographic account of the field of psychology is typically narrated as a "seamless progression from social philosophy to laboratory experimentation,"[13] implying that the shift away from a sociological, Marxian, problem-solving emphasis was inevitable and progressive. Jahoda's work suggests an alternative trajectory. The marginalization of this tradition was neither inevitable nor accidental, but rather reflected the growing anti-communism of the Cold War. Instead of abstract theorizations characteristic of conventional academic thought, Jahoda demanded an approach that begins with problems and standpoint, uncovering "habits of thought [which] are powerful factors which occasionally interfere with the discovery of the new and unexpected." As Unger put it, even into the twenty-first century Jahoda provided a "model of the scholar-activist that could well be emulated by future generations."[14]

Excerpt: Jahoda, Marie, "Anti-Communism and Employment Policies in Radio and Television," *Report on Blacklisting* **(New York: The Fund for the Republic, 1958)**

Cynicism

Most of our respondents believe that the "blacklisting" procedures, initiated and defended in the name of national security, have no bearing whatsoever on national security. They were all aware of the watertight system of control over content before it goes on the air which excludes possibilities of direct subversion. Some of them pointed out that engineers, who are in the most crucial position to do harm in an emergency, were not affected by these policies. None of them mentioned an argument which is often made elsewhere, namely that outstanding performers might use a good deal of their income to help the cause of communism financially. Most of them, as already indicated, had doubts about the motivation of the listers. When this doubt was voiced in a more charitable spirit, the listers were called misguided or crazy; in a less charitable mood the adjectives were insincere, profiteering, money-greedy, hypocritical, and the like.

Such an evaluation of the motivation behind the "blacklisting" procedures, and of their ineffectiveness, taken together with the sense of frustration with regard to decency in human relations, the constriction of activities without a justifying conviction, and the belief that unfair and unintelligible criteria are used which get people into serious trouble—collectively, these add up to an attitude of cynicism. It is not surprising, therefore, that when the question was raised as to why powerful networks and sponsors complied with the requests made by such doubtful characters, the answer was, as a rule: money.

There are some practices cited by respondents which lend support to this all-embracing cynical explanation. One major employer, for example, allegedly checks on personnel not once and for all, but insists that every new assignment of a person be confirmed only after a new check has been performed. One person in the sample, commenting on the need for repeated clearance, declared he could understand it only in terms of a rumor he had heard: there was an alleged fee of $7.50 a person had to pay to one of the outside organizations which had set up its own machinery for "clearing" personnel, whenever a question was raised. More open support for the assumption that it is all a question of money derives from several statements, allegedly made to personnel by some networks and advertising agencies, that it is in the financial interest of the sponsor to avoid the use of "controversial" persons.

This is not to assert that the persons we interviewed were blind to the general trend of public opinion. On the contrary, they mentioned again and again that what was happening in the entertainment industry fitted well into the national climate of thought— or "the national hysteria", according to some—and was possible only because of it. But what they felt was that here it was the catering to a mood rather than the fulfillment of a good purpose, and for reasons of personal profit.

Of the persons who expressed an opinion as to whether anyone should be excluded from work in the industry because of his political beliefs, the great majority felt that no one should be; qualification for the job is the criterion which they repeatedly stressed. As they perceive those who pay for their services to hold very different views, they keep quiet for the sake of the job in the conviction that there is in this respect little room for fairness in the entertainment industry. They submit to what they believe to be wrong.

Excerpt: Ackerman, Nathan W. and Jahoda, Marie, "Anti-Semitism in Context," *Anti-Semitism and Emotional Disorder: A Psychoanalytic Interpretation* **(New York: Harper & Brothers, 1950). Adapted and reprinted with permission from** *Anti-Semitism and Emotional Disorder: A Psychoanalytic Interpretation,* **by Nathan W. Ackerman and Marie Jahoda (New York: American Jewish Committee, 1950) www.AJC.org. All rights reserved.**

Throughout the preceding discussion, one question, implicitly raised at several points, has remained unanswered. Given these emotional predispositions and their history, this pattern of defense mechanisms and their interaction with cultural factors—is anti-Semitism then inevitable? In other words, is anti-Semitism as a particular hostility pattern specifically determined by this complex of factors?

No simple "yes" or "no" answer can be given. The evidence has led to the conclusion that psychological specificity is a relative factor; in the case of some anti-Semitic personalities it is high, in others low. The anti-Semitic reaction was highly specific, for example, in the case of the person (*Case 11*) who hated Jews because he saw them combining success with a happy emotional life. Color prejudice would not have fulfilled as well the same emotional function.

Specificity of a somewhat lesser degree existed in the case of the white-collar worker (*Case 29*) whose hatred of the Jews was an expression of his feeble rebellion against authority and his own economically underprivileged status. The pseudo-liberal (*Case 18*), on the other hand, whose occasional outbursts of anti-Semitism were based on his identification with the underdog whom he rejected along with himself, might well have selected the Negro for the same purpose of projection. Underdog identification, however, is not necessarily unspecific. The patient (*Case 2*) whose anti-Semitism contained the element of identification with a Jewish victim, was particularly incensed by encountering Jews in positions of authority. That he himself had betrayed the identification with the underdog mattered little compared to the Jewish "betrayal" in escaping the underdog position and assuming a position of power. The chances are that in the American culture no other target group of hatred and prejudice could have provided him with these two significant experiences.

Finally, the least degree of specificity was met in those for whom anti-Semitism primarily served the function of emphasizing "difference" per se. The sixteen year old boy, for whom "Jew" was synonymous with name calling, could easily have substituted any other prejudice for anti-Semitism.

The psychological specificity of anti-Semitism thus varies from case to case. That is why an attempt must be made to broaden the context of the problem, to regard the wider implications of anti-Semitism along with its relation to other disturbances of group living and other social ills. For despite its historical uniqueness, the selection of anti-Semitism—from the psychodynamic point of view—is in several instances a more or less *accidental* manifestation of the prejudiced person's deficiencies. Anti-Semitism may occasionally be due to a historical accident in individual cases, independent of the relative degree of emotional specificity; but the disturbance in intergroup relations in such persons appears to be psychologically determined.

A psychologically comprehensive description of attitudes in intergroup relations demands consideration of four dimensions. If members of group A and group B are interacting (say, Jews and Gentiles) these dimensions are: the attitude of a member of group A to group A and group B; the attitude of a member of group B to group B and group A. In the case of anti-Semitism, disturbances occur not only in the attitude of Gentiles to Jews and Jews to Gentiles, but also in the attitude of each to his own group. As we have demonstrated, the concept of self is continuously modified by one's own group and, in turn, the group is modified by the concept of self of its members, which finds expression in the relation to other groups.

While the suffering of the Jew as a victim is of a special brand, it is not only he who suffers. As our case studies have shown, the anti-Semite also suffers. Jew and Gentile, when they are driven by insecurity in themselves, resort to irrational hostility against outgroups. Thus, disturbances in each of these four dimensions in intergroup relations are ubiquitous in modern society.

The question then arises: Which factors in society, interacting with intrapsychic anxiety, contribute to such disturbances and the concomitant suffering?

[...]

To answer it comprehensively would demand a detailed critique of these times for which we have neither the qualifications nor the space.

All we can do is to refer again to our material and examine it once more from a new angle. Assuming, in order to limit unfounded speculation as much as possible, that our forty case histories are the only available source of information about American culture, what general deductions about the discontent in this culture can we make? The picture will be sketchy and one-sided, but it remains the best approach available in the context of this study toward finding an answer to such a question.

It appears that the most outstanding feature of the culture as seen in the lives of these patients is its intense economic and social competitiveness. An indication of this competitiveness is contained in the content of the anti-Semitic stereotype. There are but a very few cases in which economic and social status qualities are not attributed to Jews: "low class, inferior, not belonging to good society," or "powerful, superior, exploiters, pushers, social climbers." These and other accusations, whether they express rejection or envy of the Jew, are all modeled according to the competitive world in which these people live.

But there are further indications of the pressure for economic success. Most of the mothers of our cases—so far as we know about them—apparently did not tell their children "be happy" but rather: "make money," "outdo your father," "get a good job."

The mother of one man (*Case 22*) spurred all her children on to scholastic achievement in order to acquire eventual material success and to become better providers than their father. Another mother was snobbish and ever critical of her husband for being unambitious and making a poor living. Since she could not succeed in pushing him she wanted her son (*Case 9*) to become a person of wealth and social prestige. One patient (*Case 1*), as will be remembered, was driven from one profession to another by her desperate longing to achieve social security.

It is the essence of competitiveness that success is measured by comparison with others rather than by actual achievement. That is why a strongly competitive society gives permanent cause for social anxiety to everyone, even to those who have achieved material success. There are always some who have done better, who have more money and more social prestige; and there is always the danger of being pushed down the social ladder by a competitor.

For some of the social-service agency cases, the economic anxiety was realistically justified. Lack of food in some cases, crowded living quarters and continuous quarrels between the parents about money are the normal background factors that strengthen the importance of economic success as a goal in life. But the social anxiety in this competitive culture caught hold even of the economically privileged. Indeed they are often much more vulnerable to competitive anxiety because of their extreme concern with money; when they have it, they live in constant dread of losing it.

One man (*Case 10*), who had inherited so much money that he never did a stroke of work, was plagued by fear that he would lose his money and was quite convinced that whatever pleasures he could get out of life were in direct proportion to the money he paid for them. A woman (*Case 3*), who to all appearances was a highly successful business woman, was continuously worried about losing her position. Another (*Case 4*) was unable to work unless she felt she was at the top of a hierarchy, and a third (*Case 30*), who had made a remarkable ascent from utter poverty to a position of comfort, always felt insecure in her achievement. A fourth woman (*Case 12*), who came from a wealthy family, expressed her insatiable status drive by attempts to get into the circles of French and British aristocracy.

Where economic gain or social status become the only yardstick for success, acquisition of money is a virtue, poverty a crime. The acquisitive society is reflected in the patients' attitudes toward money in the analytic situation. Several analysts reported that their patients quibbled over analytic fees despite their highly privileged economic situation. Their material acquisitions, however, must be displayed to the world as a sign of success, so that others should be driven to comparison and to realize their own inferiority. Many patients seem to combine two contradictory trends in our culture: the trend for acquisition and the trend for conspicuous consumption. This was particularly evident for the man (*Case 9*) who cheated his newspaper man out of small change but at the same time felt compelled to give expensive banquets to his business friends.

Even where generosity appears in these cases—which does not happen too frequently—it was motivated by the same desire for conspicuous consumption that would prove to others that the individual was not a failure.

To regard poverty as a crime and as a sign of degradation is a natural correlate in a society that considers money a virtue. One woman (*Case 4*) was convinced that poor people and laborers get their support to a large extent from stealing the pocketbooks of the "better" people.

Inherent in the competitive and acquisitive features of society, with its concomitant social insecurity, is a progressive alienation from the satisfactions of work. This problem has often been presented as the curse of mass production for factory workers. Judging from our cases this process of alienation is by no means restricted to monotonous work, because a large proportion of these professional people and business executives are as alienated from their work as if they stood at a conveyor belt. As a matter of fact, with one exception (*Case 18*) none derive any satisfaction from their actual work performance. The cultural climate is such that no importance is attached to *what* is being done, but rather the importance arises from how much one makes out of it.

The atomization of man, judging from the social life of these patients, is highly advanced in this society. Individuals are isolated; families are isolated. There does not seem to exist a meaningful group belongingness, unless it is organized around an issue of social prestige. The country club fulfills such a function, but a function without positive content.

There is, to be sure, an urge for group cohesion. But the culture places no premium on the realization of such an urge. If the deep loneliness of people in this society were in some way to be overcome, this achievement, apparently, would be considered of small consequence. It is little wonder that the father of one patient (*Case 3*) is reported to have had the best time of his life while serving in the army during the First World War, for there he found purpose and companionship. Two other patients joined the Communist Party, not because they shared its ideology, but because they were drawn by its promise of group cohesion and purposefulness.

These persons have learned from their work-life that to know other people as human beings is of no profit. Spontaneous friendliness is hamstrung by the fact and the fear of exploitation, and human relations are consequently evaluated according to their utility. Thus society debases friendship for its own sake, and debases group membership for any purpose but prestige or utility. So much is this the case that one man (*Case 31*), who was himself conservative and anti-union, worked during an election campaign for a liberal politician because this was the best way to meet the "right people."

[...]

There is, in this society, a lack of capacity for relaxation, pleasure, or the creative use of leisure time. Fundamentally, all these people are "bored" by what is going on around them, unless they can set it into a relation to their own success strivings. This boredom is, indeed, a symptom of their deep anxiety. All activity becomes patterned by the need to control this anxiety, which emerges in part from unconscious self-hatred. So preoccupied are they with this driven activity, that they lose the capacity to enjoy themselves. To be interested in something for its own sake appears a waste of time, however heavily free time presses on such empty lives.

Notes

1   Rhoda Unger, "Obituaries: Marie Jahoda (1907–2001)," *American Psychologist* 56, no. 11 (November 2001): 1040–1041.

2   Marie Jahoda, "Introduction," in *The Authoritarian Personality* (Glencoe, IL: The Free Press, 1954), 11.

3   David Fryer and Marie Jahoda, "The Simultaneity of the Unsimultaneous: A Conversation between Marie Jahoda and David Fryer," *Journal of Community & Applied Social Psychology* 8, no. 2 (1998): 99.

4   Alexa Rutherford, Rhoda Unger, and Frances Cherry, "Reclaiming SPSSI's Sociological Past: Marie Jahoda and the Immersion Tradition in Social Psychology," *Journal of Social Issues* 67, no. 1 (2011): 48, x.

5 Unger, "Obituaries: Marie Jahoda (1907–2001)," 1040.
6 Rutherford, Unger, and Cherry, "Reclaiming SPSSI's Sociological Past."
7 Fryer and Jahoda, "The Simultaneity of the Unsimultaneous," 50.
8 Rutherford, Unger, and Cherry, "Reclaiming SPSSI's Sociological Past."
9 Unger, "Obituaries: Marie Jahoda (1907–2001)," 1040.
10 Fryer and Jahoda, "The Simultaneity of the Unsimultaneous," 91.
11 Nathan Ward Ackerman and Marie Jahoda, *Anti-Semitism and Emotional Disorder: A Psychoanalytic Interpretation*, 1st ed., Studies in Prejudice (New York. NY: Harper & Brothers Publishers, 1950), 1.
12 Ackerman and Jahoda, *Anti-Semitism and Emotional Disorder*, 2.
13 Rutherford, Unger, and Cherry, "Reclaiming SPSSI's Sociological Past," 43.
14 Unger, "Obituaries: Marie Jahoda (1907–2001)," 1041.

Bibliography

Ackerman, Nathan W. and Marie Jahoda. *Anti-Semitism and Emotional Disorder: A Psychoanalytic Interpretation*. Studies in Prejudice. New York, NY: Harper & Brothers Publishers, 1950.

Christie, Richard and Marie Jahoda. *Studies in the Scope and Method of "The Authoritarian Personality."* Continuities in Social Research. Glencoe, IL: Free Press, 1954.

Fryer, David and Marie Jahoda. "The Simultaneity of the Unsimultaneous: A Conversation between Marie Jahoda and David Fryer." *Journal of Community & Applied Social Psychology* 8, no. 2 (1998): 89–100.

Jahoda, Marie. "Anti-Communism and Employment Policies in Radio and Television." In *Report on Blacklisting II*, ed. John Cogley, 221–281. New York, NY: Arno Press, 1956.

_____. "Confronting the Unanswerable." *Nature* 298, no. 5869 (1982): 103.

_____. *Employment and Unemployment: A Social-Psychological Analysis*. Psychology of Social Issues. No. 1. Cambridge, UK: Cambridge University Press, 1982.

_____. "Introduction." In *The Authoritarian Personality*, 11–23. Glencoe, IL: The Free Press, 1954.

_____. "The Meaning of Psychological Health." *Social Casework* 34, no. 8 (1953): 349–354.

_____. "Predicting the Past." *Nature* 306, no. 5938 (1983): 96.

_____. "Psychological Issues in Civil Liberties." *American Psychologist* 11, no. 5 (1956): 234–240.

_____. *Research Methods in Social Relations, with Especial Reference to Prejudice*. New York, NY: Dryden Press, 1951.

Jahoda, Marie, and Stewart W. Cook. "Ideological Compliance as a Social-Psychological Process." In *Totalitarianism*, ed. Carl J. Friedrich, 203–222. The Universal Library. New York, NY: Gosset and Dunlap, 1964.

_____. "Security Measures and Freedom of Thought: An Exploratory Study of the Impact of Loyalty and Security Programs." *The Yale Law Journal* 61, no. 3 (1952): 295–333.

Jahoda, Marie, Paul Felix Lazarsfeld, and Hans Zeisel. *Marienthal: The Sociography of an Unemployed Community*. New Brunswick: Transaction Publishers, 2002.

Paul, Karsten I. and Bernad Batinic. "The Need for Work: Jahoda's Latent Functions of Employment in a Representative Sample of the German Population." *Journal of Organizational Behavior* 31, no. 1 (2010): 45–64.

Rutherford, Alexa, Rhoda Unger, and Frances Cherry. "Reclaiming SPSSI's Sociological Past: Marie Jahoda and the Immersion Tradition in Social Psychology." *Journal of Social Issues* 67, no. 1 (2011): 42–58.

Selenko, Eva, Bernad Batinic, and Karsten Paul. "Does Latent Deprivation Lead to Psychological Distress? Investigating Jahoda's Model in a Four-Wave Study." *Journal of Occupational and Organizational Psychology* 84, no. 4 (2011): 723–740.

UNESCO. *The Race Question in Modern Science; Race and Science*. New York, NY: Columbia University Press, 1961.

Unger, Rhoda. "Obituaries: Marie Jahoda (1907–2001)." *American Psychologist* 56, no. 11 (2001): 1040–1041.

Chapter 9
Romana Javitz (1903–1980)

By Diana Kamin

Romana Javitz was a visionary librarian whose contributions to theories of photography, image classification, and public culture are newly resonant in a contemporary image economy in which circulating digital image collections controlled by private platforms increasingly structure our visual experience. Javitz was Superintendent of the Picture Collection at the New York Public Library from 1928 to 1968, during which time the collection circulated millions of clipped pictures, cut by hand out of discarded books and magazines and available to be checked out by anyone with a library card. Users of the collection ranged from avant-garde artists including Diego Rivera and Andy Warhol to US State Department researchers to advertising professionals to schoolchildren; Javitz endeavored to make the collection accessible to all. To this end, Javitz pioneered a system in which pictures are organized in open stacks and catalogued under thousands of alphabetical subject headings, empowering user-directed searches and rejecting artist- and author-centered schemes dominant in museum and library settings, which she explicitly challenged as forms of knowledge gatekeeping. All classification schemes represent values: Javitz argued that the classification of pictures should be drawn from the language of the public, eschewing hierarchical order or specialized knowledge. Further, she advocated for libraries to take picture organization as seriously as books, warning that the absence of library leadership would leave a vacuum that would be filled by commercial enterprise. This critique has proved prescient as concerns mount that free platforms like Google lack accountability and commitment to the public interest. As a librarian whose progressive politics shaped her sense of what should be preserved and who should have access, Javitz offers a vital model for the role of libraries in public culture.

Javitz immigrated to the United States from Minsk, Russia with her Polish Jewish parents when she was three.[1] She grew up in New York City and began working part-time in 1919 at the Children's Collection at the New York Public Library to support her painting study at Cooper Union, and then moved to the Picture Collection in 1924. A trip to Europe to study library and museum picture collections in 1925 and 1926 intensified her interest in the organization of pictures as historical documents. When she began as Superintendent of the Picture Collection in 1929, she had a clear vision of the collection as a vital resource to the creative industries of New York City and to the general user. She regularly advocated for its use amongst working class and immigrant populations, arguing that the public's appreciation of images was more wide-ranging than the narrowly aesthetic views presented by the museum, or by the library's print collections.[2]

Javitz's social milieu shared her belief in the political potential of democratic modes of disseminating and interpreting visual culture. Though her own publishing and political activities were circumscribed in library work, her circle included activists, writers, and artists who embraced radical politics like poet and activist Muriel Rukeyser and documentary filmmaker Jay Leyda.[3] Javitz was also close with the family of anthropologist Franz Boas; she had a decades-long affair with his son, physician Ernst Boas, and was a friend of his daughter, dancer Franziska Boas.[4] The three shared a concern with racial justice and worked publicly to integrate their professions. Javitz recognized the role of imagery in combatting racism and regularly wrote about the importance of building up their representations of Black history and life. She assisted Arturo Alfonso Schomburg in building out the Library's Division of Negro History, Literature and Prints in the 1930s.[5]

Through the Picture Collection, Javitz developed relationships with artists Walker Evans, Ben Shahn, Dorothea Lange, Helen Levitt, Joseph Cornell, and Andy Warhol, among others. In part through these connections, Javitz conceived and helped to implement the American Index of Design (1935–1942), a visual archive of 18,000 watercolor renderings produced by Works Progress Administration artists of American decorative arts objects.[6] She also surreptitiously preserved photographs created for the famed Farm Security Administration when, at the suggestion of Shahn, Roy Stryker (head of the Information Division) sent copy prints of the program's documentary photographs to Javitz for use in the Picture Collection for fear that they would be otherwise discarded.[7] Through these activities, Javitz influenced the New Deal investment in the documentation of national history and current events, while driving her contemporaries towards a more inclusive and expansive vision and making those documents more readily available to the public. In 1967, Shahn presented Javitz with the American Institute of Graphic Arts Gold Medal.

While Javitz promoted her ideas through teaching, lecturing, writing, and publishing in professional journals, much of her thinking appeared in bureaucratic genres like the annual report or the grant application. In 1940 she received a grant from the Carnegie Foundation to produce a manual for the classification of pictures; while it led to three years of research and interim reports, she never completed the manual. Instead, across disparate reports and lectures, her writing takes on broad themes while remaining grounded in her direct experience as a public librarian. In the excerpts that follow she narrates the cultural shifts wrought by the availability of indexed "visual knowledge," and wrestles with the potential for democratization versus propagandistic power of images. She coins valuable concepts such as the "picture as document," and the "picture at work."[8] She calls for a national pictorial service with picture services in every community, and relentlessly centers the user in her plans. Javitz's voice offers an essential perspective at our present historical juncture in which the flows of images (their production, classification, and indexing) are increasingly black-boxed and privatized, instead offering a model of a public, indexed image collection that is user-centered, flexible, and scalable without commercial influence. Further, her work predicts the currency of postmodern conceptions of the image, in which meaning emerges in acts of interpretation and images cross-mediate across platforms, from the decidedly modernist milieu of 1930s America.

Excerpt: Javitz, Romana, "A Report on the Picture Collection for Mr. Ralph A. Beals," Picture Collection records (permission of Picture Collection Records. New York Public Library Archives. The New York Public Library. Astor, Lenox, and Tilden Foundations)

REPORT   on the picture collection of The New York Library

PURPOSE   to provide a basis for the formulation of policy on pictures as an integral part of the Library

> Pictures defined: throughout this report, the word *pictures* is used to describe pictorial documents: films, "stills," lithographs, engravings, photographs, and photomechanically reproduced illustrations of images, primarily looked upon for their factual content. This term does not include "fine prints," the work of artist-printmakers, collected and judged on aesthetic content, and technical and artistic merit—of museum caliber. In this report, pictures are documents.

PROPOSED   That a picture collection be established to serve the interests of the Library as a whole. This presupposes a change in the status of the present picture collection to embrace reference and circulation services, and presupposes a pooling of the picture holdings of both departments to form one coordinated archive.

That policy be formulated favoring the development of a picture collection to gain for the public a pictorial archive and information center of the scope and effectiveness New York requires.

That the policy take account of the unique and strategic location of the Library in the center of education, creative work and performance in the arts; of publishing, advertising, broadcasting and fashion. Agencies of government, private enterprise and research, the painter, the physician and the lawyer all need pictures, and turn to the Library for visual documents.

[...]

A favorable directive would give the New York Public Library leadership in the use of pictures to increase the compass of recorded knowledge.

❖ ❖ ❖

[...]

III. SPECIFICATIONS for a proposed PICTURE COLLECTION

A. FUNCTION

TO form a picture library that would parallel in images the printed record in words

maintain an iconographic archive as an adjunct to the other divisions of the library

organize pictures for the purposes of study, information and display

act as a center of pictorial information

give consultation service in the classification of pictures

give direction to and encourage picture service

develop areas of picture service within the scope of the Library, and in line with the picture needs of local groups and activities

promote interest in the use of pictures and act as a guide in the establishment of picture collections outside of the Library's sphere, e.g. for the Board of Education.

B. SUBJECT COVERAGE

The subject coverage may be likened to a general encyclopedia, brief, but generally inclusive on all subjects; which, for detailed treatment, refers the reader to bibliographic sources listed at the end of each article. Similarly, the over-all coverage in pictures would be broad but linked through referrals to collections of greater depth.

[...]

C. FORMAT

Comprehensive in types of printed pictorial documents:

Page-size: Clippings; photographs; "stills;" lithographs; advertisements; cartoons;

Card-size: Stereos; postcards; greeting cards; trade cards; labels;

Over-size: Posters; car cards; displays; color facsimiles;

Films: Filmstrips; documentary films; microfilms.
[...]

D. ACQUISITIONS

The intent would be to raise the standard of the picture stock to that of the general book collections. To do this it would be necessary to seek out and acquire several private clippings collections. More material on the commercial and applied arts, the history of trade and industry, and particularly on American history and the American scene would be needed.

Photographs should be obtained covering the life, events and personalities recorded in the first hundred years of photography. As a public service, some of the great news-agencies could be invited to contribute a cross-section of their collections for incorporation in the Library's archive. The copyright would not be endangered and the gift would publicize their holdings.

Systematic acquisitions would be planned to round out the collections, with emphasis on keeping the subject coverage abreast of contemporary trends. Areas of the categories in the circulation picture files would be microfilmed so that the original clippings and photographs could be reserved for reference use while the photo-copies would replace them for circulation.

Excerpt: Javitz, Romana, "Words on Pictures: An Address by Romana Javitz, Superintendent of the Picture Collection," New York Public Library, Before the Massachusetts Library Association, Boston, Mass., January 28, 1943 (permission of the Massachusetts Library Association)

The mounting flood of pictures is permeating all of our lives, and its impact leaves deep impression on our minds. This unexploited pool of power can be tapped to produce ideas, stimulate processes of thinking and provoke action.

Libraries seem to worship the printed word as the sole conveyor of knowledge; they leave the pictorial aspects of the world to the museums. Satisfied with the power of words, they have slighted the great infiltration of pictures and left their use to commercial channels of sensationalism and advertising. Librarians should not depend on printed words alone but should utilize the printed picture as an adjunct to books. The physicist Clerk Maxwell, said "there is no more powerful method for introducing knowledge into the mind than that of presenting it in as many ways as we can." Instead of scorning pictures, libraries should take full advantage of their power in the communication of ideas.

These pictures are not art, they are not pictures on exhibition, they are pictures at work. They are documents, momentarily cut off from their aesthetic functions to be employed for their subject content. Any picture is a document when it is being used as a source of information instead of being searched for its content of beauty.

We have inherited a tremendous mass of pictorial representations from past centuries. The camera has brought us the image of the world today and fixed a record of it for the future. Through photo-mechanical methods all of the art works of the past have been reproduced in print in countless copies. We now have a full-bodied pictorial history of man, the outer aspects of his living—the face of human events. From prehistoric times, we have the hunted exhausted bison, copied from a cave drawing; percussion instruments of Ancient China photographed from tomb figurines; the martyrdom of saints pictured in medieval prints which once were sewn into garments of pilgrims to stave off evils; we have "stills" from newsreels showing a sailor crouched against the deck expanse of an aircraft carrier, darkened by the shadow of a Zero's flight overhead. At the moment the consideration of whether these are good art or not is secondary, the subject alone is important. These are the pictures that keep for us the appearance of the past, the visages of people and their rulers, the contour of their lands, the shape of their bread and their tools, the mechanism of war machines and the features of gods.

[...]

Most pictorial representation in the past and most photographs today, were made without aesthetic purpose, they were made as illustrations. The mere attempt to communicate an idea graphically should not be claimed to be art. Most pictures have as their purpose the recording of a visual experience, the rendering of the appearance of things.

While some pictures have been made solely as records, the pictures that were made for aesthetic ends may also serve a utilitarian purpose, may function at times as sources of information. All works of art mirror the world in which they were conceived, the life and the community from which the artist sprung. The artist rarely escapes reflecting his own times.

[...]

It is difficult to imagine ourselves without our common lifelong exposure to pictorial experiences, without the family snapshot, the Sunday rotogravure, the newsreel, the history of art illustrated with photographs; to relive a time when the appearance of individuals in the public fields of government and social reform, the famous author and the notorious criminal, was unfamiliar to all those who had never seen them face to face. When the image of the world could be fixed by light, trapped forever on a surface and then reproduced mechanically in mass duplication, we were presented with a great educational force and a rich, unlimited source of social influence.

[...]

Since a picture by its nature, can depict only a fixed moment of time, it has no continuity of action. Only one scene, one aspect is visible at a time and what preceded a recorded moment cannot be discerned. [...] Pictures without labels and identification are useless as a source of information. [...] The written and spoken words amplify the meaning of pictures. [...] The interpretation and the meaning of pictures is dependent on the user and on the captions.

[...]

The use of the camera in pictorial recording and as an educational medium is still in its beginning stage; it is as revolutionary in effect as the invention of movable type in printing. We are only at the rim of a far-reaching extension of our visual knowledge, and it is impossible to envisage what this will do to books and libraries. Future pictorial libraries will probably include miniature positive prints of pictures as subject indices, documentary moving pictures such as instruction film and newsreels. Stroboscopic photographs and film in slow motion will be available for the public who will probably be able to study them in book-size individual projection devices. All kinds of pictures will be organized for research use, and for their fullest potentiality they will circulate, entering laboratories, homes, schools and studios.

Pictures organized as sources of information are as necessary to a library as dictionaries and encyclopedias. They enhance and amplify the content of the book stock, they serve the library as exhibit material with which to attract the public and stimulate interest in subjects of communal and universal importance. They help dispel the dimness of the past and animate the words of history. With pictorial data, the playwright recreates a period, an orthopedist traces the shape of hand supports on crutches; an anthropologist disproves false concepts of racial physical characteristics; a camouflage worker learns the appearance of factories from the sky; obscure scientific and technical writings are clarified for the general public.

The documentary picture collection in a library should be organized on a basis of comprehensiveness, with emphasis on the clear definition and visibility of a picture rather than its artistic content. Since these are documents, the selection by the librarian should be kept at minimum. In a library, the public selects and chooses; in a museum the staff sets up standards since it is the function of a museum to guide the public and set up what the public may see to improve their taste. The library has a different role. With the vigor of impartiality it marshals documentary pictures and through classification and editing, offers the public an impartial pictorial record of man's cultural heritage, his life and history which they may use as they see fit.

[...]

A picture that is a straightforward, simple statement of observation is an effective medium for the dissemination of ideas. It can be a dangerous and a benign influence; it can be the source of facts and of lies, it is an insidious source of propaganda. It is always useful for conveying messages to all of the people because it is the most specific, easily understood and cheaply available record of human living.

We can hardly comprehend the immenseness of this medium of words and pictures. The full effect of the constant infiltration of edited visual printed images is too frequently slighted by those who work with words. Pictures are an active force in education and should be harnessed to the highest purposes, to stimulate the present and succeeding generations. Pictures are essential to libraries where they should join books and serve as documents of man's own aspect and that of the changing times he has lived in.

Notes

1 Biographical information drawn from Romana Javitz Papers, New York Public Library (NYPL) archives, New York. Biography can also be found in Anthony Troncale, "Worth Beyond Words: Romana Javitz and The New York Public Library's Picture Collection," *Biblion: The Bulletin of The New York Public Library* 4, no. 1 (Fall 1995): 115-138. Troncale, a former NYPL photography librarian, is working on a biography of Javitz, and recently published an invaluable selection of her writing in *Words on Pictures: Romana Javitz and the New York Public Library's Picture Collection* (New York, NY: Photo Verso Publications LLC, 2020).

2 Javitz often included anecdotes about these populations in her annual reports. As one example, in *Picture Collection Annual Report for 1931*, in Romana Javitz Papers, she discusses a new policy encouraging non-English users to draw requests.

3 See correspondence with Ernst Boas referencing time spent with Rukeyser in Box 1, Folder 4, Series 1: Correspondence, Romana Javitz Papers, NYPL, and Romana Javitz correspondence file in the Jay Leyda and Si-Lan Chen Papers, Tamiment Archive and Library, New York University, New York.

4 See decades of correspondence in Series 1: Correspondence, Romana Javitz Papers, NYPL.

5 She references this work in Romana Javitz, Typewritten transcript, n.d., in Box 4 "Audio tape transcriptions—Javitz class at Pratt[?] n.d.", Picture Collection records, and "A

Report on the Picture Collection" for Mr Ralph A. Beals (July 1951), in Box 3, Folder 21, Series 1, Picture Collection Records. See also Javitz to Arthur Schomburg, May 25, 1937, in Arthur A. Schomburg Papers, Schomburg Center for Research in Black Culture. Historian Mary Panzer is exploring the connection between Javitz and Schomburg further (Mary Panzer, "Romana Javitz, Arturo Schomburg, and the Farm Security Administration Search for Usable Pictures of African American Life," panel presentation for Special Libraries Association, New York Chapter, March 23, 2021).

6 This history, and Javitz's role, is confirmed by Holger Cahill's introduction to *The Index of American Design*, by Erwin O. Christensen (New York, NY: Macmillan, 1950). Javitz had discussed interest in American design, and the dearth of materials to support the budding demand, with many artist-users of the collection. One, Ruth Reeves, had contacts at the New York City Emergency Relief Administration, and relayed Javitz's idea for a comprehensive source index of American design. A proposal was solicited from Javitz in 1935, and the project was realized over the seven years that followed.

7 See Correspondence—General U.S. Resettlement Admin. (Roy Stryker) 1936–1937 in Picture Collection Records, NYPL.

8 Javitz uses both phrases in "Words on Pictures. A Speech to the Convention of the Massachusetts Library Association, Boston, Massachusetts, January 28, 1943," *The Massachusetts Library Association Bulletin* (1943): 19–23, excerpted in this volume. The phrases are also littered across her annual reports from 1929 to 1968.

Bibliography

Bronfield, Jerry. "Just Ask for it: In this Collection You Can Find a Picture of Anything ..." *New York Herald Tribune*, November 26, 1944, 7.

Bugbee, Emma. "Miss Romana Javitz Shepherds Collection of 1,000,000 Pictures." *New York Herald Tribune*, May 10, 1943, 7.

Cahill, Holger. "Introduction." *The Index of American Design*, by Erwin O. Christensen, 1–15. New York, NY: Macmillan, 1950.

Doud, Richard. "An Interview with Romana Javitz 23 February 1965." *Archives of American Art Journal* 41, no. 1/4 (2001): 2–17.

Hill, May D. "Prints, Pictures, and Photographs." *Library Trends* 4, no. 2 (October 1955): 156–163.

"Interesting People: She Keeps the Past: Romana Javitz." *American Magazine*, February 1950.

Javitz, Romana. "Images and Words." *Wilson Library Bulletin* 18, no. 3 (November 1943): 217–221.

_____. "The Library and the Anniversary of Printing." In *500 Years of Printing – A Collection of Articles on the History of Printing Since the Invention of Movable Type: Reprinted from the Publishers' Weekly*, ed. Frederic G. Melcher. New York, NY: Gardner Press, 2012 (originally published 1940).

_____. "Pictures from Abacus to Zodiac." *The Story of Our Time: An Encyclopedic Yearbook, 1955*. New York, NY: The Grolier Society, Inc, 1955.

_____. "Picture Research." *Special Libraries* 43, no. 6 (July–August 1952): 209–210.

_____. "The Public Interest." *Work for Artists. What? Where? How?*, ed. Elizabeth McCausland, 27–35. New York: American Artists Group, 1947.

_____. "Put Accent on Pictures." *Library Journal* 74 (September 15, 1949): 1235–1236.

_____. "Still Pictures." *Picturescope* 15, no. 1 (1967): 2–6.

_____. "Words on Pictures. A Speech to the Convention of the Massachusetts Library Association," Boston, Massachusetts, January 28, 1943. *The Massachusetts Library Association Bulletin* (1943): 19–23.

Kamin, Diana. "Mid-Century Visions, Programmed Affinities: The Enduring Challenges of Image Classification." *Journal of Visual Culture* 16, no. 3 (2017): 310–336.

_____. "Picture Work: On the Circulating Image Collection." PhD diss., New York University, 2018.

_____. "Total Recall." *Artforum*, August 30, 2021. Web only, www.artforum.com/slant/ diana-kamin-on-the-new-york-public-library-s-picture-collection-86403, accessed April 9, 2023.

Kellogg, Cynthia. "Searchers for Unusual Pictures Can Find Them at Main Library." *New York Times*, November 3, 1960, 41.

"Library not Art Snob, Picture Chief Says." *Toronto Globe and Mail*, November 30, 1965, 11.

Noble, Safiya Umoja. *Algorithms of Oppression: How Search Engines Reinforce Racism*. New York: New York University Press, 2018.

Panzer, Mary. "Pictures at Work: Romana Javitz and the New York Public Library Picture Collection." In *The "Public" Life of Photographs*, ed. Thierry Gervais, 129–151. Cambridge, MA: MIT Press, 2016.

_____. "Romana Javitz, Arturo Schomburg, and the Farm Security Administration Search for Usable Pictures of African American Life." Presentation at the Special Libraries Association, New York Chapter, New York, March 23, 2021.

Troncale, Anthony T. *Words on Pictures: Romana Javitz and the New York Public Library's Picture Collection*. New York: Photo Verso Publications LLC, 2020.

_____. "Worth Beyond Words: Romana Javitz and The New York Public Library's Picture Collection." *Biblion: The Bulletin of The New York Public Library* 4, no. 1 (Fall 1995): 115–138.

Van Haaften, Julia. "Original Sun Pictures: A Check List of the New York Public Library's Holdings of Early Works Illustrated with Photographs, 1844–1900." *The Bulletin of the New York Public Library* (Spring 1977), 355–415.

Van Haaften, Julia and Anthony Troncale. *Subject Matters: Photography, Romana Javitz and the New York Public Library*. Exhibition pamphlet. New York Public Library, 1998.

Chapter 10
Claudia Jones (1915–1964)

By Hadil Abuhmaid

Claudia Jones in London in the 1960s (permission of Schomburg Center for Research in Black Culture, Photographs and Prints Divisions)

"You dare not, gentlemen of the prosecution, assert that negro women can think and speak and write!"[1]

Claudia Jones was a Black woman, an activist, a journalist, a communist theorist, a revolutionary, a fighter, and an intersectional feminist. She spent most of her life challenging racist national policies and oppressive gender roles. Class was central to Jones' understanding of identity, a category she understood to be structured by race and migration. These concerns were reflected in her politics and her fearless challenges to US class exploitation, White supremacy, gender subordination, and many forms of discrimination on the part of US government and society.[2]

Jones was born Claudia Vera Cumberbatch in Trinidad in February 1915. In 1924, her family immigrated to the United States. After graduating from Harlem's Wadleigh High School in 1935, Jones held several jobs, which shaped her understanding of US racism. As smart and talented as she was, she realized that she might never find anything other than the most menial jobs because of her skin color. College was both financially and practically inaccessible, so Jones began to study and analyze social issues revolving around suffering and injustice.

Jones joined the Young Communist League (YCL), a working-class youth organization devoted to Marxist-Leninism, in 1936 at the age of 18. Using the pseudonym "Claudia Jones," she began writing for the YCL's *Weekly Review* and became its associate editor in 1938, only two years after joining the League.[3] She became an editor-in-chief in 1943. While working for the YCL, Jones became a voice for the nine Black teenagers charged with raping two White women in Scottsboro, Alabama. She occupied several other political positions, including that of secretary of the National Women's Commission of the Communist Party USA (CPUSA).[4] During that time, Jones' writings infused racial justice with an anti-fascist agenda, especially during World War II as she tackled US intervention in the world and the contradictory nature of the fight against fascism abroad and its enforcement domestically through Jim Crow practices. Linking anti-capitalism, global struggles for national independence, and colonial oppression, Jones promoted solidarity among nations suffering at the hands of imperialism.

In 1953, Jones became the *Daily Worker*'s Negro Affairs editor. Her writings for the *Daily Worker* were distinct insofar as they were directed to Black working-class women, who she described as "the most oppressed stratum of the whole population."[5] As a Black working-class woman herself, Jones, along with her mother and sister and other working-class Black women, were not only exploited for financial gain, but also not allowed to live their lives to the fullest. As Jones wrote, "[c]apitalists exploit women doubly, both as workers and women. Woman has to face special oppression in every field in capitalist society—as a worker—a wife, a homebuilder and a citizen."[6]

By the 1940s, Jones had become one of the major theoreticians for the Communist Party. Jones published nine essays on women and ran her bi-weekly column "Half the World" for the *Daily Worker*. In "Half the World," Jones focused on women's rights and presented arguments discussing how women represent half of the world's population and should therefore receive half of its resources.[7] Jones' work challenged mainstream media representations of women and Black people and her work significantly influenced the cultural left in the US and Britain.

The US government recognized Jones' influence. Along with other Black radicals (see Chapter 5 of this volume on Shirley Graham and Chapter 18 on Fredi Washington), Jones was subjected to increasing surveillance during the 1940s. On January 19, 1948, Jones was arrested and imprisoned on Ellis Island under the 1918 Immigration Act. She was released on $1,000 bail on January 20, only to be threatened with deportation six days later, accused of calling for a violent overthrow of the government.

Despite intensifying government harassment, in 1949, Jones published one of her most well-known and influential essays, "An End to the Neglect of the Problems of the Negro Woman!" (1949). In it, Jones identified Black women's unique place within the Marxist-Leninist theorization of the mode of production and called for organizing against White chauvinism and imperialism (see the excerpt that follows this essay).[8] The essay is considered pivotal to the history of Black feminism and made Jones a pioneer thinker within the field of intersectional feminism, long before intersectionality was even a word.

In December 1955, Jones was deported to England, where she founded the first black newspaper in London, the *West Indian Gazette and Afro-Asian Caribbean News* (*WIG*) in 1958. Founding the *WIG* and the Notting Hill Carnival are considered the high points of Jones' British career.[9] Jones wrote editorials for the *WIG*, maintaining that labor movements and trade union organizing were the only ways to fight the national bourgeoisie developed by imperialism as a "reliable bulwark to protest its interests for as long as possible even after national independence is won."[10]

Fighting for Black women's rights put Jones at the center of debates among trade unionists and other progressives about class and race. Understanding class as being structured also by relations of gender and race, along with other Black members like Lucy González Parsons, Jones provided intellectual and political leadership within the Communist Party about the insights afforded by Black women's unique standpoints.[11] As a critical theorist and journalist, Jones provided a different kind of reality that opened a conversation within Marxist theory and political organizing about the multiple forms of oppression experienced by Black women and immigrants.[12]

Creating a space for Black women's leadership within the Left was a crucial task for Jones, who believed that once Black women are radicalized, "the militancy of the whole Negro people, and thus of the anti-imperialist coalition is greatly enhanced."[13] Jones' work placed these groups of "the super-exploited," as she referred to them, at the core of the conversation about race, gender, nationhood, and militarized imperialism.[14] Journalism, for Jones, was one of the ways in which she expressed anti-imperialist politics, about which became even more passionate after her deportation to England.

Jones remained devoted to her radical beliefs and fought for them until her life was cut short in 1964. As her biographer Carole Boyce Davies puts it, Jones was buried to the left of Karl Marx at Highgate cemetery in London. The inscription on her grave's tombstone, which was erected in

1984, reads: "Claudia Vera Jones, Born Trinidad 1915, Died London 24.12.64, Valiant Fighter against racism and imperialism who dedicated her life to the progress of socialism and the liberation of her own black people."[15] Her papers are archived at the Schomburg Center for Research in Black Culture at the New York Public Library.

Through challenging the imbalance of power in media and as a Black journalist, Jones was able to introduce the intersectional perspectives of Black women into the world of communication, which like most social movements of her era, failed to connect and analyze race, gender, class, and nation. She also succeeded in re-presenting herself and her community as activists, citizens, and members of the nation, influencing the world of media with her courage, skills, and devotion.

Excerpt: Jones, Claudia, "An End to the Neglect of the Problems of the Negro Woman!" *Political Affairs*, Communist Party USA, June 1949

An outstanding feature of the present stage of the Negro liberation movement is the growth in the militant participation of Negro women in all aspects of the struggle for peace, civil rights and economic security. Symptomatic of this new militancy is the fact that Negro women have become symbols of many present-day struggles of the Negro people. This growth of militancy among Negro women has profound meaning, both for the Negro liberation movement and for the emerging anti-fascist, anti-imperialist coalition.

To understand this militancy correctly, to deepen and extend the role of Negro women in the struggle for peace and for all interests of the working class and the Negro people, means primarily to overcome the gross neglect of the special problems of Negro women. This neglect has too long permeated the ranks of the labour movement generally, of left-progressives, and also of the Communist Party. The most serious assessment of these shortcomings by progressives, especially by Marxist-Leninists, is vitally necessary if we are to help accelerate this development and integrate Negro women in the progressive and labour movement and in our own party.

The bourgeoisie is fearful of the militancy of the Negro woman, and for good reason. The capitalists know, far better than many progressives seem to know, that once Negro women undertake action, the militancy of the whole Negro people, and thus of the anti-imperialist coalition, is greatly enhanced.

Historically, the Negro woman has been the guardian, the protector, of the Negro family. From the days of the slave traders down to the present, the Negro woman has had the responsibility of caring for the needs of the family, of militantly shielding it from the blows of Jim-Crow insults, of rearing children in an atmosphere of lynch terror, segregation and police brutality, and of fighting for an education for the children. The intensified oppression of the Negro people, which has been the hallmark of the post-war reactionary offensive, cannot therefore but lead to an acceleration of the militancy of the Negro woman. As mother, as Negro, and as worker, the Negro woman fights against the wiping out of the Negro family, against the Jim-Crow ghetto existence, which destroys the health, morale and very life of millions of her sisters, brothers and children.

Viewed in this light, it is not accidental that the American bourgeoisie has intensified its oppression, not only of the Negro people in general, but of Negro women in particular. Nothing so exposes the drive to fascisation in the nation as the callous attitude, which the bourgeoisie displays and cultivates toward Negro women. The vaunted boast of the ideologists of big business— that American women possess "the greatest equality" in the world is exposed in all its hypocrisy when one sees that in many parts of the world, particularly in the Soviet Union, the New Democracies and the formerly oppressed land of China, women are attaining new heights of equality. But above all else, Wall Street's boast stops at the water's edge where Negro and working-class women are concerned. Not equality, but degradation and super-exploitation: this is the actual lot of Negro women!

Consider the hypocrisy of the Truman administration, which boasts about "exporting democracy throughout the world" while the state of Georgia keeps a widowed Negro mother of 12 children under lock and key. Her crime? She defended her life and dignity—aided by her two sons—from the attacks of a "white supremacist." Or ponder the mute silence with which the Department of Justice has greeted Mrs Amy Mallard, widowed Negro school teacher, since her husband was lynched in Georgia because he had bought a new Cadillac and become, in the opinion of the "white supremacists," "too uppity." Contrast this with the crocodile tears shed by the US delegation to the United Nations for Cardinal József Mindszenty, who collaborated with the enemies of the Hungarian People's Republic and sought to hinder the forward march to fuller democracy by the formerly oppressed workers and peasants of Hungary. Only recently, President Truman spoke solicitously in a Mother's Day Proclamation about the manifestation of "our love and reverence" for all mothers of the land. The so-called "love and reverence" for the mothers of the land by no means includes Negro mothers who, like Rosa Lee Ingram, Amy Mallard, the wives and mothers of the Trenton Six, or the other countless victims, dare to fight back against lynch law and "white supremacy" violence.

Negro women in mass organisations

This brief picture of some of the aspects of the history of the Negro woman, seen in the additional light of the fact that a high proportion of Negro women are obliged today to earn all or part of the bread of the family, helps us understand why Negro women play a most active part in the economic, social and political life of the Negro community today. Approximately 2,500,000 Negro women are organised in social, political and fraternal clubs and organisations. The most prominent of their organisations are the National Association of Negro Women, the National Council of Negro Women, the National Federation of Women's Clubs, the Women's Division of the Elks' Civil Liberties Committee, the National Association of Colored Beauticians, National Negro Business Women's League, and the National Association of Colored Graduate Nurses. Of these, the National Association of Negro Women, with 75,000 members, is the largest membership organisation. There are numerous sororities, church women's committees of all denominations, as well as organisations among women of West Indian descent. In some areas, NAACP chapters have Women's Divisions, and recently the National Urban League established a Women's Division for the first time in its history.

Negro women are the real active forces—the organisers and workers—in all the institutions and organisations of the Negro people. These organisations play a many-sided role, concerning themselves with all questions pertaining to the economic, political and social life of the Negro people, and particularly of the Negro family. Many of these organisations are intimately concerned with the problems of Negro youth, in the form of providing and administering educational scholarships, giving assistance to schools and other institutions, and offering community service. The fight for higher education in order to break down Jim Crow in higher institutions, was symbolised last year, by the brilliant Negro woman student, Ada Lois Sipuel Fisher of Oklahoma. The disdainful attitudes which are sometimes expressed—that Negro women's organisations concern themselves only with "charity" work—must be exposed as of chauvinist derivation, however subtle, because while the same could be said of many organisations of white women, such attitudes fail to recognise the special character of the role of Negro women's organisations. This approach fails to recognise the special function which Negro women play in these organisations, which, over and above their particular function, seek to provide social services denied to Negro youth as a result of the Jim-Crow lynch system in the US.

The Negro woman worker

The negligible participation of Negro women in progressive and trade-union circles is thus all the more startling. In union after union, even in those unions where a large concentration of workers are Negro women, few Negro women are to be found as leaders or active workers. The outstanding exceptions to this are the Food and Tobacco Workers' Union and the United Office and Professional Workers' Union.

But why should these be exceptions? Negro women are among the most militant trade unionists. The sharecroppers' strikes of the 1930s were sparkplugged by Negro women. Subject to the terror of the landlord and white supremacist, they waged magnificent battles together with Negro men and white progressives in that struggle of great tradition led by the Communist Party. Negro women played a magnificent part in the pre-CIO days in strikes and other struggles, both as workers and as wives of workers, to win recognition of the principle of industrial unionism, in such industries as auto, packing, steel, etc. More recently, the militancy of Negro women unionists is shown in the strike of the packing-house workers, and even more so, in the tobacco workers' strike—in which such leaders as Moranda Smith and Velma Hopkins emerged as outstanding trade unionists. The struggle of the tobacco workers led by Negro women later merged with the political action of Negro and white, which led to the election of the first Negro in the South (in Winston-Salem, NC) since Reconstruction days.

It is incumbent on progressive unionists to realise that in the fight for equal rights for Negro workers, it is necessary to have a special approach to Negro women workers, who, far out of proportion to other women workers, are the main breadwinners in their families. The fight to retain the Negro woman in industry and to upgrade her on the job, is a major way of struggling for the basic and special interests of the Negro woman worker. Not to recognise this feature is to miss the special aspects of the effects of the growing economic crisis, which is penalising Negro workers, particularly Negro women workers, with special severity.

Excerpt: Jones, Claudia, "We Seek Full Equality for Women," *Daily Worker*, Communist Party USA, September 4, 1950

Taking up the struggle of the suffragists, the communists have set new tasks, new objectives in the fight for a new status for women. The special value of William Z. Foster's contribution: the leading role of the Communist Party in the struggle to emancipate women from male oppression is one of the proud contributions, which our party of Marxism-Leninism, the Communist Party, US, celebrates on its 30th anniversary.

Marxism-Leninism exposes the core of the woman question and shows that the position of women in society is not always and everywhere the same, but derives from woman's relation to the mode of production.

Under capitalism, the inequality of women stems from the exploitation of the working class by the capitalist class. But the exploitation of women cuts across class lines and affects all women. Marxism-Leninism views the woman question as a special question, which derives from the economic dependence of women upon men. This economic dependence as Friedrich Engels wrote over 100 years ago, carries with it the sexual exploitation of women, the placing of women in the modern bourgeois family, as the "proletariat" of the man, who assumes the role of "bourgeoisie".

Hence, Marxist-Leninists fight to free woman of household drudgery, they fight to win equality for women in all spheres; they recognise that one cannot adequately deal with the woman question or win women for progressive participation unless one takes up the special problems, needs and aspirations of women—as women.

It is this basic principle that has governed the theory and practice of the Communist Party for the last three decades.

As a result, our party has chalked up a proud record of struggle for the rights of women. American literature has been enhanced by the works of Marxists who investigated the status of women in the US in the 1930s. Its record is symbolised in the lives of such outstanding women communists as Ella Reeve Bloor and Anita Whitney and others who are associated with the fight for women's suffrage, for the rights of the Negro people, for working class emancipation.

Our party and its leadership helped stimulate the organisation of women in the trade unions and helped activize the wives of workers in the great labour organising drives; built housewives' councils to fight against the high cost of living; taught women through the boycott and other militant actions how to fight for the needs of the family; helped to train and mold women communist leaders on all levels, working-class women inspired by the convictions and ideals of their class—the working class.

A pioneer in the fight for the organisation of working-class women, our party was the first to demonstrate to white women and to the working class that the triply oppressed status of Negro women is a barometer of the status of all women, and that the fight for the full, economic, political and social equality of the Negro woman is in the vital self-interest of white workers, in the vital interest of the fight to realise equality for all women.

But it remained for the contribution of William Z. Foster, national chairman of our party, to sharpen the thinking of the American Communist Party on the woman question. Comrade Foster projected in a deeper way the basic necessity for the working class and its vanguard party to fight the obstacles to women's equality, evidenced in many anti-woman prejudices, in the prevalent ideology of male superiority fostered by the monopolists imbibed by the working class men.

The essence of Foster's contribution is that it is necessary to win the masses of American women for the over all struggle against imperialist war and fascism by paying special attention to their problems and by developing special struggles for their economic, political and social needs. Basing himself upon the Marxist-Leninist tenet that the inequality of women is inherently connected with the exploitation of the working class, Foster called on the party and the working class to master the Marxist-Leninist theory of the woman question, to improve our practical work on this question and to correct former errors, errors of commission and omission with regard to this fundamental question.

Foster's special contribution lies in his unique exposé of the mask placed on the status of women in every sphere in the US by American imperialism. Comrade Foster exposed the bourgeois lie that women in the US have achieved full equality and that no further rights remain to be won. He shows that the ideological prop used by reactionary propagandists to perpetuate false ideas of women's "inferiority" is to base their anti-social arguments as regards women on all kinds of pseudo-scientific assumptions, particularly the field of biology.

Any underestimation of the need for a persistent ideological struggle against all manifestations of masculine superiority must therefore be rooted out. If biology is falsely utilised by the bourgeois ideologists to perpetuate their false notions about women, communists and progressives must fare boldly into the biological sciences and enhance our ideological struggle against bourgeois ideas and practices of male superiority.

Notes

1 Claudia Jones, "Speech to the Court, February, 1953," in *"I Think of my Mother": Notes on the Life and Times of Claudia Jones*, ed. Buzz Johnson, 121–126 (London: Karia Press, 1985). This quote is from Claudia Jones' statement after a nine-month trial of 13 Communist leaders in 1953.

2 Carole Boyce Davies, *Left of Karl Marx: The Political Life of Black Communist Claudia Jones* (Durham, NC: Duke University Press, 2008).

3 Jones' autobiography shows that she had already been working with a Black newspaper and a community publication before joining the League. See also Mary Davis, "Claudia Jones: Communist, Anti-Racist and Feminist," *Morning Star*, March 8, 2015, https://morningstaronline.co.uk/-anti-racist-and-feminist-1, accessed April 11, 2022.

4 She also compared Black people's struggle from liberation to colonial struggles around the world.

5 Davies, *Left of Karl Marx*, 41.

6 Ibid., 46–47.

7 Ibid., 78.

8 Claudia Jones, "We Seek Full Equality for Women," *Daily Worker*, September 4, 1950.

9 Notting Hill Carnival is the second largest street festival in the world that celebrates multiculturalism. Held annually, the carnival started as Claudia Jones' attempt to unify a community that was divided by racism and xenophobia. See Sagal Mohammed, "Marxist, Feminist, Revolutionary: Remembering Notting Hill Carnival Founder Claudia Jones," *British Vogue*, July 25, 2020, www.vogue.co.uk/arts-and-lifestyle/article/claudia-jones-notting-hill-carnival, accessed April 11, 2022.

10 Davies, *Left of Karl Marx*, 63.

11 Lucy Eldine González Parsons was an Afro-Indigenous Latina labor organizer, journalist, and anarcho-communist. She was an outspoken defender of free speech and was persecuted by state agents who opposed her militancy.

12 Denise Lynn, "Socialist Feminism and Triple Oppression: Claudia Jones and African American Women in American Communism," *Journal for the Study of Radicalism* 8, no. 2 (2014): 1–20.

13 Davies, *Left of Karl Marx*, 38.

14 Cristina Mislán, "The Imperial 'We': Racial Justice, Nationhood, and Global War in Claudia Jones' Weekly Review Editorials, 1938–1943," *Journalism* 18, no. 10 (November 2017): 1415–1430.

15 Davies, *Left of Karl Marx*, xxvii.

Bibliography

Davies, Carole Boyce. "Deportable Subjects: US Immigration Laws and the Criminalizing of Communism." *South Atlantic Quarterly* 100, no. 4 (2001): 949–966.

_____. *Left of Karl Marx: The Political Life of Black Communist Claudia Jones*. Durham, NC: Duke University Press, 2008.

Davis, Mary. "Claudia Jones: Communist, Anti-Racist and Feminist." *Morning Star*, March 8, 2015. https://morningstaronline.co.uk/-anti-racist-and-feminist-1, accessed April 11, 2022.

Jones, Claudia. "An End to the Neglect of the Problems of the Negro Woman!" *Political Affairs* (June 1941): 51–67.

"Speech to the Court, February, 1953." In *"I Think of my Mother": Notes on the Life and Times of Claudia Jones*, ed. Buzz Johnson, 121–126. London: Karia Press, 1985.

_____. "We Seek Full Equality for Women." *Daily Worker*, September 4, 1950.

Jones, Claudia, and Boyce Davies, Carole. *Claudia Jones: Beyond Containment: Autobiographical Reflections, Essays, and Poems*. Oxford, UK: Ayebia Clarke Publishing Limited, 2011.

Lynn, Denise M. "Socialist Feminism and Triple Oppression: Claudia Jones and African American Women in American Communism." *Journal for the Study of Radicalism* 8, no. 2 (2014): 1–20.

Mislán, Cristina. "The Imperial 'We': Racial Justice, Nationhood, and Global War." *Journalism* 18, no. 10 (November 2017): 1415–1430.

Mohammed, Sagal. "Marxist, Feminist, Revolutionary: Remembering Notting Hill Carnival Founder Claudia Jones." *British Vogue*, July 25, 2020. www.vogue.co.uk/arts-and-lifestyle/article/claudia-jones-notting-hill-carnival, accessed April 11, 2022.

Chapter 11

Dorothy Blumenstock Jones (1911–1980)

By Rafiza Varão

Dorothy Blumenstock Jones (permission of David Evan Jones)

Dorothy Blumenstock Jones, a pioneer in film analysis, was born in Saint Louis, Missouri, on March 29, 1911. She attended the University of Chicago from 1930 to 1934 as an undergraduate student of political science.[1] During her studies, she did not receive financial support from her parents to study "because of her gender."[2] So, she worked as a typist during the first year of her BA studies, sometimes not having enough even to eat.[3] But Jones soon engaged in research activities at the University of Chicago. She received a grant from the Payne Fund, from 1931 to 1932, as a statistical clerk, working with the psychologist Louis Leon Thurstone (1887–1955). In 1932, she worked as an assistant to the examiner in social sciences for the Board of Examinations of the University of Chicago and as a research associate with the American political scientist Frederick Schuman (1901–1981) from 1932–1933. Finally, from 1933 to 1937, Jones worked as a research assistant for the political scientist Harold Lasswell.[4]

By the mid-1920s, propaganda had become one of the most important subjects of research in the emerging social sciences, mainly because of its increasing relevance after World War I. From the mid-1930s until the end of the Cold War, the most prominent figure in these studies was Harold Lasswell, professor of political science at the University of Chicago. He took on Jones and a few other students, such as Bruce Lannes Smith,[5] as apprentices and collaborated with them on research.[6]

In their early work, Jones and Lasswell analyzed communist propaganda. As was common at the University of Chicago's Department of Social Sciences, Lasswell and Jones immersed themselves in a deep search on their topic, participating in meetings of local communist groups. It was not yet the McCarthy years, but the fear of communism was already pervasive among Americans. Lasswell and Jones were disinterested in persecuting communists; instead, they were interested in science itself and in creating an objective method to scrutinize messages as means of communication.

In 1939, the result of their research was published as *World Revolutionary Propaganda: A Chicago Study*, and was the first major effort to use content analysis to understand a corpus of propaganda in the US. Lasswell intended to promote content analysis to give political science a method of neutral judgment and so to approximate political science to the natural sciences. Jones undertook a substantial part of the field research for *World Revolutionary Propaganda*. Lieutenant Mike Mills, who worked at the Chicago Police Department and helped Jones with the research of their archives, attests that she spent a year and a half analyzing the Chicago Police Department's files.[7] By the time the book was published, Jones had married Jack Evan Jones in 1938, yet chose to publish under her maiden name, Blumenstock.

After *World Revolutionary Propaganda: A Chicago Study*, Jones and Lasswell faced accusations of communism that they both tried to refute. Jones even had to ask friends to write letters attesting to her patriotism and proving that she was not a communist sympathizer.[8] Despite accusations of communism/communist sympathies, from 1940 until 1946, Lasswell served as the Chief of the Experimental Division for the Study of War Time Communications at the Library of Congress. Concurrently, in 1942, Jones became chief of the Motion Picture Analysis Division of the Office of War Information's (OWI) Bureau of Motion Pictures in Hollywood. President Franklin Delano Roosevelt had created the OWI as a central agency of propaganda to provide people in the US with information about the war. The OWI was highly controversial insofar as it threatened to control the flow of wartime information. She remained in the position until the OWI was dissolved in 1945.

Working in the OWI, Jones was responsible for research on films, the medium that Roosevelt believed to be "the most effective means of reaching the American public."[9] As the chief of Motion Picture Analysis, she built the methodological foundation for examining films using content analysis. One of her projects included a monumental analysis of 1,313 films. This tremendous effort popularized the use of content analysis among film researchers. In 1945, Jones published an essay entitled "The Hollywood War Film: 1942–1944." The paper analyzed war films released during 1942, 1943, and 1944, trying to understand Hollywood's representations of World War II. As the OWI ended its activities in 1945, Jones earned a grant from the Rockefeller Foundation to continue researching films.[10]

In 1955, Jones wrote *The Portrayal of China and India on the American Screen, 1896–1955: The Evolution of Chinese and Indian Themes, Locales, and Characters as Portrayed on the American Screen*. The study analyzed 325 films using content analysis to assess Hollywood representations of Chinese and Indian minorities. Although the study lacked nuance, and relied on stereotypes, it is considered a classic study of Hollywood representation.

Jones also conducted studies to determine whether there was content related to communist propaganda in movies. In 1956, she wrote her seminal study "Communism and the Movies: A Study of Film Content" (1956), where she analyzed 159 films made by the Hollywood Ten, a group of motion picture professionals who testified before the House Un-American Activities Committee in October 1947, and refused to answer questions about their sympathies or affiliations to communism. In "Communism and the Movies: A Study of Film Content" Jones concluded that none of the 159 films showed any trace of communist propaganda.

Jones' research on Hollywood gave her extensive networks among artists in the film industry.[11] These close relationships led to work in Warner Brothers Studios from 1945 to 1947, and later to engage with the group Another Mother for Peace (AMP), with Donna Reed and Barbara Avedon. The organization, which Jones directed, was a grassroots anti-war group founded in opposition to the Vietnam War. She "worked tirelessly and passionately" on behalf of the AMP.[12]

Jones died in 1980, aged 69, after a fight with cancer. While I was writing this entry about her, I noticed that one of Jones' sons had commented on the Amazon entry for the book *World Revolutionary Propaganda: A Chicago Study*. In the comment, he noted that the name of the co-author (Jones) had been omitted from the sales page.[13] The name of the other author, Harold Lasswell, was clearly visible on it, though. The absence of Jones' name gives a small idea of how she was erased from the history of communication studies, especially in relation to content analysis and film studies. Throughout her career, however, she established a scientific method of film analysis and, by doing so, also helped to create the field of motion picture research in the US.

Excerpt: Jones, Dorothy B., "The Hollywood War Film: 1942–1944," *Hollywood Quarterly* 1, no. 1 (1945)

Traditionally, the motion-picture industry has maintained that the primary function of the Hollywood film is to entertain. However, in a world shattered by conflict it has become increasingly evident that only through solidly founded and dynamic understanding among the peoples of the world can we establish and maintain an enduring peace. At the same time it has become clear that the film can play an important part in the creation of One World. The motion picture can help the people of the world to share and understand one another's viewpoints, customs, and ways of living; it can interpret the common needs and hopes of all peoples everywhere. It is well within the power of the film to reduce psychological distance between people in various parts of the world, just as the airplane has reduced physical distance.

Whether or not the picture makers of the world will meet this challenge remains to be seen. In the case of the Hollywood picture makers perhaps some indication of the answer to this question may be found in an examination of the way in which they met their responsibilities to their nation and to the United Nations during wartime.

The present article reviews the Hollywood feature product of three years of war. It makes no attempt to examine or evaluate any other part of Hollywood's many-faceted war program.

Furthermore, it does not presume to explore the entertainment function of the film in wartime as such, although the entertainment quality of films is taken into account in assessing their value to the war program. By an analysis of the war features released during 1942, 1943, and 1944 an attempt will be made to evaluate how far Hollywood has aided in interpreting the war at home and giving a better understanding overseas of America's role in the conflict.

WHAT IS A WAR FILM?

Any analysis of war films immediately raises the question, What is a war picture? The term "war film" has been bandied about very loosely in Hollywood. Usually it has referred to films depicting battle action. When Hollywood producers said, "The public is tired of war pictures," this is usually what they meant. By this definition *Wake Island* would be considered a war film, whereas *Forever and a Day*, which was produced in the hope of increasing Anglo-American understanding, would not.

Topics relating to the war were much more broadly defined by the late President Roosevelt in his address to Congress on the State of the Union one month after Pearl Harbor. Emphasizing the necessity for increased public information and understanding about the war, he outlined six aspects which needed to be more fully understood: the Issues of the War; the Nature of the Enemy; the United Nations and Peoples; Work and Production; the Home Front; and the Fighting Forces. This classification was subsequently adopted by the Office of War Information, and, because of its comprehensive nature, has proved useful generally in the dissemination and analysis of war data.

[...]

In order to segregate war films for the years 1942–1944 it was necessary to review the entire feature product of this period, a total of more than 1,300 films. Most of these films were viewed before being classified. The classification of some was made on the basis of a final script, and, of a much smaller number, from reviews appearing in the press. Approximately two-thirds of the entire three-year product was either viewed or read in the final script.

HOW MANY WAR FILMS?

During the three years following American entry into World War II the motion-picture industry released a total of 1,313 feature films. Of this number 374, or approximately three in every ten, were directly concerned with some aspect of the war. These were distributed over the three-year period as follows:

	1942	1943	1944
Number of war films [...]	126	133	115
Per cent of total releases	25.9	33.2	28.5

[...]

FILMS TELLING WHY WE FOUGHT

When the Japanese bombed Pearl Harbor on December 7, 1941, the American people were psychologically unprepared for war. Relatively few people understood why the conflict in Europe, like the war in Asia which had been going on since 1931, had inevitably been our concern from the beginning—why the very existence of fascist nations anywhere in the world was a threat to our

democracy. Once this country had been attacked, most people favored a dec-
laration of war. But unless Americans could come to a true understanding of
what the shooting was all about, there was little hope that they could wage an
all-out war and win an all-out peace.

[...]

	1942	1943	1944
Number of films dealing with the issues of the war. [...]	10	20	13
Per cent of total war films	7.9	15.0	11.3

[...]

FILMS ABOUT THE ENEMY

Films dealing with the ideology, objectives, and methods of fascism, both at
home and abroad, have been included under The Enemy. Such films were
most acutely needed during the days immediately following Pearl Harbor,
when Americans not only knew little about the nature of fascism, but also had
small comprehension of the fact that we faced enemies much stronger and
better prepared for war than ourselves.

During 1942–1944, Hollywood released 107 motion pictures depicting
the enemy. These films represented 28.6 per cent of the war product of these
years and more than 8 per cent of the total output of Hollywood:

	1942	1943	1944
Number of films depicting the enemy [...]	64	27	16
Per cent of total war films	50.8	20.3	13.9

[...]

Although there were more films about the enemy than in any other category, this
subject by and large received a distorted and inadequate portrayal on the screen.
Features of this type were the first to be produced in any quantity in Hollywood,
because they required only a slight adaptation of the usual mystery formula and
thus provided an easy means for capitalizing at the box office on interest in the
war. As the war proceeded, films treating the enemy more seriously began to
appear. When taken in relation to the total number of films about the enemy,
however, such constructively oriented pictures were relatively few.

FILMS ABOUT OUR ALLIES

The United Nations theme in pictures is important for several reasons. With
American entry into the war, it was necessary that the American public to

whom the war was a distant, far-off event should come to a more intimate understanding of the role that was being played by allied nations.

[...]

Films about our allies were needed to broaden American understanding of the many aspects of the United Nations battle. They were needed abroad as testimony of our appreciation of the role these people had played in our mutual fight against the enemy.

During the first three years of the war, the motion-picture industry produced a total of 68 films about the United Nations and peoples. This number represented 18 per cent of the war films released during these years, and 5 per cent of the total product. These 68 films were released as follows:

	1942	1943	1944
Number of films treating United Nations [...]	14	30	24
Per cent of total war films	11.1	22.6	20.9

[...]

FILMS ABOUT THE HOME FRONT

In a country like ours, which did not actually witness the hostilities, one of the most difficult problems was the mobilization of the home front. Early in the war, civilians were called upon to volunteer for civilian defense. American families were asked to conserve food, save scrap metal and waste paper, and in many other small ways to assist in the war effort. The public was asked to cooperate in the prevention of inflation and to buy war bonds. To mobilize the country for these and other war activities was no small task. There was a place for films which would stimulate interest in and dignify these chores, and convince the public of their importance. In addition, it was extremely important that films destined for overseas audiences which depicted America in wartime should tell something about these home-front activities [...].

During 1942–1944 the industry released 40 features concerned primarily with home-front problems. These pictures accounted for 11 per cent of all war films produced during these years, and for 3 per cent of the entire film product of this period.

	1942	1943	1944
Number of home-front features [...]	4	15	21
Per cent of total war films	3.2	11.3	18.3

[...]

During 1944, Hollywood released a cycle about delinquency in wartime America: *Where Are Your Children?*, *Are These Our Parents?*, *Youth Runs Wild*, *I Accuse My Parents*, etc. These films gave a sensational treatment of this problem, and offered little or nothing constructive toward a solution. Rather, such pictures caused concern because they tended to hinder the recruitment of women to industry. Conscientious mothers, fearful that their children might become delinquent, refused to enter industry where they were badly needed to release men for the armed services. It was generally agreed that delinquency films of the type produced by Hollywood created fear and hysteria, thereby intensifying the delinquency problem.

Thus the feature film did little to dignify and interpret for American audiences the home-front war. Instead, Hollywood pictures tended to ridicule, exaggerate, or sensationalize these problems. This treatment was particularly unfortunate in its effect on audiences abroad.

FILMS ABOUT OUR FIGHTING FORCES

With the exception of films about the enemy, more features dealing with the American fighting forces were produced by Hollywood during 1942–1944 than on any other war topic. In these years, 95 pictures about the Army, Navy, and Merchant Marine were released:

	1942	1943	1944
Number of films about American fighting forces [...]	29	32	34
Per cent of total war films	23.0	24.1	25.4

Approximately one out of every four war films produced during the three years following American entry into the war dealt with the fighting man, his training, his combat experiences, his adventures when on leave, etc. [...]

HOLLYWOOD'S WAR JOB

The analysis of Hollywood's war product shows that, of a total of 1,313 motion pictures released during 1942, 1943, and 1944, there were 45 or 50 which aided significantly, both at home and abroad, in increasing understanding of the conflict. This means that approximately 4 per cent of the film output of these three years, or about one out of every ten war pictures, made such a contribution. There were many causes for Hollywood's failure to make maximum use of the feature film in the war effort. To begin with, the Hollywood industry, like most others in America, was unprepared for the war emergency.

For years, motion-picture studios had been turning out six or seven hundred films a year, the great majority of which were musicals, domestic comedies, westerns, and murder mysteries based on well-worn formulas. For years producers had been adamant in their opinion that what the American public wants, above all else, is to be entertained. It is small wonder, then, that, faced with the task of making films which would educate the public about the war, most Hollywood movie makers did not know where to begin. They lacked experience in making films dealing with actual social problems. And, like the rest of America, they themselves lacked real understanding of the war.

The formula picture, and the tendency of many producers to cling to it as a safe and sure bet at the box office, proved a serious handicap during the war years. Whenever Hollywood lapsed into its usual formulas in the making of war pictures, the results were disastrous, since the material itself became secondary to the development of the stereotyped plot. That is one reason why most of the war films produced by Hollywood were inconsequential, misleading, or even detrimental to the war program (for example, the spy series, or the blood-and-thunder combat pictures).

Another important factor limiting Hollywood's effectiveness was lack of knowledge and concern about audiences abroad. Primary attention in production has always been focused on domestic box office, the main source of industry revenue. With the advent of the war, however, Hollywood's indifference about foreign audiences became a critical factor. Every film made in Hollywood either contributes to or detracts from the reputation of America and the American people overseas. In the case of pictures portraying the role of this nation and of our allies during this war, the influence of Hollywood was multiplied a thousandfold. Yet most film makers failed to realize that the melodramatic blood-and-thunder combat film, with the American hero single handedly disposing of a score of Nazis, would bring jeers and hisses in a London movie house, or that a musical singing out that the Yanks had done it once and would do it again would cause a riot between American and British soldiers in a theater in Bombay.

The problem of timing was perhaps the most difficult one facing the industry in its production of useful war films. A feature film cannot be written, photographed, edited, and released overnight. Production of an "A" feature takes from nine to twelve months, sometimes longer. The releasing problem itself caused further delays, particularly in recent years when the large backlog of unreleased pictures meant that completed films might stay in the can for many months before reaching the screen. As a result, by the time they reached the screen many war films were outdated, or the time when they would have had maximum usefulness was passed. The industry as a whole did little about meeting this serious problem. It might have been possible to speed up production on a series of "B" pictures treating immediate problems, and let the "A"-budget war films treat long-range subjects which would not become outdated. Then, too, the releasing structure could have been adapted to bring timely films to the screen more rapidly. However, the release of some important war films was excellently timed, notably *Mrs. Miniver, Wilson*, and *Mission to Moscow*.

Hollywood's experience with the making of war films has led forward looking writers, producers, story editors, and others to the realization that something must be done about these problems if the film is to play the vital role in world affairs for which it is so admirably suited. There are many indications that important changes are taking place in the motion-picture capital, that the traditional notions about film making which have so long governed the industry are slowly yielding to more progressive ideas about the function of the film in the world today. This is reflected in some of the fine films which were produced during the war, and in certain noticeable changes in the content of films generally (a more constructive portrayal of minority groups, more films realistically portraying American life for foreign audiences, etc. The changes taking place in Hollywood will be accelerated by the return of film makers who have been in the Armed Services making day-to-day use of the film as a dynamic weapon of war.

Hollywood has gained immeasurably in social awareness and in new techniques of film making as a result of the war. Now that the smoke of battle is clearing away, a world public is waiting to see whether Hollywood will accept the greater responsibilities and opportunities that lie ahead by helping to create One World dedicated to peace, plenty, and the pursuit of happiness.

Notes

1 Dorothy B. Jones never received an advanced degree or gained a permanent academic position.
2 Rafiza Varão, "A First Glance at the work of Dorothy Blumenstock Jones," *Mediterranean Journal of Communication* 12, no. 2 (2021): 33.
3 Ibid.
4 From Dorothy B. Jones, application form for a Rockefeller Fellowship in Humanities, Document Box 12, Folder 398, Rockefeller Archive Center, NY. Unpublished, 1950.
5 Bruce Lannes Smith (1909–1987) was an American political scientist and communication theorist.
6 Gabriel Almond, *A Discipline Divided: Schools and Sects in Political Science* (London: Sage, 1989), 323.
7 Mike Mills, Letter, unpublished manuscript, 1955. Permission of David Jones (personal collection).
8 Varão, "A First Glance," 33.

9 Clayton R. Koppes and Gregory D. Black, "What to Show the World: The Office of War Information and Hollywood, 1942–1945," *The Journal of American History* 64, no. 1 (1977): 89.

10 Dorothy B. Jones, "William Faulkner: Novel into Film." *The Quarterly of Film Radio and Television* 8, no. 1 (1953): 51.

11 Varão, "A First Glance," 33.

12 Ibid.

13 This entry would not be possible without the help of Jones' sons, Kim (born 1945), David (born 1946) and Kelvin Jones (born 1949).

Bibliography

Almond, Gabriel. *A Discipline Divided: Schools and Sects in Political Science.* London: Sage, 1989.

Jones, Dorothy B. "Communism and the Movies: A Study of Film Content." In Cogley, J., *Report on Blacklisting,* Vol 1. Movies. New York: Fund for the Republic, 1956, 196-305.

"The Hollywood War Film: 1942-1944." *Hollywood Quarterly* 1, no. 1 (1945): 1-19.

_____. "Hollywood's International Relations." *The Quarterly of Film Radio and Television* 11, no. 4 (1957): 362-374.

_____. "The Language of Our Time." *The Quarterly of Film Radio and Television* 10, no. 2 (1955): 167-179.

_____. *The Portrayal of China and India on the American Screen, 1896-1955: The Evolution of Chinese and Indian Themes, Locales, and Characters as Portrayed on the American Screen.* Cambridge, MA: Center for International Studies, MIT, 1955.

_____. "Quantitative Analysis of Motion Picture Content." *Public Opinion Quarterly* 6, no. 3 (1942): 411-428.

_____. " 'Sunrise': A Murnau Masterpiece." *The Quarterly of Film Radio and Television* 9, no. 3 (1955): 238-262.

_____. "War without Glory." *The Quarterly of Film Radio and Television* 8, no. 3 (1954): 273-289.

_____. "William Faulkner: Novel into Film." *The Quarterly of Film Radio and Television* 8, no. 1 (1953): 51-71.

Koppes, Clayton R. and Gregory D. Black. "What to Show the World: The Office of War Information and Hollywood, 1942-1945." *The Journal of American History* 64, no. 1 (1977): 87-105.

Lasswell, Harold D. and Dorothy Blumenstock. *World Revolutionary Propaganda: A Chicago Study.* New York, NY: Knopf, 1939.

Varão, Rafiza. "A First Glance at the Work of Dorothy Blumenstock Jones." *Mediterranean Journal of Communication* 12, no. 2 (2021): 17-34.

Chapter 12
Patricia Louise Kendall (1922–1990)

By Elena D. Hristova

Patricia Louise Kendall (photograph, Rockefeller Foundation Records Fellowships, © and Courtesy of Rockefeller Archive Center)

From 1943 to 1965 Patricia L. Kendall worked as a researcher at the Bureau of Applied Social Research, Columbia University. There she was one of the few women who climbed the Bureau's career ladder to direct research studies, develop viable research methods for the study of audiences and teach them to graduate students, and produce key ideas about persuasion.

Kendall was born in Pueblo, Colorado on June 12, 1922. In 1932, she began attending Friends Seminary, a private day school rooted in Quaker values. After graduating in June 1938, she began a BA degree at the liberal arts Smith College, in Northampton, Massachusetts. Between September 1942 and June 1945, she studied for an MA at Columbia University's Sociology Department. By 1943, she had completed all the coursework requirements, but needed to still write her thesis. In June 1943, aged 22, with Paul Lazarsfeld's support, she applied for and received a Rockefeller Foundation fellowship to work as assistant in what was still named the Office of Radio Research. For the duration of the fellowship, her annual salary would be $1700. On the application form she explained: "My plans for the future are indefinite, but I am anxious to do social research which will contribute to the war effort now, and, following the war, to the period of reconstruction."[1] Kendall's words were typical of the wartime push to undertake socially useful research.

After six months on the fellowship, Lazarsfeld wrote a glowing report of Kendall's work and recommended that her fellowship be extended by a further six months: "All of us who have worked with K. feel that she has rulfilled [sic / fulfilled] all of our expectations. As a matter of fact, it is quite surprising how such a young person does so balanced and reliable work on quite difficult subject matters. I think she is one of the best fellowship cases we ever had. Things move slowly because of so many people involved, but without K. they wouldn't move at all."[2] Kendall became one of the key researchers to head studies at the Bureau, ensuring that projects involving numerous people were undertaken in a timely, consistent, and productive manner. By 1949 she was among the seven women listed as members of the BASR on the Bureau's letterhead: Jeanette Green, Marie Jahoda (see Chapter 8 of this volume), Babette Kass, Rose Kohn, Louise Moses, and Patricia J. Salter.[3] In 1949 Kendall also married Lazarsfeld (who had been previously married to Marie Jahoda and Herta Herzog, Chapter 6).

Kendall received a PhD in Sociology from Columbia University in 1954, more than 12 years after beginning her graduate studies at the institution. Her dissertation "Conflict and Mood: Factors Affecting Stability of Response" was published by the Free Press. While at the Bureau, she authored 15 research and methodology articles, the second highest publication record of any woman affiliated with the BASR, after Carol H. Weiss' 25 publications.[4]

In 1965, Kendall left her senior research associate position at the Bureau to join the Sociology faculty of Queens College, City University of New York.[5] By July 1966, the Rockefeller Foundation staff recorded that she was a housewife, ignorant of her teaching position. In fact, Kendall's career progressed, and she chaired the Department of Sociology at Queens College between 1970 and 1971.[6]

The Bureau's publication and research records show that women tended to publish academic research individually—usually a revision of their master's theses, and most often conducted academic research in male-led teams. Women, on the other hand, dominated the Bureau's commercial studies.[7] The abridged report of one such commercial study reproduced here, *The Personification of Prejudice as a Device in Educational Propaganda: An Experiment in Product Improvement* (New York: Bureau of Applied Social

Research, 1946) is a product of a team of women: Patricia Kendall, who headed the project; Dr. Katherine Wolf, who worked as a consultant; and some 20 female interviewers—a rare example of a women-only research team.[8] It is one of the many commercial studies undertaken at the Bureau, most often by female researchers. Funded by the American Jewish Committee (AJC), the study's goal was to understand how audiences comprehend visual anti-prejudice propaganda at the time of seeing it.[9]

The study itself and the report accompanying it are notable in terms of sample selection, method of interviewing, and findings. First, the sample was of working-class white men who interviewers had to visually identify as such; the sample was therefore presumed to be homogenous despite ethnic diversity notable in interview transcripts. These working-class white men were the presumed audience for anti-prejudice cartoons that appeared in the labor press. The study, therefore, always already understood that prejudice was situated within and could be studied in the opinions of working-class white men. These men inevitably became a stand in for prejudice in the population at large. This is similar to the way in which the partner study in Decatur, Illinois (which led to the formation of the two-step flow of communication model) used white middle-class women as a stand-in for the population at large, all the while falling short from acknowledging the particularities of women's experiences, especially as white, middle-class, stay-at-home wives experiencing changes in gender relations at the end of World War II.[10]

Second, the method of interviewing gave substantial power to interviewers in the way in which they negotiated gender, femininity, class, and education status in the interview situation, found and assessed their subjects, and related back the answers given. Interviewers took it upon themselves to find respondents who visually matched the sample description, used their femininity and age to compel answers (by playing on being young and clueless), recorded answers from memory, and gave their own assessment of the respondent and the validity of his answers. The interviewers, therefore, had a substantial power to represent their subjects on the interview transcript. Kendall negotiated with the interviewers on the best approach for subject selection, on interview technique, on answer recordings, and she also monitored their work.[11]

Third, the study is notable for its findings on the "boomerang" understanding of satirical anti-prejudice propaganda cartoons, which found that a third of the sample recognised the cartoon's concern with the problem of prejudice, yet the element of satire was overlooked.[12] This was an important finding which showed that satirical visual messages, rather than persuading those with similar beliefs to abandon them due to ridicule, have the opposite effect of entrenching the very beliefs being ridiculed. These findings were also present in the Decatur sample,[13] and were later explored and pathologized by Eunice Cooper and Marie Jahoda as a misfunctioning of the brain due to prejudice.[14] In combination, these works questioned the effectiveness of anti-prejudice propaganda. Kendall's initial findings were a step towards understanding how persuasion works on different audiences; further, through the association between the AJC and Nelson Rockefeller's Office of Inter-American Affairs, these ideas would contribute to the development of strategies for propaganda campaigns from the United States to Latin America.

We cannot overestimate the impact Kendall had at the Bureau and on the development of interviewing techniques and survey methods for the study of audiences. She researched radio audiences with Lazarsfeld, articulated the methodology for the focused interview with Marjorie Fiske (see Chapter 4 of this volume) and Robert Merton, and with Merton illuminated the audience's co-authorship of meaning which anticipated Stuart Hall's ideas of encoding and decoding media messages. After her husband's death in 1976, she edited a collection of his works.[15] Kendall's social scientific training enabled her to devise complex questionnaires and interview techniques to be used at the BASR and in her own research in the sociology of medicine for years to come.[16] Moreover, Kendall trained graduate students in research methods, thus influencing the next generation of scholars who would use focused interviews and surveys in their own research and further refine the methodologies Kendall had helped create.

Excerpt: Kendall, Patricia and Katherine Wolf, *The Personification of Prejudice as a Device in Educational Propaganda: An Experiment in Product Improvement* (New York: Bureau of Applied Social Research, 1946) (permission of Robert Lazarsfeld)

Contributor's note: Footnotes from the original. I have preserved the style of the original notes. Underlining has been changed to italics throughout.

CHAPTER I *THE PROBLEM, THE PEOPLE, AND THE PROCEDURE*

There are three ways of studying propaganda documents such as the series of Mr. Biggott cartoons. One type of study investigates simply the *audience* of the material: how many people actually see, hear, or read the document, and who are these people? A second type of research studies the *effects* of the document on the attitudes, behavior, or habits of people who are exposed to it.

A third type of study examines the *experiences* of the subjects as they see or hear the material. It provides a dynamic "X-ray" picture of understanding, reactions, association, all in relation to certain predispositions of the subjects.

The present study is of the third type. In it we observed and analyzed how a group of specially selected respondents behaved when they were confronted with three of the Mr. Biggott cartoons. What did they think the cartoons were about? Was it possible to observe how certain factors in the respondents themselves influenced their understanding? What were their reactions to Mr. Biggott? Did these reactions also influence understanding? Finally, what features of the cartoons themselves were related to understanding?

In order to attempt answers to any of these questions we must know, first of all, what it was which the subjects should have understood. We must, therefore, state briefly the message which the cartoons were intended to convey to their readers.

In the second place, if we are going to be able to relate understanding and reaction to predispositions of the respondents, we must have a clear picture of just what sort of people these respondents were.

Finally, we must give a brief description of the interview technique used in the study so that the dynamic character of the "X-ray" picture will be clarified.

The Message of the Mr. Biggott Cartoons

Since the Mr. Biggott cartoons are intended as a series, their general message should be a consistent one. The only major variation should be in the specific situations depicted in each of the cartoons, and in the text which accompanies the drawing.

The Series in General

The purpose of the nine cartoons which we have been able to analyze is to *ridicule prejudice as an old-fashioned and unattractive type of* behavior. But the ridicule is not always accomplished in the same way. In some cartoons, Mr. Biggott appears as a foolish and stupid individual. In others, he is a vicious person who feels no compunction in offending other people when he asserts his prejudices. And in still other cartoons, his statements are just simply ridiculous.

More consistent than the message in which the series is the central character himself. In every cartoon, Mr. Biggott appears as a desiccated and sickly looking man of indeterminate old age. In each cartoon, his name, with its invidious connotations, labels him (for those who notice the name and understand the word "bigot") as an undesirable character. And Mr. Biggott's unattractiveness and lack of modernity are further accentuated by the cobweb which he trails from his oddly shaped head in each cartoon. In fact, the only feature which could be counted in Mr. Biggott's favor is the rather elegant clothing which he wears: his well-tailored suit, his clean white shirt, his starched — if old-fashioned—collar, and, in two of the nine cartoons, his gloves and cane. Mr. Biggott is quite clearly a city man of at least moderate income.

[...]

The Test Public

Since the study was to be limited to approximately 150 cases, it was necessary that the public be a relatively homogenous one in order to permit meaningful statistical comparisons. In consultation with the sponsors, therefore, we selected as our sample a representative group of *white, non-Jewish men in the laboring class of New York City.*[3]

[...]

The Interviewing Technique

Finally, we must describe in some detail the procedures which we used. Only when we know the way in which we "photographed" the members of our test public can the results of the "X-ray picture" be appraised.

Focus on Understanding

In studying cartoons —or any other material—which deal with racial prejudices, one is always tempted to devote the larger part of the interview to questions concerned specifically with prejudices. Anti-minority attitudes are an important and highly interesting area of investigation, and the research worker who has an opportunity to study problems tangentially related to such attitudes is always somewhat inclined to center his attention on the prejudices themselves.

But a split in the focus of research has more serious drawbacks. The first is the quite obvious one that depth of material is sacrificed. Almost every non-therapeutic interview has definite time limits. One cannot expect a respondent to discuss cartoons, anti-minority attitudes, or the state of the nation for an indefinite length of time. Every study director, therefore, is faced with the necessity for making the best possible use of the time which he can expect a respondent to spend with him. This means that the larger the range of topics to be considered in any one interview, the more superficial will be the coverage of each.

---

3 The considerations which led us to select this group, rather than any other, are discussed in Appendix A, part I.

But a second drawback has even more serious implications. It is a well-known fact that *by answering questions on any given topic a respondent's attention becomes directed toward that topic.* Supposing, for instance, that we devote a large part of an interview to questions about the possibility of unemployment, to opinions concerning the best ways to handle unemployment, and so on. If we then suddenly ask our respondents what they consider the major social problem facing the country, it is probable that many of them will mention unemployment.

It was important in the present study to prevent any such channeling of attention by the questions we asked. The sponsors of the study were interested primarily in finding out just what the members of our test public thought the cartoons were meant to be about. How many of them saw their connection with the problem of race prejudices? How many of them thought they were meant to be nothing more than jokes? How many related them to problems other than those of racial prejudices?

In other words, the respondents' understanding of and reaction to the cartoons was to be examined in an entirely neutral framework. Because of this, questions which might have influenced comments concerning understanding and reaction were reduced to a minimum. And it was primarily the questions which sought out the respondents' prejudices and attitudes toward racial minorities which had thus to be sacrificed, for these would have had a direct influence on understanding.

Throughout the study, then, *our interest has centered on the degree to which the cartoons were understood and the variety of reactions which they evoked. Only secondarily have we investigated the prejudices of our respondents.*

Focus on Process

We made the claim at the beginning of this report that the picture which we obtained, both of understanding and reaction, is a dynamic one. In other words, our interest is in the *processes* by which the respondents come to understand the cartoons or the *processes* through which they shut off any understanding. Similarly, our interest is in the dynamic features of the reaction to Mr. Biggott and the cartoons in which he appears.

Understanding was not considered a static phenomenon which could be judged at any one point in the interview. Rather we hoped that it would turn out to be a process in which either improvement or deterioration could be observed. For this reason, the same or similar questions were asked at different stages in the interview.[4]

The respondents' reactions to Mr. Biggott were treated in a similar fashion. Although we incorporated all of the interview material into rough overall picture of each respondent's predominant reaction and predominant attitude to Mr. Biggott, our main interest was in the processual features of such reaction. For this reason, again, questions, eliciting reactions to the central character in the cartoons were asked at different stages in the interview, and were separately analyzed.

Focus on Specificity

A final feature of the interview guide was the many-sided characterization of Mr. Biggott which it ensured. We felt confident that the respondents' unelaborated emotional reactions to Mr. Biggott could be determined from their spontaneous comments regarding the cartoons. But, we were not as confident that each respondent would voluntarily describe in detail what sort of a person he thought Mr. Biggott to be. We decided, therefore, not to rely on spontaneous comments concerning Mr. Biggott, but to ask each member of the test public what personal attributes he assumed Mr. Biggott would have, what his political sympathies and affiliations might be, whether or not he was prejudiced, and how representative of a class of people he was.

To summarize: the interview guide used in the present study was, first of all, focused on the problem of *understanding* the cartoons rather than on the prejudices or related attitudes of the individuals to whom the cartoons were shown. It was designed, secondly, to make possible analysis of the

---

4 The questions in the interview guide pertaining to the understanding of the material are reproduced below, along with an indication of where in the interview they were asked:

Question	Stage in Interview when asked
#8: Who do you think might put out such cartoons? For what purpose?	Asked after respondents had seen *two* cartoons.
#14: What do you think about cartoons like this in general? Do you think they are a good idea? (Probe for purpose)	Asked after respondents had seen *all three* cartoons, but before any general discussion.
#19: Would you like to see more of these cartoons? Have you ever heard any stories that could be used for these cartoons? (Probe for purpose)	Asked after respondents had been asked to characterize Mr. Biggott, and after he had answered two checklist questions.
#29: What do you think the artist is trying to do?	Asked as last question in the interview.

In addition to these questions which probed specifically for an understanding of the cartoons, the interview guide contained questions which indirectly tested the respondents' understanding. The interview guide used in our study is found in Appendix C.

processes of understanding and reaction, and therefore contained questions which were repeated at different stages in the interview. Finally, our interview guide enabled the *respondents to elaborate their pictures of Mr. Biggott.* [...]

APPENDIX C

INTERVIEW GUIDE

In order to make certain that we would obtain comparable information from all of our respondents, we furnished the interviewers with a guide which outlined the major areas of response to be covered in each interview. Briefly these areas were:

1. The respondent's *understanding* of the cartoon;
2. His *reaction* to Mr. Biggott;
3. His *characterization* of Mr. Biggott;
4. His *own prejudices and attitudes toward prejudices*;
5. His own *awareness* of political and social platforms;
6. Background characteristics.

The guide was never used as a fixed questionnaire, however. In a detailed interview, the interviewer allows himself to be led from one topic to another by the respondent. Therefore, there was no fixed order for any but a few of the questions dealing specifically with understanding. Rather, the interviewers were instructed to ask questions logically suggested by the respondents' comments, whether or not these questions were in order indicated in the guide.

Furthermore, the questions contained in the guide were usually just the starting point for the discussion of any topic. Generally, they did no more than start the respondent talking about his reactions to Mr. Biggott, his understanding of the cartoons, or some other topic. In order to make the comment as complete and as detailed as possible, then, the interviewers followed up these initial questions with appropriate probes. None of these are included in the guide, of course.

Finally, the interviewers were free to change the wording of any question when they felt there was a need to do so. The questions contained in the guide were those which a series of pretests had shown to be most successful, but an occasional rephrasing of them helped to elicit material not obtained originally. This freedom in the wording of questions had the additional advantage of making interviewers less dependent on the guide, therefore decreasing the probability that they would use it as a questionnaire rather than as a skeleton outline.

Notes

1 Patricia Kendall Rockefeller Fellowship application, RG 10.1, Series 200E, Box 13, Folder 414, Rockefeller Foundation Archives, New York.

2 Patricia Kendall Rockefeller Fellowship application, RG 10, Subgroup 2: Fellowship Recorder Cards, 1917–1970s, Box 6, Rockefeller Foundation Archives, New York.

3 Dean Manheimer to Leland DeVinney, September 7, 1949. Record Group 1.1 Projects, Series 200 United States, Box 317, Folder 3777, Rockefeller Foundation Archives, New York.

4 Elena D. Hristova, "The Speculative in Communication Research: Data, Identity, and the Pursuit of Professionalism, 1940–1960" (PhD diss., University of Minnesota, 2020), fig. 13, 102.

5 Report to the Council for Research in the Social Sciences, December 11, 1946, Box 317, Folder 3774, Rockefeller Foundation Archives, New York.

6 Peter Simonson and Lauren Archer, "Patricia Kendall." Women in Media Research, Out of the Question, www.outofthequestion.org/Women-in-Media-Research/Office-of-Radio-Research-Bureau-of-Applied-Social-Research.aspx#KENDALL, accessed April 25, 2023.

7 Elena D. Hristova, "Research and Publishing at the Bureau of Applied Social Research: The Gendering of Commercial and Academic Work," *International Journal of Communication* 16 (January 2022): 655–663.

8 At the BASR women-only teams held the lowest research and publication record with only 2.8% of studies conducted between 1941 and 1977; Hristova, "The Speculative in Communication Research," 102.

9 For further discussion of the study, see Hristova, "The Speculative in Communication Research," 136–296.

10 See: Susan J. Douglas, "Notes Toward a History of Media Audiences," *Radical History Review* 52 (1992): 127–138; Susan J. Douglas, "Personal Influence and the Bracketing of Women's History," *Annals of the American Academy of Political and Social Science* 608 (2006): 41–50.

11 This is explored at length in Hristova, "The Speculative in Communication Research," 166–238.

12 Patricia Kendall and Katherine Wolf, *The Personification of Prejudice as a Device in Educational Propaganda: An Experiment in Product Improvement* (New York, NY: Bureau of Applied Social Research, 1946), 8.

13 Kendall and Wolf note in the report: "The results of the two studies are compared in Appendix D. When we say that the techniques used in Decatur minimized the possibility that understanding would be 'cued,' we refer, of course, only to the free-answer parts of the questionnaire. The check-lists did provide the same sorts of aids to comprehension which result from extensive probing. In fact, one type of understanding which was found in the Decatur study was actually called 'checklist aided': the free-answer was corrected when the subject was given an opportunity to study the alternative suggested in the check-list." Kendall and Wolf, *The Personification of Prejudice as a Device in Educational Propaganda*, 15, ft. 12.

14 Eunice Cooper and Marie Jahoda, "The Evasion of Propaganda: How Prejudiced People Respond to Anti-Prejudice Propaganda," *Journal of Psychology* 23, no. 1 (1947): 15–25.

15 Patricia Kendall, *The Varied Sociology of Paul F. Lazarsfeld* (New York, NY: Columbia University Press, 1982).

16 See bibliography for list of publications.

Bibliography

Cooper, Eunice, and Marie Jahoda. "The Evasion of Propaganda: How Prejudiced People Respond to Anti-Prejudice Propaganda." *Journal of Psychology* 23, no. 1 (1947): 15-25.

Douglas, Susan J. "Notes Toward a History of Media Audiences." *Radical History Review* 52 (1992): 127-138.

_____. "Personal Influence and the Bracketing of Women's History." *Annals of the American Academy of Political and Social Science* 608 (2006): 41-50.

Hristova, Elena D. "Research and Publishing at the Bureau of Applied Social Research: The Gendering of Commercial and Academic Work." *International Journal of Communication* 16 (January 2022): 655-663.

_____. "The Speculative in Communication Research: Data, Identity, and the Pursuit of Professionalism, 1940-1960." PhD diss., University of Minnesota, 2020.

Kendall, Patricia. "The Ambivalent Character of Nationalism among Egyptian Professionals." *Public Opinion Quarterly* 20, no. 1 (1956): 277-292.

_____. "Clinical Teachers' Views of the Basic Science Curriculum." *Journal of Medical Education* 35, no. 2 (1960): 148-157.

_____. *Conflict and Mood: Factors Affecting the Stability of Response.* Glencoe, IL: Free Press, 1954.

_____. "Consequence of the Trend Toward Specialization." In *Psychosocial Aspect of Medical Training*, ed. Robert H. Coombs and Clark E. Vincent, 498-523. Springfield, IL: Charles C. Thomas, 1971.

_____. "Evaluating an Experimental Program in Medical Education." In *Innovation in Education*, ed. Matthew B. Miles, 343-360. New York, NY: Teachers College Bureau of Publications, 1964.

_____. "Impact of Training Programs on the Young Physician's Attitudes and Experiences." *Journal of the American Medical Association* 176, no. 12 (1961): 992-997.

_____. "The Learning Environments of Hospitals." *Journal of the American Medical Association* (1961): 195-230.

_____. "Medical Sociology in the United States." *Social Science Information* 2, no. 2 (1963): 1-15.

_____. "Medical Specialization: Trends and Contributing Factors." In *Psychosocial Aspect of Medical Training*, ed. Robert H. Coombs and Clark E. Vincent, 449-497. Springfield, IL: Charles C. Thomas, 1971.

_____. *The Relationship Between Medical Educators and Medical Practitioners*. Evanston, IL: Association of American Medical Colleges, 1965.

_____. "Student Evaluation of the Cornell Comprehensive Care and Teaching Program." In *Comprehensive Medical Care and Teaching: A Report on the New York Hospital—Cornell Medical Center Program*, ed. George G. Reader and Mary E. W. Goss, 312–344. Ithaca, NY: Cornell University Press, 1967.

_____, ed. *The Varied Sociology of Paul F. Lazarsfeld*. New York, NY: Columbia University Press, 1982.

Kendall, Patricia and James A. Jones. "General Patient Care: Learning Aspects." In *Comprehensive Medical Care and Teaching: A Report on the New York Hospital—Cornell Medical Center Program*, ed. George G. Reader and Mary E. W. Goss, 73–120. Ithaca, NY: Cornell University Press, 1967.

Kendall, Patricia and Robert K. Merton. "Medical Education as Social Process." In *Patients, Physicians, and Illness: Sourcebook in Behavioral Science and Medicine*, ed. E. Gartley Jaco, 321–350. Glencoe, IL: Free Press, 1958.

Kendall, Patricia and Katherine Wolf. "The Analysis of Deviant Cases in Communications Research." *Communications Research, 1948–49* (1949): 152–179.

_____. *The Personification of Prejudice as a Device in Educational Propaganda: An Experiment in Product Improvement*. New York, NY: Bureau of Applied Social Research, 1946.

Lazarsfeld, Paul, and Patricia Kendall. "The Listener Talks Back." In *Radio in Health Education*, 48–65. New York Academy of Medicine. New York, NY: Columbia University Press, 1945.

_____. *Radio Listening in America: The People Look at Radio—Again*. New York: Prentice-Hall, 1948. Reprinted. New York, NY: Arno Press, 1979.

Maas, Jane. *Mad Women: The Other Side of Life on Madison Avenue in the '60s and Beyond*. London: Transworld, 2012.

Merton, Robert K. "Working with Lazarsfeld." In *Paul Lazarsfeld (1901-1976): La Sociologie de Vienna à New York*, ed. Jacques Lautman and Bernard-Pierre Lécuyer, 163–212. Paris: L'Harmattan, 1998.

Merton, Robert K. and Patricia Kendall. "The Boomerang Response: The Audience Acts as Co-author—Whether You Like It or Not." *Channels, National Publicity Council* 21, no. 7 (1944): 1–7.

_____. "The Focused Interview." *American Journal of Sociology* 51, no. 6 (1946): 541–557.

Merton, Robert K., Marjorie Fiske, and Patricia L. Kendall. *The Focused Interview: A Manual of Problems and Procedures*. Glencoe, IL: Free Press, 1956.

Merton, Robert K., Patricia P. Kendall, and Marjorie Fiske. *The Focused Interview: A Manual of Problems and Procedures*. 2nd ed. New York, NY: Free Press, 1957.

Merton, Robert K., George G. Reader, and Patricia Kendall. *The Student Physician: Introductory Studies in the Sociology of Medical Education*. Cambridge, MA: Harvard University Press, 1957.

Patricia Kendall Rockefeller Fellowship application, RG 10, Subgroup 2: Fellowship Recorder Cards, 1917-1970s, Box 6, Rockefeller Foundation Archives, New York.

Patricia Kendall Rockefeller Fellowship application. RG 10.1, Series 200E, Box 13, Folder 414. Rockefeller Foundation Archives, New York.

Report to the Council for Research in the Social Sciences. December 11, 1946. Box 317, Folder 3774, Rockefeller Foundation Archives, New York.

Rockefeller Foundation Archives, Record Group 1.1 Projects, Series 200 United States, Box 317, Folder 3777.

Rowland, Allison L. and Peter Simonson. "The Founding Mothers of Communication Research: Toward a History of Gendered Assemblage." *Critical Studies in Media Communication* 31, no. 1 (2014): 3–26.

Simonson, Peter and Lauren Archer. "Patricia Kendall." *Women in Media Research, Out of the Question*. www.outofthequestion.org/Women-in-Media-Research/Office-of-Radio-Research-Bureau-of-Applied-Social-Research.aspx#KENDALL, accessed April 9, 2023.

Chapter 13

Eleanor Leacock (1922–1987)

By Tiffany Kinney

Eleanor Burke Leacock was a Marxist-feminist anthropologist who studied capitalism and colonialism's impact on indigenous groups, especially by analyzing how egalitarian societies transformed into ones marked by structural inequalities.[1] Active from the 1940s to the 1980s, Leacock influenced feminist anthropology by drawing from her findings on pre-classed, indigenous groups to challenge essentialist, ahistorical theories of women's subordination. Leacock's work influenced communication studies as she detailed how the Jesuits disseminated information, specifically crafting stories about socially acceptable behaviors as part of their pedagogical program to educate the Montagnais-Naskapi. Additionally, Leacock spoke at length about the psychological ramifications of the Jesuits' pedagogical/colonialization efforts: "conflicting ideologies caused profound [...] psychological turmoil for these individuals [...] who made an often-agonizing decision to give up traditional beliefs and practices and adhere to new codes of conduct and commitment."[2] Importantly, Leacock's work considered not only how storytelling played a role in converting these indigenous groups into Christianity but also the psychological ramifications of these pedagogical efforts.

Leacock was born on July 2, 1922 in Weehawken, New Jersey. Her father was social philosopher and rhetorician Kenneth Burke and her mother was Lily Mary Batterham, a mathematics teacher. Her parents introduced Leacock to a world of radicals, writers, and artists at a young age.[3] She spent her youth living in two locations—her family farm in New Jersey and an apartment in Greenwich Village. Later, Leacock attended Radcliffe College on a scholarship, where she became more immersed in radical politics and Marxism.[4] Leacock eventually transferred to Barnard College and earned a BA in anthropology in 1944. After graduating, fellow anthropologists Ruth Benedict and Rhoda Metraux attempted to hire her at the Office of War Information in Washington, D.C., but the FBI refused to give her security clearance because of her support of Marxism and other "radical" political causes.[5]

Instead, Leacock continued her education as a graduate student in anthropology at Columbia University where she was mentored by Gene Weltfish (see Chapter 19). Leacock attests that Weltfish was "the person to whom [she] fe[lt] closest in [her] work. [She] learned from her at many levels.

She set a forceful example in helping [her] go through graduate school and retain the attitude toward learning that many young people lose."[6] While Leacock earned "A's" in many of her graduate seminars, she was confronted by the extreme sexism of her male professors, who often excluded her from research opportunities because of her gender, thereby rendering Weltfish's mentorship all the more significant. Towards the end of her graduate education, Leacock focused her dissertation research on an ethnographic study of the Montagnais-Naskapi of Labrador, Canada.[7] Here, Leacock gathered evidence to challenge universal notions of private property, women's subordination, and misguided assumptions surrounding indigenous kinship systems. In terms of methodology, Leacock "blended archival research with ethnographic field research" and she took an unprecedented feminist approach when she "shared her results with the community she studied."[8] This revolutionary approach—sharing results with the studied community to effectively level the power dynamics between researcher and subjects—would later become foundational to feminist anthropology.

Despite her innovative research methods, Leacock did not receive the same kinds of support as earlier female anthropologists from Columbia University—such as Zora Neale Hurston and Margaret Mead. While Leacock received a grant to conduct her dissertation research in Canada, she did not receive the same level of feminist mentorship provided to these earlier women, especially in terms of guiding her "in practices of community formation that created a network of recruitment."[9] In fact, while attending Columbia, Leacock experienced a suppression of feminist mentorship likely because her mentor, Weltfish, was suddenly fired from her position as a result of McCarthyism and the "Red Scare." After graduating, Leacock spent 11 years seeking a full-time position and was frequently passed over because she was a political radical, a mother, and a wife, and therefore not considered a "serious scholar." During this time, she accepted various part-time teaching positions which allowed Leacock to "synthesize and test out [her] own thinking" while also providing her with the opportunity to continue her research and contribute to anthropology.[10]

In 1963, Leacock finally secured a full-time position in anthropology at the Brooklyn Polytechnic Institute. With financial security and intellectual freedom, Leacock became far more prolific. She published over 80 articles and ten book manuscripts exploring the foundations of racism, classism, and sexism, and subsequent forms of social and cultural resistance to these organizing systems.[11] While research was important to Leacock, she credits her academic success to her love of "writing—with all of its difficulties—in and of itself."[12] Leacock continued to attain academic accolades through her writing and teaching, eventually becoming chair of the Anthropology Department at City College of New York.[13]

While her private life should not overshadow Leacock's public accomplishments, she was also a devoted mother to four children, a wife, and a vocal, political radical. Although critical of the inequitable, societal structures which influence women's lives, Leacock was successful at combining her various roles. For example, Leacock merged her professional and personal responsibilities by bringing her newly born son, Robert, to conduct onsite field research in Labrador, Canada for her dissertation.[14] While this is but one instance, Leacock often integrated her public and private roles by functioning as a mother and researcher, and later she drew from this experience to critique anthropological findings. On this point, when Leacock first learned about famous anthropologist Margaret Mead's ideas concerning women's inherent passivity, she forcefully rejected them, stating: "I was not persuaded, but became more aware of myself as a rebel."[15] Leacock later expressly rebelled against Mead's notion of women as "passive" by drawing examples from her active life as a mother: "rush to the subway, stop at the market [...] dash home, [relieve] the babysitter, straighten things up [...] start throwing supper together."[16] In her writing, she juxtaposes this dynamic portrayal with the experience of her passive, male colleagues arriving home to a prepared supper. It was through her own experience as a female academic, *actively* and successfully navigating various roles, and her research on matrilineal, indigenous social structures, that Leacock was able to refute previously accepted understandings of gender essentialism.

Beyond integrating her private and public roles, Leacock's work is noteworthy in its multidisciplinary nature and its political commitment. She was an outspoken critic of social injustice, especially within the hierarchical confines of academia. In fact, she is known for personally mentoring junior colleagues and professionally for writing what became required reading for Marxist-feminist scholars, specifically her introduction to Friedrich Engels' *The Origin of the Family, Private Property, and the State.*[17] Her research spans diverse fields, including "anthropology of education, women cross-culturally, foraging societies, ethnohistory, urban anthropology, and Marxist anthropology" and diverse regions, including North America, Europe, Africa, and Asia.[18] And in her interdisciplinary work, Leacock built bridges between various academic communities to help them understand the role of intersectionality in exploitation and preventing effective resistance.[19]

While published within one year of each other, these two excerpts from Leacock's extensive oeuvre are emblematic of her major theoretical contributions which collectively focus on challenging the myths of male dominance. These two texts exemplify the two primary methods Leacock used to critique the ahistorical nature of gender essentialism: 1) by illustrating the independence of women in pre-classed societies and 2) by exploring how organizing structures undercut women's power.[20] Leacock admits her research on "matrilocality represents a basic element in [all her] thinking," which is highlighted throughout both excerpts. More specifically, in the first excerpt, "Society and Gender," Leacock distills her findings on indigenous tribes, their matrilocal organizational patterns, and women's subsequent power.[21] Here, she deconstructs the myth of indigenous societies as male dominated to establish that native women assumed respected roles and were treated as equals to their male counterparts. In the second excerpt, entitled "Women, Development, and Anthropological Facts and Fictions," Leacock again draws from her findings on matrilocality and indigenous societies to critique the prevalence and primacy of male dominance, colonialism, and capitalism, in order to illustrate how these organizing structures work in tandem to undercut women's autonomy.

Ultimately, Leacock's work challenged accepted understandings of women's subordination, especially by deconstructing the ahistorical nature of gender essentialism. Even beyond her revolutionary findings, Leacock's impact was widespread as her scholarship inspired generations and her mentorship helped guide the careers of countless female anthropologists.

Excerpt: Leacock, Eleanor, "Society and Gender," in *Myths of Male Dominance: Collected Articles on Women Cross-Culturally* (New York: Monthly Review Press Classics, 1981). Originally published in *Genes and Gender*, ed. Ethel Tobach and Betty Rosoff (New York: Guardian Press, 1978) (permission *Monthly Review Press*)

Contributor's note: Footnotes from the original. I have preserved the style of the original notes.

One can take one's pick among conflicting generalizations made about women cross-culturally and about the role of women in any specific society; e.g., that "all real authority is vested" in the women of the Iroquois of New York. [...] Or another statement made a century later, that the Iroquois men "regarded women as inferior, the dependent, and the servant of men" (Morgan 1954).

Steven Goldberg, author of *The Inevitability of Patriarchy* (1973), pre-dictably chose the second statement [...] That it was written in the nineteenth century, when the Iroquois lived in single-family houses, and women were dependent on wage-work done by men, was of no moment to him. The first statement was written when the Iroquois still retained a measure of political and economic autonomy. Then they lived in the "long house," in multifamily collectives. The women owned the land, farmed together, and controlled the stores of vegetables, meat, and other goods. They nominated the sachems who were responsible for intertribal relations, and had the power to recall those who did not represent their views to their satisfaction.

[...]

A much studied, reported on, and filmed people living today on the bor-derline between Brazil and Venezuela, the Yanomamö, are characterized in a widely read anthropology textbook (Harris 1975) as having a style of life that "seems to be entirely dominated by incessant quarreling, raiding, dueling, beating, and killing." [...] "Yanomamö men are as tyrannical with Yanomamö women as Oriental monarchs are with their slaves." In explanation, the author cites increasing population density and struggle over new hunting lands (279).

In a study of another Yanomamö group, however, one reads that these people may have first gained their reputation for fierceness when they fought off a Spanish exploring party in 1758 (Smole 1976). In that period, Spanish and Portuguese adventurers were ranging throughout the Amazon area searching for slaves. The author of the account worked with a relatively peaceful high-land group, and he suggested that the exaggerated fierceness of the lowland Yanomamö is not typical, but may have been developed for self-protection. In the village he studied, elder women, like elder men, are highly respected. When collective decisions are made, mature women "often speak up, loudly, to express their views" (70).

[...]

Skipping to another major area, one can read of "the traditional ideal of male domination characteristic of most African societies" (LeVine 1966). Or one can read that in most of the monarchial systems of traditional Africa, there were "either one or two women of the highest rank who participated in the exercise of power and who occupy a position on a par with that of the king or complementary to it" (Lebeuf 1971). According to Lebeuf, women's and men's positions were complementary throughout the various social ranks of African society. Women formed groups for "the purpose of carrying out their various activities," and these could become "powerful organizations." An example of how such groups have functioned even in recent times is given in an account of the Anaguta people of Nigeria. When news spread among the women that a new ruling might cut off their income they made from the sale of firewood, they

marched down from the hills and assembled before the courthouse in a silent, formidable, and dense mass, unnerving the chief and council, all of whom made speeches pledging sympathy; and similar demonstrations took place when it was rumored that women were going to be taxed in the Northern Region. (Diamond 1970: 476)*

A recurrent theme in contemporary anthropological literature is that men's activities are always in the public and important sphere, while women's concerns are limited to the private, familiar, and subsidiary sphere. LeVine (1966: 187), who wrote of the traditional male domination in African society, stated that "women contribute very heavily to the basic economy, but male activities are much more prestigeful." By contrast, Lebeuf (1971: 114) wrote, "neither the division of labour nor the nature of tasks accomplished implies any superiority of the one over the other."

[...]

The structure and images of contemporary Western society are often projected onto other cultures uncritically when women's roles are being discussed, and historical changes that took place with the spread of colonialism and imperialism are ignored. The sheer lack of information on the activities of women and decisions made by them has encouraged this ethnocentrism. However, evidence now being gathered indicates that "male dominance" is not a human universal, as is commonly argued; that in egalitarian societies the division of labor by sex has led to complementarity and not female subservience; and that women lost their equal status when they lost control over the products of their work.

[...]

Today, the age-old *practical* basis for a sex division of labor according to reproductive roles and responsibilities has all but vanished. Assertion of past inferiority for women should therefore be irrelevant to the present and future developments.

[...]

Today the humanistic goal of a peaceful and cooperative world has become an urgent need if we are to survive as a species. Generalizations about women are, in effect, generalizations about men and about human society in general. It is important to pick right.

---

* This event took place in the early 1960s. The famous women's demonstrations in Nigeria took place in the 1920s, in one of which thirty women were shot.

Excerpt: Leacock, Eleanor, "Women, Development, and Anthropological Facts and Fictions," *Latin American Perspectives*, 4, no. 1/2 (Winter 1977) (reprinted by permission of Sage Publications, Inc)

The view is commonly held that women have traditionally been oppressed in Third World societies, and that "development" is the key to changing their situation. The opposing view is that women's status was good in many (not all) Third World societies in the past, and that the structure and ideology of male dominance were introduced as corollaries of colonialism. Furthermore, accumulating evidence shows that, although contemporary development may afford political and professional roles for a few token women, given its imperialist context it continues to undermine the status and autonomy of the vast majority (Boserup, 1970; Bossen, 1975; Nash, 1975; Remy, 1975; Rubbo, 1975; Trigger, 1969). To discuss the impact of development on women's status in society, therefore, means to confront the reality that women's oppression is inextricably bound with a world system of exploitation.

[...]

To analyze the status of women in order to change it, is to analyze the need for and possibility of the most fundamental social transformation.

Real development would mean bringing an end to the system whereby the multinational corporations continue to "underdevelop" Third World nations by consuming huge portions of their resources and grossly underpaying their workers. [...] To talk of development also means facing the reality that "under-developed" national groups exist in the heart of the "developed" industrial world—Black, Chicano, Hispanic, and Native American minorities in the United States, and immigrant workers from Third World nations in Europe.

[...]

Third World women suffer manifold forms of oppression: as virtual slave labor in households, unpaid for their work as mothers who create new generations of workers, and as wives or sisters who succor the present one; as workers, often in marginal jobs and more underpaid than men; and as members of racial minorities, or of semi-colonial nations, subject to various economic, legal, and social disabilities. All the while, women bear the brunt, psychologically and sometimes physically, of the frustration and anger of their menfolk, who, in miserable complicity with an exploitative system, take advantage of the petty power they have been given over the women close to them. Perhaps the most bitter reality lies with the family, which is idealized as a retreat and sanctuary in a difficult world. Women fight hard to make it this, yet what could be a center of preparation for resistance by both sexes is so often instead a confused personal battleground, in which women have little recourse but to help recreate the conditions of their own oppression.

[...]

Although women bear the heaviest burden of national and of class oppression, they are often told that they must subvert their own cause at this time in the interest of the "larger" goals of national, racial, and class liberation from exploitation. [...] The problem of ultimately transforming world capitalist society is so vast, so enormous, that to consider it seriously calls for the recognition of the need to combine the special drive for liberation of half of humanity, women *as women*, with the drive of women and men as workers and as members of oppressed races and nations.

[...]

True, women's oppression today is virtually world-wide, and though much decreased, it has yet to be eradicated in socialist countries. Therefore bio-psychological arguments about women's greater "passivity" or men's greater competitive aggression sound persuasive. Furthermore, to project the conditions of today's world onto the totality of human history and to consider women's oppression as inevitable, affords an important ideological buttress for those in power.

[...]

The image of women as naturally the servitors of men, and men as naturally the dominators of women, reinforces the myth that traditional family relationships in Third World nations were based on the male dominance that characterized Europe, where the Calvinist entrepreneurial family was of great importance to the rise of capitalism. The idea of women's autonomy is then presented as a Western ideal, foreign to the cultural heritages of Third World peoples. The fact, however, is that women retained great autonomy in much of the pre-colonial world.

[...]

For descriptions of how women and men related in egalitarian societies in the early colonial period, one must turn to history [...] A detailed study of the seventeenth and eighteenth century Cherokee in the southeast United States, written recently by a lawyer (Reid, 1970) and describing women's autonomy, has not found its ways into discussions of female status, and a report by the early anthropologist, John Wesley Powell (1880), that documents women's political role among the Wyandot of the Great Lakes, is not mentioned in a recent ethnography on the related Huron (Trigger, 1969). The Cherokee and Wyandot were both matrilineal and matrilocal, that is, men married into households that passed down in the female line.

[...]

Powell wrote of Wyandot society that there were four levels: the family, the gens (or clan), the phratry (or group of gens), and the tribe, and he stated, "the head of the family is a woman" (1880: 59). These family heads chose four women to serve on the gens council, and these four women, in turn, chose a "chief [...] from their brothers and sons" (1880: 61). [...] Powell was explicit about the responsibilities of the women councilors to partition and mark gens land every two years; settle the inheritance of household goods that passed down to female kin; and consent to marriages proposed to them by mothers of young women.

[...]

In his account of the Cherokee, John Phillip Reid (1970) stresses the absolute equality of women and men in tribal, village, and personal affairs. The town councils that met nightly except during the hunting season consisted of "an assembly of all the men and women" (1970: 30). Everyone could speak and be heard. Some Cherokee women chose to become prominent in military affairs, and receive a title translated as "Beloved Woman," "Pretty Woman," or "War Woman" (Reid, 1970: 197). In 1781, the Beloved Woman Nancy Ward was made responsible for negotiating a peace with an invading American army. A generation earlier her uncle, Little Carpenter, had startled a council meeting of white Carolinians by asking why they were all male. Among the Indians, women attended the councils, he said, and he asked why this was not the custom of white people as well (Reid, 1970: 69).

[...]

As women continue to seek effective forms of organization against oppression, anthropologists who study cultural evolution and cross-cultural comparisons have the choice: either to document the autonomous roles women played in egalitarian societies, for the perspectives they lend to organizational strategies and socialist goals; or to spin out ever more elegant rationales for exploitation.

Notes

1 Christine Gailey, "Leacock, Eleanor. July 2, 1922–April 2, 1987," in *Notable American Women: A Biographical Dictionary Completing the Twentieth Century*, eds. Susan Ware and Stacy Braukman (Cambridge, MA: Harvard University Press, 2004), 373; Constance Sutton and Richard Lee, "Eleanor Burke Leacock (1922–1987)," *American Anthropologist* 92, no. 1 (March 2016): 201.

2 Eleanor Leacock and Jacqueline Goodman, "Montagnais Women and the Jesuit Program for Colonization," in *Women and Colonization: Anthropological Perspectives*, ed. Mona Etienne and Eleanor Leacock (New York, NY: Praeger, 1980), 55.

3 Gailey, "Leacock, Eleanor," 373.

4 Sutton and Lee, "Eleanor Burke Leacock," 202.

5 Gailey, "Leacock, Eleanor," 373.

6 Eleanor Leacock, "Preface," in *Myths of Male Dominance: Collected Articles on Women Cross-Culturally* (New York, NY: Monthly Review Press Classics, 1981), 11.

7 Juli McLoone, "Eleanor Burke Leacock, Feminist Anthropologist," University of Michigan, www.apps.lib.umich.edu/blogs/beyond-reading-room/eleanor-burke-leacock-feminist-anthropologist, accessed February 22, 2021.

8 Gailey, "Leacock, Eleanor," 374.

9 Risa Applegarth, "Working with and Working for: Ethos and Power in Women's Writing," in *Rethinking Ethos: A Feminist Ecological Approach to Rhetoric*, ed. Kathleen Ryan, Nancy Meyers, and Rebecca Jones (Carbondale: Southern Illinois University Press, 2016), 220.

10 Leacock, "Preface," 7.

11 Gailey, "Leacock, Eleanor," 374.

12 McLoone, "Eleanor Burke Leacock."

13 Sutton and Lee, "Eleanor Burke Leacock," 203.

14 McLoone, "Eleanor Burke Leacock."

15 Leacock, "Preface," 2.

16 Ibid., 2.

17 Gailey, "Leacock, Eleanor," 374; Sutton and Lee, "Eleanor Burke Leacock," 201.

18 Sutton and Lee, "Eleanor Burke Leacock," 201.

19 Gailey, "Leacock, Eleanor," 374.

20 Sutton and Lee, "Eleanor Burke Leacock," 203.

21 Leacock, "Preface," 3.

Bibliography

Applegarth, Risa. "Working with and Working for: Ethos and Power in Women's Writing." In *Rethinking Ethos: A Feminist Ecological Approach to Rhetoric*, ed. Kathleen Ryan, Nancy Meyers, and Rebecca Jones, 216–236. Carbondale, IL: Southern Illinois University Press, 2016.

Boserup, Ester. *Women's Role in Economic Development.* London: Allen and Unwin, 1970.

Bossen, Laurel. "Women in Modernizing Societies." *American Ethnologist* 2 (November 1975): 587–601.

Diamond, Stanley. "The Anaguta of Nigeria: Suburban Primitives." *Contemporary Change in Traditional Societies*, ed. by Julian H. Steward, 363–505. Champaign/Urbana: University of Illinois Press, 1970.

Gailey, Christine. "Leacock, Eleanor. July 2, 1922–April 2, 1987. Anthropologist, Feminist." In *Notable American Women: A Biographical Dictionary Completing the Twentieth Century*, ed. Susan Ware and Stacy Braukman, 373–374. Cambridge, MA: Harvard University Press, 2004.

Goldberg, Steven. *The Inevitability of Patriarchy: Why the Biological Difference Between Women and Men Always Produces Male Domination.* New York, NY: Morrow, 1974.

Harris, Marvin. *Culture, People, Nature: An Introduction to General Anthropology.* New York, NY: Crowell, 1975.

Leacock, Eleanor. "The Changing Family and Lévi-Strauss, or Whatever Happened to Fathers?" *Social Research* 44, no. 2 (Summer 1977): 235–259.

_____. "Interpreting the Origins of Gender Inequality: Conceptual and Historical Problems." *Dialectical Anthropology* 7, no. 4 (February 1983): 263–284.

_____. "Introduction: Engels and the History of Women's Oppression." In *Women Cross-Culturally, Change and Challenge*, ed. Ruby Rohrlich-Leavitt. The Hague: Mouton Publishers, 1979.

_____. "Introduction to Lewis Henry Morgan." In *Ancient Society*, Parts I, II, III, IV, Gloucester, MA: Peter Smith.

_____. "Matrilocality Among the Montagnais-Naskapi." *Southwestern Journal of Anthropology* 11, no. 1 (1955): 31–47.

_____. *The Montagnais "Hunting Territory" and the Fur Trade*. Menasha, WI: American Anthropological Association, 1954.

_____. *Myths of Male Dominance: Collected Articles on Women Cross-Culturally*. New York, NY: Monthly Review Press, 1981.

_____. "Political Ramifications of Engels' Argument on Women's Subjugation," In *Myths of Male Dominance: Collected Articles on Women Cross-Culturally*, ed. Eleanor Leacock, 305–309. New York, NY: Monthly Review Press, 1981.

_____. "Preface." In *Myths of Male Dominance: Collected Articles on Women Cross-Culturally*, ed. Eleanor Leacock, 1–12. New York: Monthly Review Press Classics, 1981.

_____. "Review of Margaret Mead's Male and Female." In *Myths of Male Dominance: Collected Articles on Women Cross-Culturally*, ed. Eleanor Leacock, 205–208. New York, NY: Monthly Review Press, 1981.

_____. "Social Behavior, Biology, and the Double Standard." In *Sociobiology: Beyond Nature/Nurture?*, ed. George Barlow and James Silverberg, 475–481. Boulder, CO: Westview Press, 1980.

_____. "Society and Gender." In *Genes and Gender*, ed. Ethel Tobach and Betty Rosafa, 197–204. New York, NY: Gordian Press, 1978.

_____. "Status Among the Montagnais-Naskapi of Labrador." *Ethnohistory* 5, no. 3 (Summer 1958): 200–209.

_____. "Structuralism and Dialectics." *Reviews in Anthropology* 5, no. 1 (January 1978): 117–128.

_____. *Teaching and Learning in City Schools: A Comparative Study*. New York, NY: Basic Books, 1969.

_____. "Women, Development, and Anthropological Facts and Fictions." *Latin American Perspectives* 4, no. 1/2 (Winter 1977): 8–12.

_____. "Women's Status in Egalitarian Society: Implications for Social Evolution." *Current Anthropology* 19, no. 2 (June 1978): 225–259.

Leacock, Eleanor and Jacqueline Goodman. "Montagnais Women and the Jesuit Program for Colonization." In *Women and Colonization: Anthropological Perspectives*, ed. Mona Etienne and Eleanor Leacock, 25–42. New York, NY: Praeger, 1980.

Leacock, Eleanor and Nancy O. Lurie, eds. *North American Indians in Historical Perspective*. New York, NY: Random House, 1971.

Leacock, Eleanor and June Nash. "Ideologies of Sex: Archetypes and Stereotypes." *Annals of New York Academy of Sciences* 1, no. 285 (March 1977): 618–645.

Leacock, Eleanor and Nan Rothschild. *Labrador Winter: The Ethnographic Journal of William Duncan Strong, 1927-1928*. Washington, D.C.: Smithsonian Institutional Press, 1994.

Leacock, Eleanor and Helen Icken Safa. *Women's Work: Development and the Division of Labor by Gender*. South Hadley, MA: Bergin and Garvey, 1986.

Leacock, Eleanor, Martin Deutsch, and Joshua A. Fishman. *Toward Integration in Suburban Housing: The Bridgeview Study*. Washington, D.C.: Anti-Defamation League of B'nai B'rith, 1965.

Lebeuf, Annie. "The Role of Women in Political Organizations of African Societies." In *Women of Tropical Africa*, ed. by Denise Paulme, 93–119. Berkeley, CA: University of California Press, 1971.

LeVine, Robert. "Sex Roles and Economic Change in Africa." *Ethnology* 5, no. 2 (1966): 186–193.

McLoone, Juli. "Eleanor Burke Leacock, Feminist Anthropologist." https://blogs.lib.umich.edu/beyond-reading-room/eleanor-burke-leacock-feminist-anthropologist, accessed April 9, 2023.

Morgan, Lewis Henry. *League of Ho-De-No-Sau-Nee or Iroquois*. New Haven, CT: Human Relations Area Files, 1954.

Nash, June. "Certain Aspects of the Integration of Women in the Development Process: A Point of View." Mexico City: United National World Conference of the International Women's Year, 1975.

Powell, John Wesley. *Wyandot Government: A Short Study of Tribal Society*. First Edition, Annual Reports of the Bureau of American Ethnology, 1880. www.gutenberg.org/files/16947/16947-h/16947-h.htm, accessed April 23, 2023.

Price, David. *Threatening Anthropology: McCarthyism and the FBI's Surveillance of Activist Anthropologists*. Durham, NC: Duke University Press, 2004.

Reid, John Phillip. *A Law of Blood: The Primitive Law of the Cherokee Nation*. New York, NY: New York University Press, 1970.

Remy, Dorothy. "Underdevelopment and the Experience of Women: A Nigerian Case Study." In *Toward an Anthropology of Women*, ed. by Rayna R. Reiter, 358-371. New York, NY: Monthly Review Press, 1975.

Rubbo, Anna. "The Spread of Capitalism in Rural Colombia: Effects on Poor Women." In *Toward an Anthropology of Women*, ed. Rayna R. Reiter, 333-356. New York, NY: Monthly Review Press, 1975.

Smole, W.J. *The Daily Life of the Aztecs on the Eve of the Spanish Conquest*. New York, NY: Macmillan, 1976.

Sutton, Constance and Richard Lee. "Eleanor Burke Leacock (1922-1987)." *American Anthropologist* 92, no. 1 (March 1990): 201-205.

Trigger, Bruce. *The Huron, Farmers of the North*. New York, NY: Holt, Rhinehart and Winston, 1969.

Chapter 14

Helen Merrell Lynd (1896–1982)

By Aimee-Marie Dorsten

Helen Merrell Lynd (courtesy of the Sarah Lawrence College Archives)

Researching Helen Merrell Lynd often implicates her husband, sociologist Robert S. Lynd, as if they are two sides of the same coin, because they are known as the husband-and-wife team of the *Middletown* studies. Yet, Lynd's scholarly career is remarkable in its own right: she completed her PhD in the 1920s at Columbia University while helping build Sarah Lawrence College and raising two children.[1] Her scholarship ranges across sociology, history, psychology, social philosophy, and other disciplines; includes seven sole-author books on history, psychology, and philosophy, numerous articles, and shared authorship on *Middletown: A Study in American Culture* (1929) and *Middletown in Transition: A Study in Cultural Conflict* (1937). Her scholarship was based in the classics and social philosophy, including Hegelian philosophy.[2] But the true pulse of her work was vigorous endorsement for critical social justice. She is cited in critical consumer studies, feminism, globalization, history, Marxism, mass communication studies, psychology, qualitative research methods, social psychology, and sociology.[3]

Helen Merrell Lynd was born in LaGrange, Illinois in 1896 to Congregational Protestant parents. Her humanist bent came from her parents' socially liberal attitudes toward race and culture and a modest upbringing in Illinois and Massachusetts. Her father's work was itinerant; her mother took in boarders.[4] Lynd entered Wellesley College in 1915, awakened to her own stratified class position. Unlike other students, she worked and lived in the dorms simultaneously: "I had no money. My clothes were all wrong."[5] But she recalled that it did not make "a scrap of difference."[6] Lynd graduated in 1919. She taught secondary school in New York until she met Robert S. Lynd on a hiking trip. They married in 1921. Lynd earned her master's degree at Columbia University the following year.

In 1924 the Lynds began the Middletown study, a ground-breaking, ethnographic research project funded by the Rockefeller Foundation. They fully embedded themselves for a year, analyzing "Middletown" life, including media and popular culture; and Lynd shared in the design and on-site research in Muncie, Indiana.[7] Yet, she was not properly credited for her contributions. There were no clear workload boundaries, because she said that "was alien to our thinking."[8] Robert Lynd used the book as his doctoral dissertation, and one requirement for his graduation was that *her* work be stricken to legitimate his degree. According to her, "there were some parts of [Middletown] that people think Bob wrote, I actually wrote," because the process was that "we would each write a chapter and then we would exchange and [...] rewrite for the other."[9] In a 1973 interview she underscores some resentment about a note on method in *Middletown*: "I wrote it [...] and that's one thing Bob didn't revise [...]. So I said that should be crossed out. He said, 'I would have written it if you hadn't.'"[10]

Yet, Lynd's critical cultural stamp on *Middletown* is evident. She saw the mass media and consumer ideology permeating Muncie. She completed the newspaper archival research representing the bulk of the third chapter that also provides "base-line" context throughout the book. She was also a key interviewer/participant for the second section, "Making a Home" and a later chapter, "Things Making and Unmaking Group Solidarity."[11] Lynd's "newspaper work" was not merely for context.[12] In the 27th chapter, "Getting Information," her research was qualitatively and quantitatively rich, providing a critical media content-analysis roadmap for future scholars. Marxist in orientation, "Getting Information" argues that the press "becomes [...] an essential community necessity in the conduct of group affairs," particularly for maintaining the status quo of Muncie-style American culture.[13] Merrell Lynd does not hesitate to clarify that the *Middletown* studies were a "deviation" from her own "thing," which was to work on the PhD she ultimately earned from Columbia in 1944.[14]

Her dissertation-turned-book, *England in the Eighteen-Eighties: Toward a Social Basis for Freedom* (1945), uses news to tap into the laissez-faire zeitgeist of 1880s England to demonstrate how the development of the social philosophies of the day shaped the class structure in discourse and practice. *England* is a basal text demonstrating how happy a marriage could be between political economy and cultural studies that established broad conclusions about the impact religious, cultural, social, political, and economic institutions and theories had on those with little class power or agency.[15]

In "Realism and the Intellectual," written seven years later, Lynd stands against McCarthy and Eisenhower's attempt to refashion educational and mass media institutions as "instruments of [...] military, business, or political interests."[16] She criticizes the hypocrisy of those—including the mass media—who accept a forced choice fallacy between hawkish realism and utopianism in both military and educational policy.[17] Her arguments around the Red Scare and the potential for atomic war in "Realism" prefigure 1980s arguments about the Cold War and the capitalistic corporatization of the mass media or education.[18] But "Realism" sparked off controversy: she received scathing criticism from conservative academics in print, local and regional news, and she drew the attention of the House Un-American Activities Committee (HUAC) who questioned her and her Sarah Lawrence colleagues.[19] She reflected that if she had to do it again, she would "take the First Amendment," and fight HUAC's investigation to the Supreme Court.[20] A decade later, Lynd signed her name to the National Committee to Abolish the House Un-American Activities Committee report titled: "House Un-American Activities Committee: Bulwark of Segregation."[21]

Six years after her public excoriation, she wrote her most influential work, *Shame and the Search for Identity* (1958), which represented her turn toward psychology and reflected her interrogation and defamation by HUAC. In *Shame*, Lynd examined the discourse on the concept of shame and its entanglement with "guilt" in order to argue that "guilt [...] is based on internalization of values—in contrast to shame, which is based upon disapproval coming from outside."[22]

It is unclear whether the impact of Lynd's work is felt more in sociology, philosophy, psychology, or communication—it cannot be saddled by concerns for canonicity because her mark is across disciplines and her prolificacy must still be reckoned with. In a draft of her husband Robert S. Lynd's eulogy, one of their close friends wrote that Robert "tried desperately to live up to Helen, knowing that it was impossible."[23]

**Excerpt: Lynd, Helen Merrell, *England in the Eighteen-Eighties:
Toward a Social Basis for Freedom* (London: Oxford University Press,
1945) (permission Staughton Lynd)**

Contributor's note: Footnotes from the original. I have preserved the style of
the original notes.

I. The Eighteen-Eighties
	[...]

England in 1880 was aware of a new apprehension about the future.
Half a decade of world depression had brought fear of foreign competition
and imperialist rivalry. While a century of world industrial supremacy had
engendered a vast complacency within England, insistent questions were now
being raised: Were the 'days of great trade profits over'? Was 'liberal enterprise'
at an end? Had the world 'at this precise year of grace come to the "end of its
tether" in regard to the development of its industrial resources'?* Looking back
from the nineteen-forties we see in the years following the Congress of Berlin
the sharp emergence of the question regarding the future of the British Empire
and even of industrial society with which we are now so familiar.

On 1 January 1880, the London *Times* began its leading editorial:

A new year begins every morning ... But there are no the less 'tides in the affairs of
men'... we have many motives for exchanging with a more than usual heartiness the
customary wishes for a 'happy New Year,' ... We leave behind us in 1879 a year which
has combined more circumstances of misfortune and depression than any within
general experience ... The combination of untoward influences during 1879 has been
unique ... War in two continents ... Commerce stagnant ... Agriculture has suffered
from an adversity so severe as to impose a heavy burden upon all the classes connected
with land ... weak points in our financial organization are revealed ... party spirit in
politics has displayed a bitterness which the most experienced politicians confess to
exceed anything within their remembrance.

[...]

---

* T.H.S. Escott, *England: Her People, Polity, and Pursuits*, London, Chapman and Hall,
  1885, pp. 123-4. This volume by the editor of the *Fortnightly Review*, covering in 600
  pages topics ranging from 'Popular Amusements' to 'Imperial England' and quoted
  frequently in this study, was reviewed as follows by *The Economist* at the time of its publication: 'Mr. Escott's subject is vast and complicated [...] he has given a wonderfully
  faithful picture of our daily life [...] The tone and spirit of the book, too, are eminently
  English [...] He is conservative without being reactionary, liberal, yet not subversive [...]'
  (31 January 1885, Vol. 43, pp. 194-5).

Reading the fears and hopes of our own time into a comparable period of the past can easily become an over-plausible occupation. But there is much in the England of the eighteen-eighties as compared with America in the nineteen-thirties and 'forties to lend support to the belief that changes in life and thought in England not infrequently precede by about half a century similar changes in the United States. Certain developments in industry and in social philosophy in the two countries have been similar. But America's later industrialization, use of the 'frontier,' and greater distance from Europe have given rise in the two nations to different timings and sets of urgencies. England from the eighteen-eighties on had to face problems that America has been able down to the present time largely to disregard. For America, too, these years of grace are now past. If we do not press the historical comparison too far some insight into possible directions of change in this country—their opportunities and hazards—may be gained from a study of this critical period in England.

Then, as now, theoretical panic was added to practical confusion. There was, as Cliffe Leslie pointed out, a new sense of being in the dark, surrounded by the unknown: 'it is the consciousness of not seeing their way on the part of the people that is new.'[1]

[...]

Accepted institutions and accepted philosophies were being sharply challenged by changes in economic conditions. A letter to *Reynolds' Newspaper* in 1880 said:

When he wrote [his] description of jobbery and callousness to the poor in aristocratic countries, it would also seem that de Tocqueville had the government of Lord Beaconsfield in view ... And it may confidently be predicted that unless we reform and renovate most of our institutions, and abolish many, nations will fast give us the go-by in commerce and other matters, and we shall no more be able to compete with America than our old stage-coaches of fifty years back could hope to run successfully against the railroads of the present.[2]

Then, as now, political 'democracy' served as a shibboleth and a symbol of hope with an accompaniment of skepticism about almost every one of its actual instruments. Re-shuffling of political alignments and of political principles to meet immediate situations seemed to be the answer to the

---

1 Thomas Edward Cliffe Leslie, 'The Known and the Unknown in the Economic World' (published in the *Fortnightly Review*, 1 June 1879) in *Essays in Political Economy*, London, Longmans, Green, 1888, p. 221.

2 4 January 1880.

disillusionment with Parliament and with parties. Liberals observed glee-
fully that the Conservative Party as a party had ceased to exist. Tory legislative
acts took on the character of political scoops. The Tories held that if reforms
must be passed in any event, they had best be effected under the auspices of
their own party, a method which the *Spectator* characterized as an effort to
turn the flank of radicalism.[3] Liberals of the old school, in revolt against their
own party, cried for leaders who would show 'that they will not slip down the
inclined plane on which we are all now standing ... letting go of all that has
hitherto been understood as sound Liberal Principles.'[4] Even before the party
split over Home Rule for Ireland in the middle of the decade it was apparent
that the right wings of the Conservative and Liberal parties and the left wings
of each were closer to each other than were the two extremes within each
party. 'Conservative' and 'Liberal' were ceasing to have any clear meaning.

[...]

England was developing increasing awareness of national and of imperial
destiny. The country was becoming more and more a part of the rest of the
world. England could not remain isolated from her own empire, which had
now reached nearly eight million square miles and 268 million people, and
from countries of the Continent and the United States, whose claims to a share
of world trade were making them rivals of British commercial supremacy. At
home Englishmen were beginning to emerge from an assured isolationism in
which to the man in the provinces 'continentals were people who provided us
with music-hall entertainers, barbers, bakers, cheap clerks, and picturesque
guests to see the recurrent Jubilee.'[5] Within Great Britain communication was
increasing and isolation diminishing. Increased literacy, cheaper printing, and
easier transportation were bringing the people of England nearer together in
large concerns of nation and empire and in small, intimate habits of daily life.

[...]

New problems were being considered. 'Liberty' was less taken for
granted; the relation between freedom and authority was of interest to others
than Matthew Arnold, and was becoming a subject of popular discussion.
'The momentous problem of our age,' wrote Bishop Westcott, 'is the rec-
onciliation of authority with freedom.'[6] T.H. Green, applying his Hegelian

---

3 Cf. William J. Wilkinson, *Tory Democracy*, New York, Columbia University Press, 1925.
4 Hon. Arthur Douglas Elliot, *The Life of George Joachim Goschen*, London, Longmans,
   Green, 1911, Vol. II, pp. 252–3.
5 E.T. Raymond, *Portraits of the Nineties*, London, T. Fisher Unwin, 1921, p. 17.
6 J.H.B. Masterman, 'Bishop Westcott,' in *Nine Famous Birmingham Men*, ed. J.H.
   Muirhead, Birmingham, Cornish Bros., 1909, p. 177.

philosophy to such questions as the Ground Game Act and the Employers' Liability Act, said that:

[...]

The discovery of the kind of social organization compatible with democratic individualism was a problem of this period as of our own.

The chief significance of the 'eighties, indeed, is that this period marked the beginning of a new phase in the recurrent struggle for individual freedom.

Excerpt: Lynd, Helen M., from "Realism and the Intellectual in Time of Crisis," *The American Scholar* 21, no. 1 (Winter, 1951–1952) (permission Staughton Lynd)[1]

Many college and university presidents have similarly endorsed the belief that education and research at this time should become instruments of public policy as defined by military, business, or political interests. President Allen of the University of Washington in his report on the tenure cases at his university made it clear that the scholarly 'pursuit of truth' must be such as not to offend the 'tough, hard-headed world of affairs.' Trends, published by the National Association of Manufacturers, has commented favorably on the advocacy by university presidents of the use of the school system for indoctrination. Mrs. Mildred McAfee Horton, former President of Wellesley, appears to view with equanimity a uniform national policy which would cause important areas of independent choice and social forces which influence choice to disappear. In urging the drafting of women, she said: "...Military services...*have a right* to as wide a basis of selection as possible." (Italics mine.) Her article "Why Not Draft Women?" was captioned: "All the social forces which make women hesitate to volunteer for military duty would vanish if women were drafted."

If such statements were isolated or exceptional, they could be disregarded; coming as they do, as part of a trend in which loyalty oaths and political screening of teachers are accepted, and in some cases actually initiated, by university presidents, there can be little doubt that they represent a tendency to give over education to political direction—a tendency new in American life. There can be little doubt, also, that in many cases American intellectuals take this position not because they like the effects of military training on the young people they are trying to educate, or because they like the idea of a garrison

---

1 This article, in somewhat different form, was given as a lecture on March 15, 1951, at the annual Phi Beta Kappa dinner at Vassar College.

state, but because they see no effective alternative to such "realism." We must be realistic, they believe, because in the present world situation attention to what ought to be done rather than what is done will, in Machiavelli's words, bring ruin rather than preservation.

Yet if utopianism is self-defeating, so also is the current practice of the realism of Edmund. The thoroughgoing utopian cuts himself off from any means of working effectively toward his ends; the thoroughgoing contemporary realist cuts himself off from any end beyond self-preservation, and, it is beginning to appear, loses even that; this contemporary realism destroys that which it would preserve.

But the choice does not lie between these two extremes, for such realism is a peculiar, limited version of realism. The difficulty with the realism of Edmund or Machiavelli is not that it rejects the easy optimism of a utopian dream world, not that it focuses on what the time is, but that it unnecessarily constricts that focus. It does not take *what is* in its full dimensions, which includes what can be. Realism that excludes the as yet unrealized possibilities of the future inherent in the present, realism that excludes the longer, enduring purposes of men, is less than full realism. Full realism includes men's dreams. Dreams need not be illusions. If utopianism which ignores what is brings ruin, it is also true that realism denies dreams of what may be will not bring preservation. Where there are no dreams, the people perish.

All realism must be selective. No person and no society can grasp the whole reality of any historical situation. But contemporary realism narrows its focus too exclusively to certain aspects of reality and ignores others. It biases selection in favor of an interpretation of reality based upon fear and hate, upon the limitation of possibilities, emphasizing what cannot be done. And this narrowed focus, this scarcity theory—applied to human nature, to understanding of other peoples and our own, to diplomatic options— constantly intensifies itself. In situation after situation, American policy begins by limiting attention to what is, or is regarded as, an immediate danger, concentrating on the most obviously coercive next steps to meet that danger and allowing no wider perspectives or more dynamic possibilities to intrude. Each successive step involves a more constricted focus, more distortion of perspective, and makes the following step seem inevitable, allowing still less choice.

[...]

At home, members of both parties increasingly, as was pointed out in a recent letter to the *Herald Tribune*, allow Senator McCarthy to make the rules, then accuse his opponents of having broken them, and the accused, instead of questioning the rules, merely deny having broken them. When intellectual leaders resign their traditional position of independent thought to support unquestioningly national policy, it is this acceptance of issues as defined by others that they are supporting.

In foreign policy our stated purpose is to preserve democratic freedoms. It has come to be accepted that the way to do this is to concentrate on, and oppose, the Soviet Union as the sole threat to freedom. This single focus has led us to adopt any methods, including some of those of the very state which the whole policy is designed to oppose. It has also led us to select allies in what we call the "free world," not on the basis of their practice of democracy and freedom, but on the basis of their hatred of and willingness to fight Russia.

[...]

For a time it seemed the absurdity of many of the current attacks on freedom of thought would make them self-defeating. When Senator McCarthy's campaign began, the term most widely used to describe his activities was "antics." This has proved, tragically, too trivial a description of the climate of opinion of which he is both symptom and cause. When such men as Owen Lattimore, Philip Jessup, Dwight D. Eisenhower, and Kingsley Martin, whose lives and works are a matter of open record, can be charged in America with following "a Communist line," we can no longer rely on the ludicrous nature of the charges to protect freedom.

The Government, in allowing its loyalty program to be oriented in terms of Senator McCarthy's definition of issues, has contributed to the suppression of free inquiry and thus deprived itself of the responsible intelligence on which democratic government must rely. The result is anti-intellectualism that leads the government to rely on the rigid, the fearful, and the irresponsible instead of on the best intelligence of its citizens.

Notes

1 Helen Merrell Lynd, "Reminiscences of Helen Lynd, 'Interviews 1–7,'" 1973, RG 10.4, Series I: Personal Papers, Box 1, Sub-series F. Miscellaneous, 110, Helen Merrell Lynd (1896–1982) Papers, Sarah Lawrence College Archives, Bronxville, NY.

2 Christine Biancheria and Susan Frietsche, "A Path Out of Middletown: The Life of Helen Merrell Lynd, 1986–1982," *The Language Exchange,* http://v1.elfieraymond.com/ccorner/exchange/lynd.html, accessed April 11, 2022.

3 Stuart Ewen, *Captains of Consciousness: Advertising and the Social Roots of the Consumer Culture* (New York, NY: Basic Books, 2001). Roland Marchand, *Advertising the American Dream: Making Way for Modernity, 1920–1940* (Berkeley: University of California Press, 1985); Nancy A. Naples, *Feminism and Method: Ethnography, Discourse Analysis and Activist Research* (New York, NY: Routledge, 2003); Mike Featherstone, *Undoing Culture: Globalization, Postmodernism, and Identity* (London: Sage, 1995); David Garland, *Punishment and Welfare: A History of Penal Strategies* (New Orleans: Quid Pro

Books, 1985); Scott Lasher and John Urry, *The End of Organized Capitalism* (Madison, WI: The University of Wisconsin Press, 1987); Elihu Katz and Paul F. Lazarsfeld, *Personal Influence, The Part Played by People in the Flow of Mass Communications* (New Brunswick: Transaction Publishers, 1955); Abraham Maslow, *Toward a Psychology of Being*, 2nd ed. (New York, NY: D. Van Nostrand, 1968); Catherine Marshall and Gretchen B. Rossman, *Designing Qualitative Research*, 6th ed. (Thousand Oaks: Sage, 2016); Axel Honneth, *The Struggle for Recognition: The Moral Grammar of Social Conflicts* (Cambridge, MA: MIT Press, 1995); Randall Collins, *The Credential Society: An Historical Sociology of Education and Stratification* (New York, NY: Columbia University Press, 2019).

4 Biancheria and Friestche, "A Path Out of Middletown," 18.

5 Ibid., 23.

6 Ibid., 55.

7 Lynd, "Reminiscences," 51–52. Helen Merrell Lynd, "Middletown," August 30, 1980, Staughton and Alice Lynd Collection, Series 1: Box 1: Robert Lynd Papers and Andrea Lynd Letters, Folder 15, Robert and Helen Lynd Family Papers, Kent State University Special Collections and Archives.

8 Robert S. Lynd and Helen Merrell Lynd, *Middletown: A Study in Modern American Culture* (New York, NY: Harvest Books, 1956), 2.

9 Lynd, "Reminiscences," 97.

10 Ibid., 98–110.

11 Ibid., 53. Lynd and Lynd, *Middletown*, 5.

12 Lynd, "Reminiscences," 53.

13 Lynd and Lynd, *Middletown*, 471, 477.

14 Lynd, "Reminiscences," 44, 101.

15 Helen Merrell Lynd, *England in the Eighteen-Eighties: Toward a Social Basis for Freedom: New Impression* (London: Frank Cass Publishing, 1965), 4–5.

16 Helen Merrell Lynd, "Realism and the Intellectual in a Time of Crisis," *The American Scholar* 21, no. 1 (1951–1952): 23.

17 Lynd, "Realism," 25–26.

18 Robert McChesney, *Corporate Media and Threat to Democracy* (New York, NY: Seven Stories Press, 2010); Edward S. Herman and Noam Chomsky, *Manufacturing Consent: The Political Economy of the Media* (New York, NY: Pantheon, 1988).

19 John Saunders, "Fourth Report of Americanism Committee Westchester County American Legion at Yorktown Heights: N.Y. May 14, 1952 RE Sarah Lawrence College," Helen Merrell Lynd (1896–1982) Papers, Sarah Lawrence College Archives RG 10.4: Series II: Box 2, Sub-series F. Miscellaneous, 110, Sarah Lawrence College Archives, Bronxville, NY.

20 Helen Merrell Lynd, *Possibilities* (Bronxville, NY: Sarah Lawrence College, 1983), 49.

21 Anne Braden, *House Un-American Activities Committee: Bulwark of Segregation* (Los Angeles: National Committee to Abolish the House Un-American Activities Committee, 1963); Civil Rights Movement Archive, www.crmvet.org/info/64_braden_huac-r.pdf, accessed April 11, 2022.

22 Helen Merrell Lynd, *On Shame and the Search for Identity* (New York, NY: Harcourt Brace & Company, 1958), 20.

23 Helen Merrell Lynd, "Draft Robert S. Lynd Eulogy," 1970, Box 1, Folder 5, 9, Helen Lynd Papers, Robert and Helen Lynd Family Papers, Kent State University Special Collections and Archives, Kent, OH.

Bibliography

Biancheria, Christine and Susan Frietsche. "A Path Out of Middletown: The Life of Helen Merrell Lynd, 1986–1982." *The Language Exchange*, 2002. http://v1.elfieraymond.com/ccorner/exchange/lynd.html, accessed April 11, 2022.

Braden, Anne. *House Un-American Activities Committee: Bulwark of Segregation*. Los Angeles: National Committee to Abolish the House Un-American Activities Committee, 1963. Civil Rights Movement Archive. www.crmvet.org/info/64_braden_huac-r.pdf, accessed April 11, 2022.

Collins, Randall. *The Credential Society: An Historical Sociology of Education and Stratification*. New York: Columbia University Press, 2019.

Ewen, Stuart. *Captains of Consciousness: Advertising and the Social Roots of the Consumer Culture*. New York: Basic Books, 2001.

Featherstone, Mike. *Undoing Culture: Globalization, Postmodernism, and Identity*. London: Sage, 1995.

Garland, David. *Punishment and Welfare: A History of Penal Strategies*. New Orleans, LA: Quid Pro Books, 1985.

Herman, Edward S. and Noam Chomsky *Manufacturing Consent: The Political Economy of the Media*. New York, NY: Pantheon, 1988.

Honneth, Axel. *The Struggle for Recognition: The Moral Grammar of Social Conflicts*. Cambridge, MA: MIT Press, 1995.

Katz, Elihu and Paul F. Lazarsfeld. *Personal Influence: The Part Played by People in the Flow of Mass Communications*. New Brunswick, NJ: Transaction Publishers, 1955.

Lasher, Scott and John Urry. *The End of Organized Capitalism*. Madison, WI: The University of Wisconsin Press, 1987.

Lynd, Helen Merrell. "Draft Robert S. Lynd Eulogy." 1970, Box 1, Folder 5, 9, Helen Lynd Papers. Robert and Helen Lynd Family Papers. Kent State University Special Collections and Archives, Kent, OH.

_____. *England in the Eighteen-Eighties: Toward a Social Basis for Freedom: New Impression*. London: Frank Cass Publishing, 1945.

_____. *Field Work in College Education*. New York, NY: Columbia University Press, 1945.

_____. *Identifications and the Growth of Personal Identity*. Detroit, MI: Wayne State University Press, 1956.

_____. "Middletown," August 30, 1980. Box 1: Robert Lynd Papers and Andrea Lynd Letters, Folder 15. Staughton and Alice Lynd Collection, Series 1: Robert and Helen Lynd Family Papers. Kent State University Special Collections and Archives. Kent, OH.

_____. *The Nature of Historical Objectivity*. New York, NY: Columbia University, 1950.

_____. *On Shame and the Search for Identity*. New York, NY: Harcourt Brace & Company, 1958.

_____. "Parent Education and the Colleges." *The Annals of the American Academy of Political and Social Science* 160, no. 1 (1932): 197–204.

_____. *Possibilities*. Bronxville, NY: Sarah Lawrence College, 1983.

_____. "Realism and the Intellectual in a Time of Crisis." *The American Scholar* 21, no. 1 (1951–1952): 21–32.

_____. "Reminiscences of Helen Lynd, 'Interviews 1–7,'" 1973, RG 10.4, Series I: Personal Papers, Box 1, Sub-series F. Miscellaneous, 110, Helen Merrell Lynd (1896–1982) Papers, Sarah Lawrence College Archives, Bronxville, NY.

_____. *Toward Discovery*. Bronxville, NY: Sarah Lawrence College, 1965.

_____. "The Truth at the University of Washington." *The American Scholar* 18 (1949): 364–353.

Lynd, Helen Merrell and Caroline B. Zachry. *Two Views of the Work of Women Today*. New York, NY: Society for Ethical Culture, 1940.

Lynd, Robert Staughton and Helen Merrell Lynd. *Middletown: A Study in Modern American Culture*. New York: Harcourt Brace & Company, 1929.

_____. *Middletown in Transition: A Study in Cultural Conflict*. New York, NY: Harcourt Brace & Company, 1937.

Marchand, Roland. *Advertising the American Dream: Making Way for Modernity, 1920–1940*. Berkeley, CA: University of California Press, 1985.

Marshall, Catherine and Gretchen B. Rossman. *Designing Qualitative Research*, 6th ed. Thousand Oaks, CA: Sage, 2016.

Maslow, Abraham. *Toward a Psychology of Being*, 2nd ed. New York, NY: D. Van Nostrand, 1968.

McChesney, Robert. *Corporate Media and Threat to Democracy*. New York, NY: Seven Stories Press, 2010.

Naples, Nancy A. *Feminism and Method: Ethnography, Discourse Analysis and Activist Research*. New York, NY: Routledge, 2003.

Saunders, John. "Fourth Report of Americanism Committee Westchester County American Legion at Yorktown Heights: N.Y. May 14, 1952. RE Sarah Lawrence College," May 14, 1952, RG 10.4: Series II. Box 2, Sub-series F. Miscellaneous, 110. Helen Merrell Lynd (1896–1982) Papers. Sarah Lawrence College Archives, Bronxville, NY.

Chapter 15

Hortense Powdermaker (1896–1970)

By Shelley Stamp

Hortense Powdermaker's 1950 study of Hollywood's motion picture industry, *The Dream Factory*, was the first anthropological research of its kind and her observations about "the social system underlying the production of movies" remain prescient.[1] Movies, she argued, played an outsized role in American life in the mid-twentieth century, where they served as "ready-made fantasies" and "collective daydreams [...] manufactured on the assembly line."[2] This factory-like mode of production, Powdermaker insisted, "significantly influences their content and meaning."

Using an approach she called "applied anthropology," Powdermaker spent a year in Hollywood in late 1946 and early 1947, conducting some 900 interviews with 300 people working at many different levels of the business.[3] She read industry trade press, Hays Office files, and records kept by the professional guilds. As a "participant-observer" she visited movie sets, attended guild meetings, and joined social gatherings.[4] Powdermaker conducted her study at a crucial juncture in Hollywood history. Box office attendance reached an all-time high in 1946, an indication of the prominent role movies held in the daily lives of many Americans. (Close to two-thirds of the population went to the cinema every week.) But by the end of the decade challenges to the industry were already evident: the rise of broadcast television, the anti-communist investigations and subsequent blacklist, and the antitrust enforcement that broke up monopolistic practices of the Hollywood studios.

Powdermaker's ethnographic research in Hollywood was part of a long career of anthropological field work. Born in Philadelphia on December 24, 1896, Powdermaker grew up in a secular Jewish family, the second of four children.[5] Her elder sister, Dr. Florence Powdermaker (1895–1966), became a prominent psychiatrist best-known for helping to pioneer group psychotherapy.[6] Powdermaker attended Goucher College in Baltimore, graduating in 1919 with a degree in history. While still a student she became active in the Women's Trade Union League and after graduation worked as a labor organizer for the Amalgamated Clothing Workers. Powdermaker moved to England in 1925 to study anthropology at the London School of Economics, where she was a student of Bronislaw Malinowski, an early proponent of "participant-observer" anthropology, a methodology that revolutionized the field. She earned her PhD in 1928.

Supported by a grant from the Australian National Research Council, Powdermaker conducted field work among indigenous people in Papua New Guinea, the results of which were published in her first book *Life in Lesu: The Study of a Melanesian Society in New Ireland* (1933). While an associate at the Institute of Human Relations at Yale University, Powdermaker embarked on her second field study, living for two years in Indianola, Mississippi, where she conducted one of the earliest participant-observer studies of race relations in the southern United States, published in her second book *After Freedom* (1939). She then co-wrote a book for high school students called *Probing Our Prejudices* (1944) examining the roots of racism, anti-Semitism, and anti-immigrant bias in the US. Following her study of Hollywood, published in 1950, Powdermaker received a Guggenheim Fellowship to conduct field work in Zambia, then called Northern Rhodesia, publishing those results in her 1962 book *Copper Town: Changing Africa. The Human Situation on the Rhodesian Copperbelt.*

Powdermaker was a professor of anthropology at Queens College in New York for 30 years, receiving the Distinguished Teaching Award there in 1965. She served as vice president of the New York Academy of Sciences between 1944 and 1946, and vice president of the American Ethnological Society in 1945–1946, then that society's president in 1946–1947. Powdermaker also served on the council of the American Anthropological Society for many years. Her memoir, *Stranger and Friend: The Way of an Anthropologist*, was published in 1966. Powdermaker died of a heart attack on June 16, 1970, two years after relocating to Berkeley, California, where she began a study of the flourishing youth culture there and activism amongst students at the University of California. That field work was never finished.

Powdermaker's field work in Hollywood remains largely unique within traditional anthropology, but marks an important precursor to contemporary ethnographic work conducted amongst media industry workers by scholars in the subfield of production studies.[7] She got the idea for her study while conducting field work in small-town Mississippi, recalling later that she was struck by the influence that movies had on the community. "I got to thinking of movies not simply as providing entertainment but as portraying culture patterns as well." She then decided to use her anthropological training "to learn how the social structure of Hollywood affects the final product."[8]

Powdermaker's research was not well received in Hollywood at the time; commentators seemed to bristle at the suggestion she might apply the same participant-observer methods to indigenous Pacific Islanders (whom they considered "primitive") and the denizens of Hollywood. Indeed, the *Los Angeles Times* reported that "the movie colony has exploded with wrath" over Powdermaker's study.[9] Reviewing Powdermaker's book for the *New York Times*, screenwriter Budd Schulberg called her approach "far-fetched and tortured."[10] *Variety* complained of the "lady doctor" who "drags her anthropology in by the scruff whenever she thinks of it."[11]

But Powdermaker's detailed descriptions of production cultures amongst producers, directors, screenwriters, actors, and Production Code enforcers in the 1940s provide an essential snapshot of the Hollywood studio system at its height—a system that would soon be challenged by the combined forces of television, the blacklist, and antitrust legislation. Much of the history of post-World War II Hollywood that we associate with more recent scholarship is captured here in Powdermaker's first-hand account. What is more, Powdermaker's method of linking production cultures to finished products remains an influential one today. She immediately grasped the relationship between Hollywood's social system and movie content, an idea newly valent in the #MeToo era. And with her deceptively modest aim, "to better understand the nature of our movies," Powdermaker placed herself amongst cinema audiences, not above us.[12]

Excerpt: Powdermaker, Hortense, "Mass Production of Dreams," from *Hollywood: The Dream Factory* (1950) (permission Alan Powdermaker)

Contributor's note: Footnotes from the original. I have preserved the style of the original notes, but have included additional citation information when available, such as publication date or subtitle.

Hollywood is engaged in the mass production of prefabricated daydreams. It tries to adapt the American dream, that all men are created equal, to the view that all men's dreams should be made equal. Movies are the first popular art to become a big business with mass production and mass distribution. It is quite obvious that movies cannot be individually produced, and that some form of mass production is inevitable. But the assumption is that for any sort of mass production more than one kind of social system is possible. The question is therefore asked, Is the Hollywood system the most appropriate one for the making of movies—one form of an ancient and popular art, storytelling, in which the storyteller's imagination and understanding of his fellow men have always been a necessary ingredient?

[...]

A feature of all mass production is the uniformity of the manufactured product. Hollywood has tried to achieve this by seeking formulas that it hopes will work for all movies and insure their success. It is ironical that this was more possible in the early days, when movies were small business, for then just the novelty of movement on the screen fascinated an audience. The common denominators of pantomime, slapstick and romance could be understood and enjoyed by uncritical audiences almost anywhere in the world. Since all members of the human species have the same basic needs and have some characteristics in common, there were certain simple forms of entertainment to which they can all respond. But now, when movies are big business, and the mass production and uniformity in the prefabricated daydreams more desirable to the manufacturers, such uniform products have become less salable.

[...]

The criteria of good entertainment might be applied to any picture, with or without a message. But good entertainment is not harmonious with the following of formulas and the use of stereotypes. Year after year, the list of top box-office hits indicated great diversity in audience tastes, and includes musicals, serious dramas, adventure and suspense stories, comedies, farces, war and historical themes.

[...]

Those movies which have been acclaimed by the more serious critics also show diversity. But in spite of this demonstrated many-sided character of the taste of movie audiences, the industry continues to look for formulas, and to produce cycles of pictures dealing with the same theme. This continues even though the exhibitors, the businessmen who operate the theaters, protest.

[...]

Theater operators say that cycles are bad business and that the law of diminishing returns starts working long before the end of one is reached. The audience gets tired of the same theme over and over again.

The industry attempts not only to use formulas for movie plots, but to use star actors as another formula for success, and to stereotype actors, those who play secondary roles as well as stars. Both these practices are considered in the discussion of actors and acting. The points are only briefly mentioned here as examples of the industry's attempt to substitute formulas for the storyteller's imagination and skill.

A well-known maxim in the industry is, "We give the public what it wants." The technique of polling organizations used to find out what the public wants is to ask members of a "sample" question, such as, "Would you like to see a movie based on a story about—?" following with a condensation of the proposed plot in a few sentences. In some polls the names of stars who will play in the films are used. Other polls are taken for preferences in titles and for the depth of audience penetration reached by the publicity and advertising campaigns.

[...]

Underlying this whole process of polls is a lack of understanding of the creative process underlying storytelling and an attempt to imitate practices of other big businesses. If a poll of prospective customers for a new automobile indicates that they prefer one with four doors rather than two, this would in no way interfere with the functioning and efficiency of the workers in an automobile factory. But a gifted writer or director loses much of his efficiency and creative skill if he works not out of his own knowledge of what is true, but according to what a polling organization tells him the public wants. The production of movies is a creative process, and this characteristic does not disappear even when it is denied. It is illogical to carry the premises underlying the manufacture and merchandising of automobiles to the making and selling of movies, because the problems involved are essentially different.

[...]

Instead of adopting the use of polls and gadgets in an undiscriminating fashion from other big businesses, the industry might find it more profitable in terms of dollars and cents if it attempted to learn about relevant changes in behavior and attitudes among the American people. A knowledge of its market, present and potential, is needed by any big industry, but this kind of study is not within the province of polling organizations. The world in which audiences lived during the first quarter of the century is obviously very different from the one of today. Therefore, they need and enjoy different kinds of daydreams, fantasies and stories. The movie audience has not only increased numerically but has become increasingly more diversified from the early days of working-class audiences who went to the first silent movies. Today, the audience differs widely in age, experience and background and all these condition the kind of quality of movies it wants to see. Nor is any individual so restricted that he can enjoy only one type of movie.

The increasing spread of college education, which received such an impetus after World War II from the financial aid extended by the government to former G.I.s, cannot help but further modify standards and tastes in all the popular arts. Likewise, one can predict changes in the future when the present generation of children becomes adults. Movies for them are confined to "entertainment" in the neighborhood theater. They are continuously being exposed to 16mm. educational and documentary films, in schools, clubs and even churches. Courses in film making and lectures on film appreciation are being given in many schools. Making movies is a pastime in some homes and a Handbook of *Basic Motion-Picture Techniques* has been published for amateur movie makers.[8] "Cinema 16" and other noncommercial movie societies continue to increase. This kind of familiarity is bound to produce innovations in both standards and attitudes concerning movies. But a knowledge of such changes cannot be gained through the use of mechanical polls and gadgets [...]

[...]

The anthropologist wonders if the general attitude to the industry towards its audience represents a survival from the past, to which it stubbornly and unrealistically clings [...]

[...]

However, when movies became big business, the head of the industry did quickly adopt some of the monopolistic characteristics of large-scale mass production. The desire or uniformity in its product and the use of formulas and of polling devices are all part of the same trend. The business functions of movie production reach far beyond Hollywood, extending not only to New York and Chicago and every town in the United States where there is a motion picture theater, but also to every part of the world where American films are shown.

The five major companies, Metro-Goldwyn-Mayer, RKO Radio Picture, Inc., Twentieth Century-Fox Film Corp., Inc., Warner Brothers Pictures, Inc., and Paramount Pictures, Inc., control a large number of subsidiaries such as film laboratories, lithographing concerns, radio manufacturing subsidiaries, music publishing houses, real estate companies, booking agencies, broadcasting corporations, recording studios and television companies.

This diversity of interest is represented on the board of directors of each large motion picture company by bankers, real estate men, theater owners and heads of production. Executive personnel are men of high finance and real estate interests, as well as those in charge of productions.

However, the real backbone of the monopoly has been in the control by one company of production, distribution and exhibition. The top executives

---

8 Emil B. Brodbeck, *Handbook of Basic Motion-Picture Techniques* (New York: Whittlesey House, 1950).

of the three departments relating to theater, sales and production have decided on "the number of pictures to be made, the total amount of money to be spent, the distribution of funds between the various classes of pictures, the budgets of the individual pictures, and the dates when they are to be finished."[12] The distributor has been the middle man who rents the film to the exhibitor or theater owner. Since the majors have owned the first-run theaters which provide a large part of the film rentals, they have been their own best customers.

This three-way control has been investigated by the Federal Trade Commission and the Anti-Trust Division of the Department of Justice for more than twenty years.[13] An antitrust suit was brought against the majors with the aim of divorcing exhibition from production and distribution. A consent decree in 1940 provided for modifications, by restricting rentals in the block-booking[14] to five films at a time, the elimination of blind selling by having trade showings of all films before their release, and an agreement by the five majors not to expand their theater holdings.[15]

A new federal decree regulating the film industry was issued in 1946. It further banned block-booking and was designed to break monopolistic practices and encourage competitive ones. It also aimed at the partial divorcement of studios from theater ownership.

[...]

The monopolistic character of the industry has been challenged not only by federal antitrust decrees, but also by the growing development of independent producers. In 1946 more than a third of all films in production were being shot by independent units,[19] and according to *Variety* (January 7, 1948) in 1947 more than one hundred independent companies were formed carrying budgets of over four million.

---

12 Mae D. Huettig, *Economic Control of the Motion Picture Industry* (Philadelphia: University of Pennsylvania Press, 1944), 59–60.

13 The first antitrust suit against legitimate theater interests was filed on February 21, 1950. This charged the Shubert Brothers with controlling thirty-seven theaters in the United States and also controlling a large part of all bookings.

14 Block-booking is "the simultaneous leasing of groups of films at an aggregate price fixed upon the condition that all the films in the given block be taken." (Huettig, *op. cit.*, p. 116).

15 Huettig, *op. cit.*, p. 140.

19 Borneman, Ernest, "Rebellion in Hollywood. A Study in Motion Picture Finance," *Harper's*, October 1946.

This development continues from two quite different causes. One comes from the Treasury Department. "The artists, dismayed by wartime income-tax rates, went into business for themselves as independent producers in order to pay a capital gains tax rather than income tax."[20] The other, according to the same writer, is the itch of the director, writer, actor, and producer to gain more control over the medium, to be in the driver's seat. However, their independence is circumscribed, since the outlets for distribution are limited to the major companies. The latter therefore exercise a considerable control, in that they still put their O.K. on the kind of pictures they wish to distribute and refuse their O.K. for others. Many of the independents use the production facilities of a big studio, and expenses and profits are shared. The independents, who have their own organization, have been active in fighting co-operative buying-booking combines, and have welcomed the decisions of the Department of Justice that favor separating the exhibition and the production activities of major companies.

Like any other big business, the motion picture industry is dependent on capital, which can be defined as a potential for production.[21] More than most, Hollywood operates on borrowed funds.[22]

[...]

The skills of the writers, directors, actors, and other artists are as necessary to the production of movies as are the funds borrowed from the banks. The question of whether Hollywood gets its money's worth from these employees, and whether it utilizes their special gift as well as do the big businesses which employ chemists, physicists or other scientists, interests the anthropologist but is rarely heard in Hollywood.

All these are the problems of any large industry. Yet of prime importance remains one fact: the production of the dream factory is not the same nature as are the material objects turned out on most assembly lines. For them, uniformity is essential; for the motion picture, originality is important. The conflict between the two qualities is a major problem in Hollywood.

---

20 Borneman, *op. cit.*, p. 337.

21 Roger Burlingame, *Backgrounds of Power: The Human Story of Mass Production* (New York: Scribner's, 1949), p. 192.

22 Mae D. Huettig, *op. cit.*, p. 98.

Notes

1 Hortense Powdermaker, *Hollywood: The Dream Factory. An Anthropologist Looks at the Movie-Makers* (Boston: Little Brown, 1950), 9.
2 Ibid., 13, 12.
3 Ibid., 7.
4 Ibid., 7.
5 Details of Powdermaker's life and career were gathered from the following sources: "Hortense Powdermaker is Dead, An Authority on Varied Cultures," *New York Times*, June 17, 1970, 47; "Long-Time Instructor at College," *Washington Post*, June 18, 1970, B10; "Dr. Hortense Powdermaker, Anthropologist," *Los Angeles Times*, June 19, 1970, B3; and Barbara C. Johnson, "Hortense Powdermaker, 1896–1970," *The Encyclopedia of Jewish Women*, https://jwa.org/encyclopedia/article/powdermaker-hortense, accessed September 4, 2020.
6 "Dr. Florence Powdermaker, 71, Group Psychotherapist, is Dead," *New York Times*, January 13, 1966, 25.
7 For an introduction to methodologies in production studies, see John Caldwell, *Production Culture: Industrial Reflexivity and Critical Practice in Film and Television* (Raleigh, NC: Duke University Press, 2008) and Miranda Banks, John Caldwell and Vicki Mayer, eds., *Production Studies: Cultural Studies of Media Industries* (New York, NY: Routledge, 2009).
8 Quoted in "Hortense Powdermaker is Dead," 47.
9 Don Guzman, "Ego-Irritating Study Sets Hollywood Tempers Aboil," *Los Angeles Times*, December 17, 1950, D6.
10 Budd Schulberg, "Hollywood Primitive," *New York Times*, October 15, 1950, BR4.
11 Herb Golden, "Hollywood as 'Dream Factory' Just Nightmare to Femme Anthropologist," *Variety*, October 18, 1950, 4, 18.
12 Powdermaker, *Hollywood*, 3.

Bibliography

Banks, Miranda, John Caldwell, and Vicki Mayer, eds. *Production Studies: Cultural Studies of Media Industries*. New York: Routledge, 2009.

Borneman, Ernest. "Rebellion in Hollywood. A Study in Motion Picture Finance." *Harper's*, October 1946.

Brodbeck, Emil B. *Handbook of Basic Motion-Picture Techniques*. New York, NY: Whittlesey House, 1950.

Burlingame, Roger. *Backgrounds of Power: The Human Story of Mass Production*. New York, NY: Scribner's, 1949.

Caldwell, John. *Production Culture: Industrial Reflexivity and Critical Practice in Film and Television*. Raleigh, NC: Duke University Press, 2008.

"Dr. Hortense Powdermaker, Anthropologist." *Los Angeles Times*, June 19, 1970, B3.

"Dr. Florence Powdermaker, 71, Group Psychotherapist, is Dead." *New York Times*, January 13, 1966, 25.

Golden, Herb. "Hollywood as 'Dream Factory' Just Nightmare to Femme Anthropologist." *Variety*, October 18, 1950, 18.

Guzman, Don. "Ego-Irritating Study Sets Hollywood Tempers Aboil." *Los Angeles Times*, December 17, 1950, D6.

"Hortense Powdermaker is Dead, An Authority on Varied Cultures." *New York Times*, June 17, 1970, 47.

Huettig, Mae D. *Economic Control of the Motion Picture Industry*. Philadelphia: University of Pennsylvania Press, 1944.

Johnson, Barbara C. "Hortense Powdermaker, 1896–1970." *The Encyclopedia of Jewish Women*. https://jwa.org/encyclopedia/article/powdermaker-hortense, accessed April 11, 2022.

"Long-Time Instructor at College." *Washington Post*, June 18, 1970, B10.

Powdermaker, Hortense. *After Freedom: A Cultural Study in the Deep South*. New York, NY: Viking Press, 1939.

_____. "The Anthropological Approach to the Problem of Modifying Race Attitudes." *The Journal of Negro Education* 13, no. 3 (July 1944): 295–302.

_____. "An Anthropologist Looks at the Movies." *The Annals of the American Academy of Political and Social Sciences* 254, no. 1 (November 1947): 80–87.

_____. "The Channeling of Negro Aggression by the Cultural Process." *American Journal of Sociology* 48, no. 6 (May 1943): 750–758.

_____. *Copper Town: Changing Africa. The Human Situation on the Rhodesian Copperbelt*. New York, NY: Harper and Row, 1962.

_____. "Feasts in New Ireland; the Social Function of Eating." *American Anthropologist* 34, no. 2 (April 1932): 236–247.

_____. "Further Reflections on Lesu and Malinowski's Diary." *Oceania* 40, no. 4 (June 1970): 344–347.

_____. *Hollywood: The Dream Factory. An Anthropologist Looks at the Movie-makers*. Boston, MA: Little, Brown and Company, 1950.

_____. "Leadership in Central and Southern Australia." *Economica*, June 1, 1928, 168–190.

_____. *Life in Lesu: The Study of a Melanesian Society in New Ireland*. London: Williams and Norgate, 1933.

_____. "Mortuary Rites in New Ireland (Bismarck Archipelago)." *Oceania* 2, no. 2 (September 1931): 26–43.

_____. "Movies and Society." *Cinema* (August 1947): 14–15.

_____. "Report on Research in New Ireland." *Oceania* 1 (January 1930): 355.

_____. "Social Change through Imagery and Values of Teen-Age Africans in Northern Rhodesia." *American Anthropologist* 58, no. 5 (October 1956): 783–813.

_____. *Stranger and Friend: The Way of an Anthropologist.* New York, NY: W.W. Norton, 1966.

_____. "Vital Statistics of New Ireland (Bismarck Archipelago) as Revealed in Genealogies." *Human Biology* 3, no. 3 (September 1931): 351–357.

Powdermaker, Hortense and Helen Frances Storen. *Probing Our Prejudices: A Unit for High School Students. Bureau for Intercultural Education Publication Series. Problems of Race and Culture in American Education.* New York, NY and London: Harper and Brothers, 1944.

Powdermaker, Hortense and Joseph Semper. "Education and Occupation among New Haven Negroes." *The Journal of Negro History* 23, no. 2 (April 1938): 200–215.

Schulberg, Budd. "Hollywood Primitive." *New York Times*, October 15, 1950, BR4.

Chapter 16
Jeanette Sayre Smith (1915–1974)

By Aimee-Marie Dorsten

Jeanette Sayre Smith on WBML Radio, c. 1942 (courtesy of the Smith family)

Jeanette Sayre's research reflected a fascination with the power and control broadcasting exerted over public perception. She was invested in broadcasting regulation's impact on the public's lived experience, whether for farmer, homemaker, or immigrant. As a research associate, Sayre was well published as part of an esteemed cadre at the Princeton Radio Research Project (PRRP) and the Radiobroadcasting Research Project (RRP) through the Harvard Littauer Center in the late 1930s–1940s under Carl J. Friedrich.[1] Sayre recognized early the power of "niche" audiences as key to the influence of radio or television programming; she was also concerned with radio's weak regulatory structure, the potential for educational broadcasting, and the public's attitude toward the medium, whether nationalized or privatized.

Sayre provided a historical and critical context for the development and use of radio. Sayre's work—often published in psychology and public opinion journals—combined qualitative audience research, extensive archival research into federal agencies, and critical analysis of current media discourse. She is often cited by scholars in the critical history of radio, those working in audience research, administrative social science, survey methods, and social psychology, among others.[2] Sayre's work, along with Mae Huettig's (see Chapter 7 of this volume), is also a forerunner of the industrial political economy of communication.

Sayre grew up in South Orange, New Jersey, graduating from Wellesley College with honors in Sociology in 1931. In 1936, she became Robert S. Lynd's master's student at Columbia University. Sayre's early experiences working with those most impacted by federal policy—juvenile delinquents, laborers, and immigrants—also likely had an impact on her critical perspective, which blends advocacy and immersive research. Sayre was a matron at the Sleighton Farm Reformatory for Girls in Pennsylvania; a worker at the Greenwich Settlement House for immigrants in New York City; an assistant at the Bryn Mawr Summer School for Women Workers in Industry in Pennsylvania; and an ethnographer studying unemployment in the glass industry with the Works Progress Administration.[3]

In her first study, "An Analysis of the Radiobroadcasting Activities of Federal Agencies" (1941), Sayre exposed the historical relationship between commercial broadcasters, federal agencies, and audiences following the Communications Acts of 1926 and 1934. Through extensive archival research Sayre argued the laissez-faire approach to the early national radio system, including lack of both government funding for non-commercial programming and regulatory standardization, were conditions that prioritized commercial over educational radio.[4] Sayre cogently traced radio's political-economic genealogy as it followed a regulatory domino-effect: just as newspapers and movies became commercially oriented entities, so would radio, simply because the government failed to steward a nationally sponsored system. Sayre argued that the government deeply discounted broadcasting in the public interest by avoiding "any thoughtful discussion of the difference" between the national broadcasting of necessary and useful information versus that of propaganda.[5] The fear of totalitarianism blinded policymakers to the possibilities a public national radio system could offer citizens; the obtuseness made commercial radio a foregone conclusion.[6]

In "Broadcasting for Marginal Americans" (1942), Sayre continued her critique of foreign-language radio as the radio industry's "step-child" whose limited programming meant a forced choice for listeners.[7] In her study of 62 subjects chosen from "every eighth house along representative streets" in northern Boston, Sayre investigated this marginalized, minority Italian audience, noting they were "engaged in a struggle against their mother country" between world wars.[8] While it is important to note that some stereotypes were used in her analysis, ultimately, Sayre argued for more objective educational broadcasting in Italian and other languages to give foreign listeners "a feeling of security in a world in which they feel very insecure and shut out."[9] She argued that the heavy influence of sponsors and brokers, and lack of regulation for programmatic record-keeping, led to programmatic paucities.[10] Thus, at World War II's peak, Sayre's arguments ran counter to US government prejudices against foreign-language programming and speakers who might represent a potential "fifth column" of fascist support.[11]

In "Radiobroadcasting and Higher Education" (1942) Sayre collaborated with Friedrich to assess the success higher education had in establishing independent, commercial radio. Through their survey of 250 broadcasting faculty, they found that educators had been running a "turtle race" in what had become a commercially oriented system by the 1920s. The greatest challenge to educational broadcasters—according to Friedrich and Sayre— whether in education, religion, or labor—was the chronic need to finance operations: requirements such as cumbersome license fees and adherence to rigorous technical standards were additional barriers to competition against commercial radio for spectrum space.[12]

Despite expertise in radio regulation, Sayre took second seat to Friedrich in collaborations. In the preface to "Radiobroadcasting," Friedrich says that Sayre "collected and digested a large part of the material for chapters II–V and helped interpret the results of the survey reported in chapter VI," yet she is credited as assistant for hire, as if her contributions were merely supplementary.[13] More oddly, in the preface to "Radiobroadcasting," Friedrich announces that Sayre's research career is over after "Radiobroadcasting," because, "Miss Sayre has left the [RRP] to become Mrs. Francis Smith."[14] The proclamation foreclosed Sayre's scholarly credentials, given the gendered assumptions about women's commitment to scholarship once they were married. Like the radio industries she explored, Sayre experienced significant barriers to entry into the research academy.

Following her exit from the RRP, Sayre moved to the other side of the microphone; she became a radio announcer and program developer at WBML in Georgia, while starting her family. Sayre also tried re-energizing her communication research career and published *Control: How to Study Control of the Media of Communications* (1945) independently in a limited run. *Control* emphasized that studying those who exert power in media industry policy— whether practitioners, executives, unions, professional organizations, or politicians—is as important as the media message itself.[15] Here, Sayre brought together the sum of her research and professional experience to map critical points of examination that would help future media scholars understand the entirety of the US media ecology. She advocated the need to determine which personnel roles tended to exert the most control either for, or across, each medium.[16] *Control* documented Sayre's innovation: to remedy the currently non-existent "industry-wide analyses" for each broadcasting medium.[17]

Undoubtedly, had Sayre been able to secure a position in the academy, she would have completed future phases of her comprehensive study on media industry mechanisms of control. Certainly, the inequities Sayre experienced during her career in communication research revealed to her that the same injustices existed in the US media industry. Despite being credentialed, like so many of the women who conducted research at the Rockefeller-funded and university-sponsored institutes of the mid-twentieth century, Sayre never found a permanent mentor or home in the nascent era of communication research. Like her friend Mae Huettig (see Chapter 7 of this volume), Sayre profoundly understood the implications of power and control, especially over people and the means of communication. Sayre deserves credit as an early architect of critical regulatory studies in the history of communication research.

Excerpt: Sayre, Jeanette, "An Analysis of the Radiobroadcasting Activities of Federal Agencies," *Studies in The Control of Radio, Numbers 1–6*, no. 3 (Cambridge, MA: Littauer Center, June 1941)

1. THE SETTING

a. Introduction

Students of political science have been concerned lately with the relations of administrative agencies to older branches of government. In the last twenty years bureaus or commissions dealing with specialized problems have been set up, either directly responsible to the Congress (in theory) or to some existing department. The officials, many of them highly skilled technicians, have been entrusted with the execution of legislation, as well as with suggesting legislation for situations about which they have information, or with helping in policy formation. The rulings of these bureaus and commissions have the force of law. Often it would be difficult to explain to Congress these rulings, which are made to carry out a policy defined so broadly by Congress that the commission or agency has been forced to act on its own responsibility. When policy has been ill defined or is outdated, the danger of difficulties between these groups and Congress is enhanced. There are at present two checks upon the independent groups: the judgment of experts in the field, and the judgment of citizens. If citizens do not fulfill the requirements made of them by a law, the agency charged with its enforcement has failed in its task. Of recent years there has been an increasing tendency toward "citizen participation" in such matters. The agencies have established offices of information which perform two tasks: keeping the citizen informed about the work of the agency, and keeping the agency informed about the reaction of citizens to its performance.[1]

[...]

This study examines the radio activities of federal agencies from three points of view: the historical setting, an analysis of the work of three representative agencies, and the broadcasters' point of view. Some conclusions will be drawn about the use of radio by government.

[...]

With the growth of advertising and other publicity functions by private business into a major industry in this period, consumers' groups have grown up to challenge these attempts to sell ideas or commodities. Such an organization as the Institute for Propaganda Analysis, which exposed as propaganda the information functions of groups, regardless of the nature of the group or its purpose, was indicative of the prevailing temper of mind. Only of very recent years has there been any thoughtful discussion of the difference between education and propaganda, between the presentation of necessary and useful information by some groups and propaganda, between propaganda by groups working constructively for the democratic way of life and that of groups which seek to undermine it.

These challenges have made especially difficult the work of governmental agencies in seeking to elicit citizens' participation in their work. Citizens have been wary of accepting information presented to help them carry out legislation passed by their Congress. Congress itself challenged the right of these agencies to use radio for publicity work. Organized groups opposing the work of the agencies have been quick to protest to Congress or to the agency itself about the publicity work undertaken to facilitate the carrying out of legislation intrusted [sic] to the agency. In using radio, the agencies have had their informational and publicity work further subjected to the scrutiny of private business, which did not wholly approve of some of the governmental policies during the Roosevelt regime.

[...]

From many points of view the essential lack is some agency to coordinate the radio work of the various departments. The Office of Government Reports,

---

1 Friedrich. C. J. "Public Policy and the Nature of Administrative Responsibility," *Public Policy*, Vol. 1. Edited by C. J. Friedrich and E. S. Mason (Cambridge: Harvard University Press, 1940) pp. 3–24.

which had hoped to be such a group, was not completely successful, because of the antagonism of broadcasters in the government who disagreed with its production methods or its theories broadcasting, or who were afraid of losing their jobs if they cooperated. The recent debate in Congress on funds for radio work for this group reflected this failure, as well as the fear of "censorship" accentuated by developments abroad. Democracy means freedom for the expression of many points of view, but it need not mean inefficiency. If the experience and personnel of the government in radio were pooled, money could be spent more expeditiously, programs would be approved, stations would be happier, and more people would listen federal programs. In a situation of national emergency such a central programming agency is more necessary than ever. Although it would seem unwise in wartime for the government to take over the operation of broadcasting stations, it must be able to reach citizens quickly and effectively.

[...]

Without some central agency to do work of coordination and to set up program standards, private broadcasters will be put in the position of passing judgment on the merits of government programs and of establishing priorities for the various agencies wanting time on the air. Broadcasters are not in a position to do this adequately, for no outsider could, and in addition, the social attitude of broadcasters is often much like that of their advertisers, one that has challenged the whole theory of the Administration in recent years. It is up to Congress to realize that the morale of the nation in a time of national emergency can hardly be left in the hands of private interests.([2])

Excerpt: Smith, Jeanette Sayre, "Broadcasting For Marginal Americans," *Public Opinion Quarterly* 6, no. 4 (Winter 1942) (permission Oxford University Press)

Contributor's note: Footnotes from the original. I have preserved the style of the original notes.

Broadcasting in the public interest is in times of war more than an editorial catchword and certainly more than a part-time activity. And when radio reaches an audience whose integration into the war effort is a pressing problem of the day, its responsibility becomes more profound. The public

---

2 For a more complete discussion of this problem, see C. J. Friedrich, "Controlling Broadcasting in War-time," *Studies in the Control of Radio*, No. 2. (Harvard University, 1940).

interest is, under such circumstances, the public safety. Foreign language broadcasts, long the step-child of the radio industry, reach just such an audience. Domestic programs in Italian can reach almost an eighth of our foreign-born population. Yet in spite of the fact that foreign language broadcasting in this country is at least a decade old, little is known about it, either as to the nature of the programs broadcast, or as to its effect upon listeners.[1]

This paper is a partial report of the findings of an investigation into social and political attitudes, and the relation of broadcasting to those attitudes, in the North End of Boston.[2] The neighborhood is densely populated, almost exclusively Italian, and consists of about twenty thousand people. In June 1941 a survey was conducted of listening habits in the district, with reference to both long and short wave radio. Interviews were made in every eighth house along representative streets to discover language preferences, program preferences, and shortwave listening habits, if any. From these interviews, respondents were divided according to constellations of listening habits, and subsequent intensive interviews, were conducted with sixty-two people chosen to represent the various constellations. These interviews were directed at the deeper lying social and psychological factors which influence and are influenced by radio listening.[3] After the outbreak of war this study would have been very difficult; it was difficult enough to conduct with the tension of the group a year ago. In spite of the fact that some of the material is dated, it does permit an appraisal of the war-time problem of foreign language broadcasting "in the public interest."

[...]

LOCAL ITALIAN BROADCASTING

The function of local Italian broadcasting, both actual and potential, must be viewed in relation to its setting, the mind of Italian Americans who now find themselves engaged in struggle against their mother country. That state of

---

1 For a recent study of the content of foreign language broadcasts see Arnheim and Bayne, "Foreign Language Broadcasts over Local American Stations," *Radio Research 1941*. Edited by P.F. Lazarsfeld and F. Stanton. (Duell, Sloan and Pearce, New York, 1941)

2 The study was financed by two grants: one from the Princeton Listening Center, a project of the Rockefeller Foundation and Princeton University and the other from the Radiobroadcasting Research Project, also a project of the General Education Board of the Rockefeller Foundation. The writer is indebted to Professors Harwood L. Childs of Princeton and C.J. Friedrich of Harvard for support in this work.

3 A part of this investigation has already been reported in the pages of this journal. For a more detailed description of the community studied, the methods used, and the questionnaires, see Bruner, J.S. and Sayre, J. "Short-wave Listening in an Italian Community," *Public Opinion Quarterly* 4, no. 5 (1941): pp. 640–656.

mind in the months preceding the war was such as to make one fear for their active enthusiasm in the struggle. Seventy-two per cent of the people asked said "This is not America's war," while less than ten per cent felt that America had a part to play in defeating Fascism. In a community strongly organized by the Democratic Party it is significant that one-third of the people disapproved of President Roosevelt merely because of his foreign policy, while another third (mostly recipients of Federal Aid) approved of his internal, but not external policies.

[...]

ITALIAN BROADCASTING IN BOSTON

During June 1941 the listener wishing to hear Italian programs in Boston might choose from thirteen hours and forty-five minutes of Italian on Station WCOP each week, one hour and forty-five minutes on station WHDH, three hours and thirty minutes on WAAB, and a one-hour program on Station WMEX, announced in English but consisting of Italian records and singing in Italian.[4] With a good radio he might hear Salem, Fall River, Providence, Hartford, and New York. If he understood only Italian there was little real choice for him, for at only one time during the day was there a chance for him to hear more than one Italian program: the 12 to 12:30 noontime period when three programs might be heard.

[...]

WHERE LIES THE BLAME?

In seeking the source of the lack of responsible leadership in the field, one is first aware that Italian broadcasting is the orphan child of the radio industry in Boston. For the most part station managers do not speak languages other than English. They have lost control over these programs by selling time on the air to brokers, who in turn create the program, find advertisers, and do pretty much as they please. Only occasionally does the station demand or offer audience surveys to find out whether anyone is listening to these programs. So long as they are paid for their time on the air little else is really important. No records are kept of most of the programs, so that it is impossible to make an accurate estimate of the content of these broadcasts. Most of the employees interviewed at the stations now carrying foreign programs in

---

4 Prior to 1940 there were several Italian programs on WMEX, but these were discontinued. Most of them shifted to WCOP.

Boston had no idea at all of the content of the programs. The manager of the station carrying the largest amount of Italian broadcasting gave the writers a completely inaccurate description of two of his programs and confessed that he had no idea what the others were about. No one at the Yankee Network could be found who knew the content of a half-hour program they broadcast every day which they pick up from Station WOV in New York.

[...]

An outsider cannot tell the broadcaster how this should be done; this is his job. We can merely point out that treatment of minority groups in this country, whether it be at the employment office or in the radio fare they are offered, is a problem whose solution is crucial to our national unity in war time and, for many of us, to the kind of world we wish to see after the war. Italian radio in Boston has essentially failed in this job. But the answer is not to stop broadcasting in Italian (this is probably true of other foreign languages as well) but to encourage broadcasters to adopt a constructive attitude toward their public.

Notes

1 Mrs. Francis G. Smith, "DATA SHEET," Smith Family Private Collection, July 1959.

2 Michele Hilmes, *Radio Voices: American Broadcasting, 1922-1952* (Minneapolis: University of Minnesota Press, 1997); Robert McChesney, "The Battle for the U.S. Airwaves, 1928-1935," *Journal of Communication* 40, no. 4 (1990): 29-57; Kathy M. Newman, *Radio Active: Advertising and Consumer Activism, 1935-1947* (Berkeley, CA: University of California Press, 2004); Sam G. McFarland, "Effects of Question Order on Survey Responses," *Public Opinion Quarterly* 45, no. 2 (1981): 208-215; Michaela Wänke and Norbert Schwarz, "Reducing Question Order Effects: The Operation of Buffer Items," in *Survey Measure and Process Quality*, ed. Lars E. Lyberg, Paul P. Biemer, Martin Collins, Edith D. de Leeuw, Cathryn Dippo, Norbert Schwarz, and Dennis Trewin (Hoboken, NJ: John Wiley & Sons, 1997): 115-140; Gordon W. Allport and Helene R. Veltfort, "Social Psychology and the Civilian War Effort," *Bulletin of the Society for the Psychological Study of Social Issues* 18, no. 1 (1943).

3 Smith, "DATA SHEET."

4 Jeanette Sayre Smith, "An Analysis of the Radiobroadcasting Activities of Federal Agencies," in *History of Broadcasting: Radio to Television. Studies in the Control of Radio*, No. 3, ed. Christopher Sterling (New York, NY: Arno Press and the *New York Times*, 1942), 114.

5 Ibid., 110.

6 Ibid.

7 Jeanette Sayre Smith, "Broadcasting for Marginal Americans," *Public Opinion Quarterly* 6, no. 4 (Winter 1942): 588.

8 Ibid., 589.

9 Ibid., 600.

10 Ibid., 601.

11 Nancy C. Carnevale, "'No Italian Spoken for the Duration of the War': Language, Italian-American Identity, and Cultural Pluralism in the World War II Years," *Journal of American Ethnic History* 22, no. 3 (2003): 3-33.

12 Carl J. Friedrich and Jeanette Sayre, "Radiobroadcasting and Higher Education," in *History of Broadcasting: Radio to Television. Studies in the Control of Radio*, No. 4, ed. Christopher Sterling (New York: Arno Press and the *New York Times*, 1942), 37.

13 Ibid., title page.

14 Ibid., 7.

15 Jeanette Sayre Smith, "How to Study Control of the Media of Communications" (draft, Smith Family Private Collection, November 1945), 1.

16 Ibid., 4.

17 Ibid., 2.

Bibliography

Allport, Gordon W. and Helene R. Veltfort. "Social Psychology and the Civilian War Effort." *Bulletin of the Society for the Psychological Study of Social Issues* 18, no. 1 (1943): 165-233.

Bruner, Jerome S. and Jeanette Sayre. "Shortwave Listening in an Italian Community." *Public Opinion Quarterly* 5, no. 4 (1941): 640-656.

Carnevale, Nancy C. "'No Italian Spoken for the Duration of the War': Language, Italian-American Identity, and Cultural Pluralism in the World War II Years." *Journal of American Ethnic History* 22, no. 3 (2003): 3-33.

Friedrich, Carl J. and Jeanette Sayre. "The Development of the Control of Advertising on the Air." In *History of Broadcasting: Radio to Television. Studies in the Control of Radio*, No. 1, ed. Christopher Sterling, 1-39. New York, NY: Arno Press and the *New York Times*, 1942.

Friedrich, Carl J. and Jeanette Sayre Smith. "Radiobroadcasting and Higher Education." In *History of Broadcasting: Radio to Television. Studies in the Control of Radio*, No. 4, ed. Christopher Sterling, 1-81. New York, NY: Arno Press and the *New York Times*, 1942.

Hilmes, Michele. *Radio Voices: American Broadcasting, 1922-1952*. Minneapolis, MN: University of Minnesota Press, 1997.

McChesney, Robert. "The Battle for the U.S. Airwaves, 1928-1935." *Journal of Communication* 40, no. 4 (1990): 29-57.

McFarland, Sam G. "Effects of Question Order on Survey Responses." *Public Opinion Quarterly* 45, no. 2 (1981): 208-215.

Newman, Kathy M. *Radio Active: Advertising and Consumer Activism, 1935-1947*. Berkeley, CA: University of California Press, 2004.

Sayre, Jeanette. "A Comparison of Three Indices of Attitude Toward Radio Advertising." *Journal of Applied Psychology* 23, no. 1 (1939): 23-33.

_____. *Control: How to Study Control of the Media of Communications*. New York: Bureau of Applied Social Research, Columbia University, 1945.

_____. "Progress in Radio Fan-Mail Analysis." *Public Opinion Quarterly* 3, no. 2 (1939): 272–278.

_____. "Radio." *Public Opinion Quarterly* 4, no. 3 (1940): 507–522.

_____. "Radio." *Public Opinion Quarterly* 4, no. 4 (1940): 674–686.

_____. "Radio." *Public Opinion Quarterly* 5, no. 1 (1941): 121–125.

_____. "Radio." *Public Opinion Quarterly* 5, no. 2 (1941): 301–305.

_____. "Progress in Radio Fan-Mail Analysis." *Public Opinion Quarterly* 2 (1939): 272–278.

Smith, Mrs. Francis G., "DATA SHEET." Smith Family Private Collection, July 1959.

Smith, Jeanette Sayre. "An Analysis of the Radiobroadcasting Activities of Federal Agencies." In *History of Broadcasting: Radio to Television. Studies in the Control of Radio*, No. 3, ed. Christopher Sterling, 1–81. New York, NY: Arno Press and the *New York Times*, 1942.

_____. "Broadcasting for Marginal Americans." *Public Opinion Quarterly* 6, no. 4 (1942): 588–603.

_____. "How to Study Control of the Media of Communications." Draft, Smith Family Private Collection, November 1945.

_____. *Television and Organized Groups*. New York: Bureau of Applied Social Research, 1953.

Wänke, Michaela and Norbert Schwarz. "Reducing Question Order Effects: The Operation of Buffer Items." In *Survey Measure and Process Quality*, ed. Lars E. Lyberg, Paul P. Biemer, Martin Collins, Edith D. de Leeuw, Cathryn Dippo, Norbert Schwarz, and Dennis Trewin, 115–140. Hoboken, NJ: John Wiley & Sons, 1997.

Chapter 17
Lisa Sergio (1905–1989)

By Carol A. Stabile and Laura Strait

Lisa Sergio on WQXR (permission New York Public Archives, WQXR Collections)

Lisa Sergio was one of the most influential women in news broadcasting during World War II. Despite her prominence, few histories of twentieth-century broadcasting discuss her role or the network of women in print and broadcast journalism of which she was a part.[1] Little has been written about her subversive activism in fascist Italy, or her attempts to prevent its global spread through expert cultural analysis. In fact, Sergio's career exemplifies a tradition of female journalists leveraging their careers to participate in the public sphere as trusted political theorists—a space otherwise occupied primarily by men.

Sergio was born in Florence, Italy on March 17, 1905. Her father, Baron Agostino Sergio, was a "dashing Italian aristocrat in his forties." Her mother, Margherita Fitzgerald, was "a lively attractive American young woman of twenty-five," from a prosperous Baltimore family.[2] While living in Rome,

Sergio worked for the newly formed Association of Mediterranean Studies, compiling bibliographies and participating on digs at Ostia, Pompeii, and Herculaneum. Fluent in English and Italian, she translated Amedeo Maiuri's guide to Pompeii into English, wrote short stories, and translated plays. She also worked for Eugenie Sellers Strong, a British archaeologist and art historian who broke new ground as a woman in a field dominated by men.[3]

In 1922, Sergio joined the editorial staff of the *Italian Mail*, the only English-language weekly in Italy. She was eventually promoted to assistant editor and then editor.[4] In March 1932, Sergio became the first woman commentator on EIAR, the single public service station allowed to broadcast by the Italian Fascist regime. At EIAR, she took what she described as "the dual position of English interpreter of il Duce and broadcaster for the government-controlled Radio-Roma," gaining a reputation as "the Golden Voice" of Rome.[5]

Sergio herself initially did not question Fascism.[6] But she became increasingly uncomfortable with "officially promulgated lies," citing as a turning point "a day when Mussolini himself wrote a press bulletin according to which many English soldiers serving in Egypt were found to have bubonic plague and were infecting the civilian population. His intention seemed clear: he was setting in motion malicious rumors with which he hoped to turn the Arabs against the English."[7] According to Sergio's account, "to remedy the distortions I saw [...] I began to skip a phrase or two, or to translate certain texts with such circumlocutions as to make them practically incomprehensible."[8] By April 1937, the Fascist government had become aware of Sergio's efforts to counter official propaganda. After she refused to resign from her post, the Fascist government ordered her deportation to one of the prison islands.[9] Alerted to her imminent arrest by an informant high up in the Fascist government, Sergio fled Italy, aided by inventor and family friend Guglielmo Marconi.[10]

Sergio arrived in New York City with a letter of introduction from Marconi, and began working for David Sarnoff at NBC. Frustrated because she believed that "NBC was not about to allow a woman to do news," and aided by Ann Batchelder, a journalist and later Sergio's adoptive mother, Sergio landed a position at New York City station WQXR in 1939, "a New York radio station willing," she wryly observed, "to let a woman broadcast news and commentaries."[11] Sergio became one of the first female news commentators on WQXR, developing her own news program, "Lisa Sergio's Column of the Air," which broadcast seven days a week, from 1939 to 1945. Sergio wrote her own scripts, providing analyses of political events and not merely reading analyses written by others. She used her unique experience of fascism to analyze its migration to South America, to criticize the support that neutral countries were providing Fascists through trade, and to offer an international perspective on the war.[12]

Because of her ties to the Italian Fascist regime and claims by Italian ex-patriates that she was promoting Fascist propaganda on her NBC news program, Sergio had been under surveillance by the FBI from the moment she arrived in the US. As Sergio's fervent anti-fascism became evident, the FBI did an about-face and justified continued surveillance of Sergio on the basis of her alleged affiliation with the Communist Party. The Bureau had an aggressive interest in Sergio and used a wide range of strategies to undermine her reputation. In the late 1930s, for example, the FBI began spreading rumors Sergio had been Fascist Galeazzo Ciano's mistress. In the pages of FBI memos, the rumors escalated: in addition to sleeping with Ciano, she had slept with other prominent (if unidentified) Fascist men as well, drinking to excess and bragging about her exploits. One source quoted by the FBI claimed, "she advertised her bedroom experiences with Ciano" and that she "was very exhibitionistic."[13]

After the war ended, Sergio supported herself by lecturing at universities and other organizations around the world. In 1949, the American Legion put Sergio's name on a list of those who should not be hired for such lectures because of their Communist affiliations. In June 1950, Sergio's name was included in *Red Channels: The Report on Communist Influence in Radio and Television*. Despite the Legion's assertion that Sergio's name had been removed from their list, as late as 1958, the American Legion was encouraging the public to protest her lectures and to organize letter-writing campaigns to prevent her from speaking on college campuses and other venues because of alleged communist ties.[14]

Anti-communist harassment may also have resulted from the fact that Sergio was part of a tightly knit group of gender non-conforming women in government, publishing, and broadcasting; her programs often featured other gender non-conforming women and self-identified lesbians including Eva Le Gallienne, Margaret Webster, and Mary Margaret McBride. *Ladies Home Journal* writer and editor Ann Batchelder adopted Sergio in 1944, ostensibly to facilitate Sergio's citizenship process, a strategy that gay men and lesbians used in the decades before marriage equality to gain access to some of the legal protections enjoyed by married heterosexuals.[15] Sergio and Batchelder divided their time between Vermont and New York until 1952, when Batchelder was diagnosed with cancer. They lived together in Woodstock, Vermont until Batchelder's death in 1955.

Sergio supported progressive causes throughout her life, especially civil rights. With activist Anna Arnold Hedgeman, Sergio helped fundraise for the

1963 March on Washington. She described herself as a feminist, writing and delivering many lectures and articles on the role of women in media and government in the years after World War II. Like other women working in media at the time, Sergio was curious about the history of women's political involvement and their resistance to patriarchy. She wrote a biography of Anita Garibaldi, partner and comrade-in-arms of Italian revolutionary Giuseppe Garibaldi. After she was blacklisted, Sergio completed a biography of Lena Madesin Phillips, a twentieth-century American feminist and early critic of the gender pay gap and crusader for wage equality.[16]

Despite the obstacles she encountered and the anti-communist harassment that dogged her throughout her years in the US, Sergio's six-year stint on "Column of the Air" put her at the center of news production at a pivotal moment in history. Her extensive career bridged the fields of journalism, global politics, media criticism, and broadcast entertainment. Her connections to other women in broadcasting and journalism—including Mary Margaret McBride and Dorothy Thompson—foreground the role of once powerful networks of women who subsequently were relegated to the background of media history.

Excerpt: Sergio, Lisa, "Brains Have No Sex," *WQXR Program Guide*, April 1943 (permission New York Public Archives, WQXR Collections)

Because many people wonder how it feels to be a woman radio commentator, we asked Miss Sergio to write the following article. She needs no introduction to the WQXR audience, which listens to her regularly at 7 o'clock every evening, Monday through Friday, nor to her morning audience at 10 A.M. on Monday and Friday.

"Brains have no sex," Madame Chiang-Kai-Shek told a press conference in Washington when asked her views on the Equal Rights Amendment. Everybody agreed with her, it seems. Everybody present, that is. But in radio broadcasting, experts will tell you that listeners classify brains according to the speaker's sex. The woman commentator who deals in current events does not come out on top. This is what the experts say: men don't like to have a woman tell them what's what; they want he-man stuff or nothing. Women, they continue, don't like to take it from another woman, for they also demand the stern voice of male authority when they learn the war news and the political issues that perplex and confuse this man-made world.

I am one who agrees with the brilliant lady from China and who takes little stock in the findings of those obliging experts. I will admit that one man in my audience, who signs his name in full and gives me his address each time, accuses me at regular intervals of being a female parrot who belongs in the kitchen. I can also boast one woman listener who remains anonymous in the mail, and who, with the same frequency, bids me get off the air and let a worthy man fill in the time with brains and common sense. However, I am glad to say that these two specimens are not typical of my audience, for thousands of others write in their criticisms, good and bad, without reference to petticoats or pants. And that is the way it should be.

Woman commentators are the product of the last few years. In the beginning sing as they would, fiddle as they would, women in radio were confined to the class known as "fillers." Eventually women broke into the cereal and macaroni game, and their cooking schools conducted over the radio called for all the mental agility of the housewife, combined with persuasive tones and convincing words. They made a hit and still retain their high-ranking place in this field. But they have also broadened out, bringing their measure of intuition, common sense, appreciation of particulars, analytical faculty, in brief their brains, to the discussion of other, graver subjects.

In time of war men and women are equally needed in the war effort, as they indubitably are, if men and women the world over are bearing the tragic burden of a war without quarter, as they are, it follows that men and women can equally contribute to the understanding of issues at stake and of the sometimes baffling trend of the events which affect us.

It so happens that I have been on the air for just ten years, a decade in which both radio and the world have revolutionized themselves. I began in Europe, commenting on the news of the day—the first assignment of this kind, it seems, ever given to a woman over there. Perhaps it was a tough one. To me it was exciting and unique. Ten years of familiarity with current events and with the microphone on both sides of the ocean, have neither dulled the excitement, nor bred contempt of the matter I deal with nor of the medium through which I reach the audience. And in all these years rarely, if ever, have I had reason to feel that being a woman was a handicap in this field. That is why I prefer not to believe the experts.

The quickened pace of the last few years, the broader freedom which America offers as compared to most countries of pre-war Europe, the stimulating contrast of opinions and clash of reactions in the heterogenous American audience, and the growing suspenses which the state of war brings into our lives, are factors that have unquestionably increased the responsibilities I recognize in the work of a commentator. But I do not believe that, as a woman, I recognize them less clearly nor accept them less honestly, than my male colleagues. Women as a whole, make a smaller fuss about accepting responsibilities, of whatever nature, than men. That is probably why they get less credit for fulfilling them, and more criticism if they fail! That is why they have to work harder to make a place for themselves and to hold it.

Frankly, the commentator's business boils down to this, I think: in hectic times it is a hectic marching step one has to keep. One must have mental energy, and some physical stamina too: a mind free from prejudice and stocked with as many facts and realities as it will hold. Whether it is a man or a woman collecting material, analyzing it, writing it up, making deductions and presenting the picture to the unseen audience, the most important single factor is sincerity. On the strength of that the audience, forgetting the sex, will condone the inaccuracies and errors when they occur, because the microphone has a strange and impolite way of sending over the air waves not only what the commentators say, but also what they think in the silent recesses of their minds.

Excerpt: Sergio, Lisa, *Radio—The Conquest of Our Time* (New York: The Town Hall, 1939)

Politics feeds radio in Europe; business feeds it here. Commercial or sponsored programs are the backbone of American radio. They are the revenue of an activity entailing enormous expenditure. Commercial programs are often the target of severe criticism. It is true that not all of them are good, and that some of them fall beneath the fair mark. But they are constructed primarily as a sales medium, and if a bad program has a buying audience the sponsor cannot be blamed for keeping it on the air. It is therefore the duty of the sustaining programs to raise radio's standards to a high all-around level, and unfortunately not all the sustaining programs remain above the mark of ordinary adult intelligence.

Incidentally, I think that the term "sustaining" is misleading, and might effectively be changed to "presentation" when applying to programs obviously broadcast by the station for the enjoyment or information of the audience, without a view to selling them to a sponsor. "Sustaining" gives the impression of merely filling in time for sale. Surely the NBC Symphony, with and without Toscanini, the WABC broadcasts from Carnegie Hall, other symphony programs from American cities, "America's Town Meeting of the Air," WOR's Sinfonietta with Alfred Wallenstein, WQXR's recorded classics, are not merely spare-time fillers! They are presentations, or gifts of the best quality, to ninety-five million American listeners.

Some first-rate presentations, which the stations hesitate to broadcast for fear of going over the head of the audience, not only proved that the audience holds its head very high, but that they found eager sponsors in spite of their excellent quality. Outstanding examples of this are NBC's "Information Please" and Columbia's "Mercury Theatre of the Air" launched as sustaining and quickly sold commercially. This latter program, incidentally, in one instance of breath-taking proof of the persuasive power of radio, of its influence on the imagination, and of the painful results of unintelligent and careless listening.

Network broadcasting, a brilliant American solution of the problem presented by the country's enormous area, facilitates the task of improving radio standards. Thanks to the networks, small or local stations are able to give to their communities the major programs from key stations, which could not be financed except through a network. Network broadcasting is democratic broadcasting. What goes to one should go to all.

Radio also enters the classroom, and is ready to become the teacher's best assistant without, of course, aiming to replace them. Radio programs can supplement textbook theories with demonstrations of their significance in everyday life. Radio opens the mind of the pupil, taking him into the world through which he will make his way in later years. The "American School of the Air" is directed towards this end, and presents a special feature devised to illustrate to teachers the use of radio in the classroom. Educational features for children and adults are heard on all stations, covering all fields. Music in radio becomes a medium of education, and radio educates all people in the appreciation of music. Dr. Damrosch's delightful musical appreciation program, intended for children and fascinating to grown-ups, proves my point. Radio gives us the essence of music and teaches us to abandon ourselves to its enchantment in the silence to our homes. Music and the ether waves are an ideal marriage, sealed in the harmony of infinite space.

Radio—art, political instrument, commercial medium, public service— is also a hobby, the most romantic of all hobbies, when it takes the name of amateur broadcasting. Sixty thousand individuals throughout the world call this hobby their own. The original Pittsburgh station, KDKA, of 1920 fame, was operated by amateurs for amateur audiences, and became the seed from which sprang the mighty tree of American broadcasting. The development of short-wave broadcasting goes to the credit of amateurs who developed this medium, their use of the ether having been confined to waves under 200 meters when regular stations were allocated the medium and longer frequencies. In the performance of public service amateurs have deserved and received universal conversation.

Radio has reserved the old saying: Mohammed goes to the mountain. It is now the mountain which goes to Mohammed. The entire world comes to us, leaping over seas and mountains, darting over continents, spanning the abyss of time, to unroll before us the miracles of nature and science; to carry us forward, united, towards greater and better achievements. We stand on the threshold of a world vaster than our ancestors dreamed of, yet a world made smaller by the pathways in the ether shortening the distance between man and the infinite.

Notes

1 See Donna L. Halper's *Invisible Stars: A Social History of Women in American Broadcasting* (New York, NY: Routledge, 2015), 92.

2 Lisa Sergio, "Autobiography" (Georgetown, DC, n.d.), 22, Box 5, Folder 6, "Autobiography," Lisa Sergio Papers, Georgetown, DC.

3 Sergio, "Autobiography," Chapter VI, 4.

4 Stacy L. Spaulding, "Lisa Sergio: How Mussolini's 'Golden Voice' of Propaganda Created an American Mass Communication Career" (PhD diss., University of Maryland, 2005), 54.

5 Sergio, "Autobiography," Chapter 6, 5.

6 Ibid., 9.

7 Ibid., 9–10.

8 Ibid., 10.

9 Sergio, "Autobiography," Chapters 2–12, 20.

10 Paul H. O'Grady, "Lisa Sergio, Was.," FBI Report (Albany, NY: FBI, December 11, 1954), 2, FBI #65-HQ-18966, National Records and Archives Administration, College Park, MD.

11 Sergio, "Autobiography," Chapter IX, 30; Spaulding, "Lisa Sergio," 299.

12 Stacy Spaulding, "Off the Blacklist, But Still a Target: The Anti-Communist Attacks on Lisa Sergio," *Journalism Studies* 10, no. 6 (2009): 792.

13 Frank L. Amprim, "Elisa Maria Alice Sergio, Alias Lisa Sergio" (Rome, Italy: Federal Bureau of Investigation, October 12, 1945), 1, FBI #65-18966-48, National Records and Archives Administration, College Park, MD.

14 M. A. Jones, "To Mr. Nease," Office Memorandum (Washington, D.C.: Federal Bureau of Investigation, April 30, 1945), FBI #65-18966, National Records and Archives Administration, College Park, MD.

15 Koa Beck, "How Marriage Inequality Prompts Gay Partners to Adopt One Another," *The Atlantic*, November 27, 2013, www.theatlantic.com/national/archive/2013/11/how-marriage-inequality-prompts-gay-partners-to-adopt-one-another/281546/, accessed April 11, 2022; Elise Chenier, "Love-Politics: Lesbian Wedding Practices in Canada and the United States from the 1920s to the 1970s," *Journal of the History of Sexuality* 27, no. 2 (May 2018); Sergio, "Autobiography," Chapter IX, 31.

16 Lisa Sergio, *I Am My Beloved: The Life of Anita Garibaldi* (New York, NY: Weybright and Talley, 1969), ix; Lisa Sergio, *A Measure Filled: The Life of Lena Madesin Phillips Drawn from Her Autobiography* (New York, NY: R.B. Luce, 1972).

Bibliography

Amprim, Frank L. "Elisa Maria Alice Sergio, Alias Lisa Sergio." Rome, Italy: FBI, National Records and Archives Administration, October 12, 1945, 1, FBI #65-18966-48, College Park, MD.

Armstrong, Jennifer Keishin. *When Women Invented Television: The Untold Story of the Female Powerhouses Who Pioneered the Way We Watch Today.* New York, NY: Harper, 2021.

Beck, Koa. "How Marriage Inequality Prompts Gay Partners to Adopt One Another." The Atlantic, November 27, 2013. www.theatlantic.com/national/archive/2013/11/how-marriage-inequality-prompts-gay-partners-to-adopt-one-another/281546/, accessed April 11, 2022.

Chenier, Elise. "Love-Politics: Lesbian Wedding Practices in Canada and the United States from the 1920s to the 1970s." *Journal of the History of Sexuality* 27, no. 2 (May 1, 2018): 294—321.

Flint, Peter B. "Lisa Sergio, Radio Commentator in Italy and New York, Dies at 84." *New York Times*, June 26, 1989. www.nytimes.com/1989/06/26/obituaries/lisa-sergio-radio-commentator-in-italy-and-new-york-dies-at-84.html, accessed April 24, 2023.

Halper, Donna. *Invisible Stars: A Social History of Women in American Broadcasting.* 2nd ed. New York, NY: Routledge, 2015.

Hosley, David H. and Gayle K. Yamada. *Hard News: Women in Broadcast Journalism.* Greenwood, CT: Greenwood, Press, 1987.

Jones, M.A. "To Mr. Nease." Office Memorandum. Washington, D.C.: Federal Bureau of Investigation. April 30, 1945. FBI #65-19966, National Records and Archives Administration, College Park, MD.

Lisa Sergio FBI Files, Federal Bureau of Investigation, College Park, MD: National Archives and Record Administration, FBI #65-18966-80.

Lisa Sergio Papers, Booth Family Center for Special Collections, Georgetown University. https://findingaids.library.georgetown.edu/repositories/15/resources/10071, accessed April 24, 2023.

O'Grady, Paul H. "Lisa Sergio, Was.," FBI Report. Albany, NY: National Records and Archives Administration, FBI. December 11, 1954. 2, FBI #65-HQ-18966, College Park, MD.

Red Channels: The Report of Communist Influence in Radio and Television. New York, NY: American Business Consultants, 1950.

Sanger, Elliott M. *Rebel in Radio: The Story of WQXR.* New York, NY: Hastings House Publishers, 1973.

Sergio, Lisa. "Autobiography." n.d., 22, Box 5, Folder 6, Lisa Sergio Papers. Booth Family Center for Special Collections, Georgetown University. Georgetown, D.C.

_____. *I Am My Beloved: The Life of Anita Garibaldi.* New York, NY: Weybright and Talley, 1969.

_____. *Jesus and Woman: An Exciting Discovery of What He Offered Her*. McLean, VA: Hawthorn Books, 1975.

_____. *A Measure Filled: The Life of Lena Madesin Phillips Drawn from Her Autobiography*. New York, NY: R. B. Luce, 1972.

Spaulding, Stacy. "Off the Blacklist, But Still a Target: The Anti-Communist Attacks on Lisa Sergio." *Journalism Studies* 10, no. 6 (2009): 789–806.

Spaulding, Stacy L. "Lisa Sergio: How Mussolini's 'Golden Voice' of Propaganda Created an American Mass Communication Career." PhD diss., University of Maryland, 2005.

Chapter 18
Fredi Washington (1903–1994)

By Malia Mulligan, Morning Glory Ritchie, and Miche Dreiling

Fredi Washington, 1931 (Philadelphia Ledger)

Born in Savannah, Georgia in 1903, Fredericka Carolyn "Fredi" Washington was a film, radio, and Broadway actor, as well as a writer, producer, and an activist. After the death of her mother, Washington was sent to a convent for orphaned Black and Indian children at St. Elizabeth's in Cornwell Heights, Pennsylvania. Washington moved to New York City in 1919 to live with her grandmother. While working at Pace and Handy's Black Swan Record Company, Washington, who had never danced professionally, auditioned for Eubie Blake's *Shuffle Along*. Choreographed by Elida Webb, and featuring Washington, *Shuffle Along* (1921) became the first all-Black Broadway hit.[1] Although Washington was best known for her role as the light-skinned Peola in John Stahl's film production of *Imitation of Life* (1934), theater was her home. In addition to *Shuffle Along*, Washington performed in *Singin' the Blues* (1931), *Run, Little Chillun* (1933), *The Emperor Jones* (1933), *Mamba's*

Daughters (1939), *Lysistrata* (1946), *A Long Way from Home* (1948), and numerous other theatrical productions. Washington also appeared in special programs and guest appearances on WCBS, WOR, WNBC, and WINS.

From the beginning of her career, Washington's commitment to civil rights shared equal billing with her aspirations as a performing artist. She co-founded the Negro Actors Guild Association in 1936 to address the exclusion of Black performers and tradespeople from unions during the Depression. While writing in support of better treatment for Black soldiers, she also advocated for the Double V campaign initiated by the *Pittsburgh Courier*, which crusaded for victory over fascism globally as well as victory over those in the US who opposed civil rights for African Americans.

Washington's work as editor and columnist for the weekly newspaper *People's Voice*, owned and edited by her then brother-in-law, Adam Clayton Powell, Jr., showcases her analyses of racism, sexism, and economic inequalities in American pop culture. Originally hired in 1942 to handle public relations for *Voice*, as the paper was known, Washington transitioned into writing for the column "Odds and Ends" and "Headlines and Footlights" in 1943 before being assigned her own column, "Fredi Says," in 1944. As the newspaper's theatrical editor, *Voice* allowed Washington free rein as a "newspaperwoman," celebrating her candor and political commitments. During World War II, Washington's columns reflected her frustration, as she put it, that "so many people in show business close their eyes to social and political developments around them—that they believe they can live in their own ivory towers without becoming an integral part of this fast changing world."[2] Despite those who criticized the political nature of her columns, Washington insisted that her columns were "written deliberately to stimulate discussion not about me or whether or not it is in my province to take as my subject this or that phase of our national life but rather for thought and discussion of the subject itself which is projected here [...] the theatre and its people are very much a part of the war, church, politics and society in general."[3]

Washington's columns covered a variety of topics, often addressed to the diverse population of Harlem. For instance, she advised her readers that, "To keep hair well groomed during the hot weather, the old fashioned corn-row (the hair braided over instead of under and pinned across the top of the head) is very convenient and satisfactory." Other times, her columns celebrated integrated cultural events, like the "Male-Female-Negro-White American Youth Orchestra." Her columns also provided essential information, for instance, for Black soldiers seeking hotel accommodations in wartime New York.[4] And she used her column to draw attention to the need to "give serious and careful thought to fighting men, physically and mentally wounded, who are returning home to try and pick up the threads of their lives."[5]

Washington reprimanded the sexism of her own critics. Responding to one letter-writer, whose letter to her ended with "What! Woman columnist? Ye, Gods!!!," Washington wrote, "Now, Mr. Roberts, is that nice? You emphatically know your jazz but your attitude toward women just ain't kosher."[6] She addressed media producers and audiences alike, arguing they shared a collaborative mission "to fight for a decent America."[7] Washington wrote, "We must work out a method whereby each artist and every member of an audience will become a committee of one to improve racial relations, so that we can get on with the business of creating a better world for all."[8]

Identifying the intersections of inequality within pop culture and politics, Washington's criticism of media content was incisive and fearless. Addressing the issue of whether Black performers should "accept 'Uncle Tom' roles in the theatre and movies," Washington recounted her experience working with script writers whose only knowledge of Black culture came "from what has been told them by the whites who are supposedly interested in Negroes and 'know all about them.' "[9] Big stars, she maintained, had power to resist, whether through working with screenwriters, using contracts to enforce anti-racist norms, or refusing "Uncle Tom" parts. Washington held a nuanced critique of racial stereotypes. It was not that Black actors should not be cast as maids or butlers, roles that were true to the segregated nature of Black employment. Instead, she objected to "the stereotype servant with his bowed head, ridiculous dialect and idiotic, brainless stupidity."[10] Taking on Disney's *Song of the South* on the eve of its release, Washington wrote, "Like 'Gone with the Wind' this new Disney opus helps to perpetuate the idea that Negroes throughout American history have been illiterate, docile and quite happy to be treated as children—without even the average child's ambition and without thought of tomorrow."[11] *Song of the South*, Washington added, directly echoed the refrains of politicians like Mississippi Senator Theodore Bilbo, who in the face of a growing civil rights movement maintained that Black people were content with the Southern status quo.

Her columns also uplifted voices of other aspiring activists. She once turned her column over to "young white writer" Earl Conrad, author of a biography of Harriet Tubman. Washington shared Conrad's still unrealized belief that "One day, when this land is free, and education is for everyone, and textbooks tell the truth, and men are decent to one another, and color is regarded as not more than the minor mutation that it is, then the stature of fighting Harriet Tubman will rank high in human achievement as the figure of any other man or woman in this land's history."[12] Washington devoted another column to dancer Josephine Baker, with whom she had performed in *Shuffle Along*. In it, she described the treatment Baker had received as "a lanky brown-skinned girl" at the hands of the "chorus girls who were on the yellow side" and how Baker had taught them all to "never consider yourself superior to any human being."[13] In another column, she praised Paul Robeson's dedication "to the cause of freedom for all underprivileged people," and his deep appreciation for the rich cultures of the world (Robeson, she noted, spoke Chinese, Russian, Spanish, and was learning several African languages).[14]

In her analysis of the links between anti-communism and White supremacy within American culture, Washington took pains to explain the interlocking interests among Hearst newspapers, the Catholic Church, and the racist forces working to oppose voting rights measures throughout the South. Calling out the racism and anti-Semitism that had allowed fascist radio host Father Charles Coughlin to promote hate-filled broadcasts, and the hypocrisy that targeted communists, while Mussolini and Hitler went uncriticized, Washington concluded, "I want a free America for all peoples and I shall work with anyone who wants the same thing, be he Communist or any other named group."[15] *Voice* allowed Washington to openly discuss the stigma associated with the words "Communist" and "Communism" in a "Headlines and Footlights" column. However, she paid for her staunch support for progressive organizations and causes, first by being fired from *Voice* along with other writers who had been blacklisted by the FBI, and then by the lack of attention paid to her work by subsequent generations of historians and critics, themselves influenced by anti-communist histories.

Washington wrote over 300 columns and features for *Voice*, from 1943 through 1947, before *Voice* was forced to close its door in 1948. Her columns for *Voice* form an archive of Black media criticism, illustrating how analyses exploring the interlocking nature of oppression were very much part of a broader, if later, suppressed conversation about media, culture, race, class, and gender in the first half of the twentieth century. The columns included in this volume show how Black women's cultural criticism, then as now, challenged the boundaries of categories that with the aid of anti-communist ideologies served to obscure relationships of power. Against the denial of freedom to all people, and in the face of significant racist retaliation, Washington firmly maintained, "I'm a Black woman and proud of it. That's the way it is, and I will fight injustices and encourage others to fight them until the day I die or there is nothing to fight against."[16]

Excerpt: Washington, Fredi, "Headlines and Footlights," *People's Voice,* June 10, 1944

MANY PEOPLE HAVE asked me whether I'm supposed to use this column for topics other than that of the theatre and its people. Seems there has been quite a lot of discussion about the fact that I have sounded off any number of times on the subject of politics, soldiers, etiquette, the church, etc. These columns are written deliberately to stimulate discussion not about me or whether or not it is in my province to take as my subject this or that phase of our national life but rather for thought and discussion of the subject itself which is projected in here.

As a matter of fact, the theatre and its people are very much a part of the war, church, politics and society in general. Therefore, whatever subject dealt with affects people of the theatre if not directly, certainly indirectly.

As an example, I am in receipt of a letter from a soldier stationed in Georgia who says, "This clipping is from the *Atlanta Journal* and I think it the most outrageous thing I've ever seen. Are those appearing so broke they must take such bookings—and humiliation? It's really a disgrace—even in Georgia." Signed: "A very indignant colored soldier."

'FOR WHITE PEOPLE ONLY'

The clipping of which the soldier speaks is a large advertisement in the *Atlanta Journal* which states that The Ink Spots, Ella Fitzgerald, Cootie Williams and his band, Moke and Poke, Eddie Vinson and Ralph Brown were appearing at the Auditorium. At the top of the ad in bold print, "For White Patrons Only," makes very clear, how jimcro laws and discrimination in its every phase, affects the theatre. It is for reasons such as these that this column tries to stay on the beam.

THE IMPORTANCE OF FIGHTING

All of the above-mentioned artists are from New York and while they have run into this kind of segregation here and there, they have had to live with it to the extent that it gnaws at their insides the same as it does the soldier's who has had to live with it.

When this troupe signed its contract in New York before starting the tour, the idea never occurred to them that they would play theatres whose policy is "white only." Mind you, these performers are not ignorant that there are such theatres. But the importance of fighting these conditions—though they are far removed from their everyday lives—has not been thoroughly impressed upon their minds.

Perhaps Southern theatrical tycoons are looking for a loophole to back up their "white only" stand. Anyway, our own youth plays right into their hands when they deport themselves badly when their favorite Negro bands and stars appear in their communities.

BEST FOOT ALWAYS AT ALL TIMES

Bookers are in a dither as to handling of the situation. Daily they receive cancellations of top attractions allegedly because a group of teen age youngsters have broken up this or that theatre. This column does not for a moment intend to suggest that Negro youth is alone in this type of vandalism. The whites are just as bad. But because we are a minority group with the finger always pointed at us, we cannot afford to indulge in anything but the strictest adherence to "the best foot forward" at all times—man, woman and child. We must not put weapons in the hands of Southern theatre managers to use against us and our performers.

On the other hand, we do have a suggestion to make to our performers. There is a method by which they can begin to break down segregation and discrimination even in Southern theatres. Paul Robeson, Hazel Scott and now Marian Anderson, have put it into effect, and certainly the results have been good. The method is simply this: those artists who are established and have box-office draw can and should have inserted into their contracts a clause stating that they will not play any theatre which does not admit Negroes. This would mean that all the lesser people in the unit could not play such a date.

THEATREGOERS MUST DO THEIR PART

On the other hand, the theatregoing public must not only do their part to breakdown discrimination but work also for the self-respect of the Negro population, as well. The artists' fight without the help of the public would only result in many of the spots which now use Negro talent, closing their doors to us and using white talent exclusively. That has been done in the largest movie and vaudeville theatres in both Chicago [and] Detroit to name but two cities.

In checking with a few musicians who played this same Auditorium a few seasons ago, I found that this "for white only" policy is new since in every case, these boys played to mixed audiences season after season.

What is the reason for the change? Have we ourselves contributed to the change? We must work out a method whereby each artist and every member of an audience will become a committee of one to improve racial relations, so that we can get on with the business of creating a better world for all.

Excerpt: Washington, Fredi, "Fredi Says," *People's Voice*, November 30, 1946

WALT DISNEY WILL, NO DOUBT, RECEIVE THE HIGHEST AWARD the Solid South has to offer, for it will be through him and the world-wide distribution of his latest efforts with animated cartoons and live actors that the picturesque south with its bandanna-headed-song-singing "darkies" will be shown through the medium of the screen. In his latest technicolor film, **Song of the South**, Disney has created some of his best cartoons to date. Based on the tales of Uncle Remus—the antics of Brer Rabbit, Brer Fox and Brer Bear— the whole is fused with an appropriate musical score which will be sheer delight to adults as well as children.

But it is the background story of these tales of the "dear old southland" and the story's enactment by the live cast which will give new courage and impetus to the discriminatory south. Like "Gone With the Wind" this new Disney opus helps to perpetuate the idea that Negroes throughout American history have been illiterate, docile and quite happy to be treated as children— without even the average child's ambition and without thought of tomorrow.

Mr. Disney, no doubt, has argued and will continue to argue that **Song of the South** is folklore, and had, of necessity, to be authentic—that, indeed, he has woven social content into his unusual film by making Uncle Remus a wise, lovable character. That Remus is allowed to walk through the front door of the stately southern mansion—that it is only Uncle Remus who can bring the little white boy out of a death grip delirium against which his mamma is helpless—that the little Negro boy is allowed to catch toad frogs with the unhappy white child—that it is Remus' fantastic tales of the "critters" coupled with his love and understanding of children which saves an otherwise fatal situation—these are all weak claims to social progress.

ALL OF THESE REASONS and some more will be proffered by Mr. Disney in defense of his new film. In addition to this Mr. Disney will lean heavily on the fact that he has been the only one in pictures to recognize and give opportunity to the undeniable talents of Jimmy Baskett who plays Uncle Remus, and that it was through the filming of this story that many Negro actors who have been idle for one reason or another for months, were given employment.

The two latter arguments are good ones and no one in his right mind would take issue with them in a purely economic sense. But it is not only economics that we are concerned with and anyone interested in human relationships and democratic principles, must take into consideration the entire broad picture of the struggle of the Negro people to gain their rights as dignified American citizens.

As a Negro living in a nation within a nation, who has some knowledge of the theatre and movie industry, I take very strong exception to the argument that one must not only be authentic but go to stereotyped extremes in presenting Negro characterization or subject matter, regardless of the time element or place in America. The argument that because the film deals with folklore, it had to be authentic, melts into thin air by the mere fact that, even though the setting is in Georgia, there is no trace of southern accent to be found in any of the dialogue used by the white characters, including the poor whites. The Negroes on the other hand, are saddled with the worst kind of dialect.

Needless to say, a plaintive song accompanies most of their action. No one has any objection to the beautiful choral singing of the players, but when it is coupled with every cliche in the book, the meaning gets to be pretty obvious. You can almost hear Bilbo say: "We in the South know how to keep our 'nigras' happy. They're content and to prove it, listen to 'em sing as they leave their cabins to pick cotton in the fields."

WHEN A PERSON OF WALT DISNEY's artistic and technical stature in an industry which is the greatest medium in the world for molding public opinion chooses to ignore the anti-social implications contained in any of his productions, then it is plain for all to see that the man's social and political consciousness has yet to be awakened.

This is a great pity, for Disney had the opportunity to produce a highly amusing and entertaining film without resorting to all the stereotype characters of the Uncle Tom era. Since Chandler Harris' Uncle Remus and his tales are all pure fantasy, the film would not have been one wit more fantastical had the locale not been in Georgia in the days of the bandanna-head-bowing-uneducated-Uncle Tom-Negro. But Mr. Disney wanted to perpetuate Mr. Harris' classical folklore tales in all their blessed Georgian glory. And to prove this, **Song of the South** had its premiere in Atlanta (a city which has been much in the news of late for its anti-Negro activities) just two weeks ago.

I'm wondering when folks with Disney's talent, power and money are going to start itching to record and dramatize some of the true and worthwhile history of the American Negro's achievements, much of which has high amusement value. The great trouble is, most of the authentic folklore of the Negro has been completely ignored while the writers have worked overtime at getting down on paper the minstrel ideas about us.

DESPITE THE DIALECT which had to be mouthed, a high word of praise should be said for Jimmy Baskett who, as Uncle Remus turns in a fine, sensitive performance. He sings several of the delightful songs in the picture and lends his fast talking spiel to the sound track for Brer Fox. Baskett will no doubt continue to do sound tracks for Disney's animated cartoons since his voice is so adaptable, but you can't help but wonder if he is ever going to get the opportunity to play roles commensurate with the high calibre of talent he showed for character acting in **Song of the South.**

Johnny Lee supplies the voice for Brer Rabbit and Nicodemus Stewart's voice is effective as Brer Bear. Hattie McDaniel is her efficient "mammy" self and there was a charming little fellow whose name is Glenn Leedy who seemed ill at ease handling the dialect.

"Song of the South" will soon be released in New York, and while you are bound to appreciate and enjoy Mr. Disney's animated characters, you no doubt will feel as I do about his story background and Negro characterizations. If you do, a letter or post card to Mr. Disney will help to acquaint him with the fact that there are paying customers who do not appreciate the idea of having the Negro perpetuated in the minds of the public as dialect-speaking-song-singing Uncle Toms.

Excerpt: Washington, Fredi, "Fredi Says," *People's Voice*, April 26, 1947

Hattie McDaniel who has managed to get herself involved time and again on the wrong side of the fence on the topic of Hollywood stereotypes, is once again sounding off on the subject. This time, through the medium of Hedda Hopper's syndicated column which appears in New York's *Daily News*. Hattie seems to be upset because several mass organizations from coast to coast, picketed *Song of the South*, Walt Disney's tale of Uncle Remus in which she plays the role of a mammy. Hattie says in her letter to Hedda Hopper, "I don't think I've disgraced my race by the roles I've played. I'm trying to fathom what an 'Uncle Tom' is. People who can afford to certainly have maids and butlers called 'Uncle Tom'? Truly, maids and butlers in real life are only trying to make an honest dollar, just as we who work in pictures. I only hope that producers will give us Negro actors and actresses more roles—even if there will be those who'll call us 'Uncle Toms.' When they speak thus, I'm sure it's only because of their frustrated minds."

This letter I think shows clearly the tremendous educational job which needs to be done among ourselves. Miss McDaniel has missed completely the crux of the argument against stereotyping the Negro on screen. And too, I think it shows the lack of confidence she has in her ability as an actress. To suggest that many Negroes do not make their living as servants would be to belie the living facts. But also, to suggest by reason of omission that there are not Negroes in all phases of government, education, white-collar professions, the sciences and in the ordinary business of every day living is a down right concealment of the truth.

No one has any objection to Miss McDaniel playing the role of a mammy when necessary but we do object to the Civil War mammy in the modern setting. And furthermore, what makes this actress think that she must be forever relegated to the "ya-sa boss" type servant?

It should not be difficult for Miss McDaniel to point out to some of her many studio contacts, which no doubt consist of writers, directors and producers, that all Negro servants do not speak in dialect. Indeed, I know from personal contact that many Negro servants have a better command of the English language than some of the people they work for. Why not match this type servant for every stereotype used? At least it would give both sides of the servant class.

I don't think there is one person who fights against stereotyping the Negro who blames the individual actor or actress for carrying out assignments handed them in pictures. These people are well aware of the fact that these artists are making a living in the only way they know how but certainly it is not expected that these artists will become so completely subjugated to the stereotype idea that they will defend it [...]

It would behoove all of us to ever keep in mind that in many sections of this world the only contact people have with the American Negro is what they get via the screen and radio and they take it literally. I wonder if Miss McDaniel wants the peoples of Africa, India and other isolated peoples to think of her only as she appears in *Song of the South*?

Since this is practically the only kind of role Hollywood hands Miss McDaniel, movie-goers who have no contact with Negroes have no other means of finding out that off the screen she and countless other Negro females live an entirely different kind of life.

Some producers have defended their position on casting Miss McDaniel by saying, you can't make a Lena Horne out of her. My answer to that one is, who asked for such an impossible transition? Hattie McDaniel is an actress and what is wrong with her portraying some one of the caliber of Mary McLeod Bethune, an educator who attained high success the hard way? There are many Negro women all over this country who answer the physical description of Hattie McDaniel who could take some of the Hollywood big shots to school.

Wake up Hattie, no one is riding you for the mammy roles you must play, but I for one am riding you for your defense of the overall picture these roles create in the minds of the movie going public.

If you readers feel that Hollywood has a responsibility to the Negro population from whom they collect a terrific revenue, then you ought to join the Cultural Division of the National Negro Congress, 307 Lenox Av. This division is out not to put Hattie McDaniel and others like her out of the business of making pictures, but on the contrary it is out to get better roles for them depicting us as part of the day to day American scene.

Notes

1 Donald Bogle, *Brown Sugar: Eighty Years of America's Black Female Superstars* (New York, NY: Harmony Books, 1980), 76.
2 MJC, "Our Four Star Washington Gal," *People's Voice*, August 14, 1943.
3 Fredi Washington, "Headlines and Footlights," *People's Voice*, June 10, 1944, 22.
4 Fredi Washington, "Fredi Says," *People's Voice*, May 26, 1945, 24.
5 Fredi Washington, "Headlines and Footlights," *People's Voice*, March 18, 1944, 22.
6 Fredi Washington, "Headlines and Footlights," *People's Voice*, January 29, 1944, 22.
7 Fredi Washington, "Fredi Says," *People's Voice*, September 7, 1946, 28.
8 Fredi Washington, "Headlines and Footlights," *People's Voice*, June 10, 1944, 22.
9 Fredi Washington, "Headlines and Footlights," *People's Voice*, April 10, 1943, 26.
10 Fredi Washington, "Headlines and Footlights," *People's Voice*, August 5, 1944, 22.
11 Fredi Washington, "Fredi Says," *People's Voice*, November 30, 1946, 22.
12 Earl Conrad for Fredi Washington, "Headlines and Footlights," *People's Voice*, April 22, 1944, 22.
13 Fredi Washington, "Headlines and Footlights," *People's Voice*, November 6, 1943, 24.
14 Fredi Washington, "Headlines and Footlights," *People's Voice*, April 15, 1944, 22.
15 Fredi Washington, "Headlines and Footlights," *People's Voice*, May 27, 1944, 26.
16 Norma Jean Darden, "Oh, Sister! Fredi and Isabel Washington Relive '30s Razzmatazz," *Essence Magazine*, September 1978, 105.

Bibliography

Bearden, Bessye. "Fredi Washington Weds Duke's Trombonist." *Chicago Defender*, August 19, 1933, 5.

"Bill Robinson Named Guild Honorary Head." *Chicago Defender*, February 18, 1939, 10.

Black, Cheryl. "Looking White, Acting Black: Cast(e)Ing Fredi Washington." *Theatre Survey* 45, no. 1 (2004): 19–40.

_____. "'New Negro' Performance on Life and Art: Fredi Washington and the Theatrical Columns of the People's Voice, 1943–47." *Theatre History Studies* 24 (2004): 57–72.

Blake, Aaron. "Republican Rep. Allen West Says Many Congressional Democrats Are Communists." *Washington Post Blogs,* April 4, 2012. www.washingtonpost.com/blogs/the-fix/post/republican-rep-allen-west-suggests-many-congressional-democrats-are-communists/2012/04/11/gIQApbZiAT_blog.html, accessed April 11, 2022.

Bogle, Donald. "The Washington Sisters: Orphans of the Storm." In *Brown Sugar: Eighty Years of America's Black Female Superstars*, 76–82. New York, NY: Harmony Books, 1980.

Bourne, Stephen. "Obituary: Fredi Washington." *The Independent*, July 4, 1994. www.independent.co.uk/news/people/obituary-fredi-washington-1411510.html, accessed April 11, 2022.

Bowdre, Karen M. "Passing Films and the Illusion of Racial Equality." *Black Camera* 5, no. 2 (2014): 21–43.

Brooks, Atkinson. "Concerning Mamba's Waters." *New York Times*, January 15, 1939, X1.

Committee on Un-American Activities. "Report on the Congress of American Women." Washington, D.C.: US House of Representatives, October 23, 1949.

Conrad, Earl. "Headlines and Footlights." *People's Voice*, April 22, 1944, 22.

Darden, Norma Jean. "Oh, Sister! Fredi and Isabel Washington Relive '30s Razzmatazz." *Essence Magazine*, September 1978, 98.

Davis, Kimberly Nicole. "Fredi Washington: Black Entertainers and the 'Double V' Campaign." PhD diss., Texas State University-San Marcos, 2006.

Dewberry, Jonathan. "Black Actors Unite: The Negro Actors' Guild." *The Black Scholar* 21, no. 2 (1990): 2–11.

Finlay, Nancy. "Remembering Fredi Washington: Actress, Activist, and Journalist." 2021, ConnecticutHistory.Org.https://connecticuthistory.org/remembering-fredi-washington-actress-activist-and-journalist/, accessed April 11, 2022.

"Fredericka Carolyn 'Fredi' Washington, Harlem," *Harlem World Magazine.* July 3, 2017. www.harlemworldmagazine.com/fredericka-carolyn-fredi-washington-harlem-video/, accessed April 11, 2022.

"Fredi Washington Bares Her Hubby's Letters from 'Other Woman' in Court." *Chicago Defender*, February 28, 1948.

G-2. "Subject: Negro Criticism of U.S.O. Entertainment Overseas." December 10, 1943. Weekly Conference Report. New York: FBI.

McCarthy, Joseph. "Speech to 25th Women's Patriotic Conference of National Defense." Washington, D.C., January 26, 1951. Marquette University, John P. Raynor, S.J. Libraries, Department of Special Collections.

_____. *Treason in Washington Exposed*. St. Louis, MI: Christian Nationalist Crusade, 1950.

McCarthy, William J. "U.S. vs. Joseph E. McWilliams, Was, et al, Elizabeth Dilling – Defendant." Form No. 1. August 2, 1944. Washington, D.C.: Federal Bureau of Investigation. FBI File #61-7055. National Archives and Records Administration, College Park, MD.

MJC, "Our Four Star Washington Gal." *People's Voice*, August 14, 1943.

Mullen, Bill and James Edward Smethurst. *Left of the Color Line: Race, Radicalism, and Twentieth-Century Literature of the United States*. Chapel Hill, NC: University of North Carolina Press, 2003.

Phelan, Joseph J. "Fredi Washington Security Matter—C." Letterhead Memo. July 11, 1946. FBI File #100-81380-4. National Archives and Records Administration, College Park, MD.

Regester, Charlene B. *African American Actresses: The Struggle for Visibility, 1900–1960*. Bloomington, IN: Indiana University Press, 2010.

Robinson, Albert. "Dear Miss Fredi Washington." Fan letter. April 1, 1935. Box 1, Correspondence 1935–1948, Fredi Washington Papers, Amistad Research Center, Tulane University, New Orleans.

Rule, Sheila. "Fredi Washington, 90, Actress; Broke Ground for Black Artists." *New York Times*, sec. Obituaries. June 30, 1994. www.nytimes.com/1994/06/30/obituaries/fredi-washington-90-actress-broke-ground-for-black-artists.html, accessed April 11, 2022.

Smith, Alfred E. "Coast Agrees that Miss Washington is Terrific." *Chicago Defender*, September 27, 1941.

Washington, Fredi. "Fredi Says." *People's Voice*, May 26, 1945, 24.

_____. "Fredi Says." *People's Voice*, September 7, 1946, 28.

_____. "Fredi Says." *People's Voice*, November 30, 1946, 22.

_____. "Fredi Says." *People's Voice*, April 26, 1947, 26.

_____. "Headlines and Footlights." *People's Voice*, April 10, 1943, 26.

_____. "Headlines and Footlights." *People's Voice*, November 6, 1943, 24.

_____. "Headlines and Footlights." *People's Voice*, January 29, 1944, 22.

_____. "Headlines and Footlights." *People's Voice*, March 18, 1944, 22.

_____. "Headlines and Footlights." *People's Voice*, April 15, 1944, 22.

_____. "Headlines and Footlights." *People's Voice*, May 27, 1944, 26

_____. "Headlines and Footlights." *People's Voice*, June 10, 1944, 22.

_____. "Headlines and Footlights." *People's Voice*, August 5, 1944, 22.

Washington, Mary Helen. "Alice Childress, Lorraine Hansberry, and Claudia Jones: Black Women Write the Popular Front." In *Left of the Color Line: Race, Radicalism, and Twentieth-Century Literature of the United States*, 183-204. Chapel Hill, NC: The University of North Carolina Press, 2003.

_____. *The Other Blacklist: The African American Literary and Cultural Left of the 1950s*. New York, NY: Columbia University Press, 2014.

Woodard, Laurie Avant. "Performing Artists of the Harlem Renaissance: Resistance, Identity, and Meaning in the Life and Work of Fredi Washington from 1920 to 1950." PhD diss., Yale University, 2007.

Chapter 19

Gene Weltfish (1902–1980)

By Marianne Kinkel

At a 1976 gathering held in honor of her contributions to anthropology, Gene Weltfish asserted that defeating prejudice and social injustice are fundamental: "Human hatred and group self-destruction must be the basis of our work, for those committed rather than merely professionalized."[1] Her committed practice was shaped much earlier by her teachers, Franz Boas and John Dewey. As Juliet Niehaus argues, Weltfish integrated their ideas of democracy, social activism, and the collective production of knowledge in her own form of pragmatic anthropology.[2] From the late 1930s to the end of her career, Weltfish sought social justice, but such a committed practice was arduous and perilous, especially when she became a leading anti-racist activist during post-war McCarthyism.

Gene Weltfish (née Regina Weltfisch) was born into a Jewish middle-class family in Manhattan in 1902. When Weltfish was 14, her father passed away and she began working to support her family. She pursued high school studies in the evenings and graduated in 1919. Soon after, Weltfish enrolled in Hunter Evening College and majored in journalism while working as a stenographer.[3] From 1922 until 1926, Weltfish worked as a teacher clerk in elementary schools, at the same time pursuing her college studies.[4] Weltfish transferred to Barnard College, where she initially studied philosophy and literature before turning to anthropology in 1923.

In 1925, Weltfish married a fellow student of Boas, Alexander Lesser, graduated from Barnard, and began graduate studies in anthropology at Columbia University, completing her dissertation in 1929.[5] Ann Lesser Margetson, her only child, was born in 1931, and four years later Weltfish began teaching anthropology at Columbia University, where she continued teaching until 1953. She divorced Lesser in 1940. Weltfish began her anti-racist activities in the late 1930s and the FBI started surveilling her as an alleged subversive.[6] Her subsequent publications, public lectures, and activities in women's organizations were deemed communistic by members of the US Senate, and Weltfish was called to testify before Congress in 1952 and 1953.[7] Following her testimony, Weltfish was fired by Columbia.[8] She later wrote two books and became a full professor at Fairleigh Dickinson University and taught at the New School for Social Research.[9]

In December of 1938 Weltfish joined her senior colleagues, Franz Boas and Ruth Benedict, in their efforts to combat racism in America. She and a small group of her colleagues in the American Anthropological Association supported a resolution denouncing Nazi racial theories.[10] It followed the publication of the "Scientists' Manifesto," which asserted that scientists have a moral obligation to oppose "false and unscientific doctrines which appear before them in the guise of science."[11] In 1939, Boas' newly formed organization, the American Committee for Democracy and Intellectual Freedom, surveyed educational textbooks and found that many presented misleading views of race.[12] Boas, Benedict, and Weltfish began collaborating with teachers to develop new curricula and textbooks on race and genetics. While serving as a research associate for the Bureau of Educational Research in Science, Weltfish provided guidance on the subjects of race and anthropology for several educational publications.

Weltfish became publicly visible in these efforts when she and Benedict co-authored a pamphlet, *The Races of Mankind* (1943). Working within a committee under the supervision of the American Association of Scientific Workers, the anthropologists marshalled facts to debunk Nazi notions of racial superiority.[13] They did not challenge the concept of biological races, which would accord with current views of race as a social and historical construct.[14] Instead, Benedict and Weltfish minimized the significance given to physical differences of the three so-called primary races and dismantled associations of race with intelligence, language, culture, and religion.[15] In so doing, they shook the foundations of prevailing racist arguments.

Written in an accessible style and featuring cartoons by the artist Ad Reinhardt, the *Races of Mankind* was originally intended for distribution in United Service Organizations (USO) clubs. Some congressmen linked its claim of racial equality to communist propaganda and attempted to block its circulation within the US military.[16] Various organizations contested the barring of the pamphlet, and the dispute escalated into a national media event.[17] It circulated widely and served as foundational material for anti-racist educational programs in many American schools.[18] Adaptations of the text appeared multiple media forms: a filmstrip, an animated film, a children's book, and school playscripts. The comic book, *There Are No Master Races*, was the subject of the first study by the Bureau of Applied Social Research on the efficacy of anti-prejudice publications.[19] In "Science and the Race Problem" (1946), Weltfish modifies *The Races of Mankind* for a radio broadcast. She expands the pamphlet's argument by explaining how prejudicial attitudes are acquired through stereotypes in schoolbooks, sustained by fluctuating Western standards of beauty, and practiced through employment discrimination.

Following the pamphlet controversy, Weltfish assumed the role of a public intellectual, presenting about 300 lectures in one year alone.[20] She opposed the myth of the disinterested scientist in "The Scientist Is a Citizen" (1944), underscoring scientists' relations to their communities and obligations to the public. In "Science and Prejudice" (1945), she condemned scientists who collaborated with the Nazis and challenged scientists to take this oath: "I pledge that I will use my knowledge for the good of humanity and against the destructive forces of the world and the ruthless intent of men; and that I will work together with my fellow scientists of whatever nation, creed, or color, for these, our common ends."[21]

In 1945, Weltfish co-edited two issues of the *Journal of Social Issues*, which brought together scientists and "practitioners," leaders of civil rights and community organizations, in an experimental project for analyzing prejudicial attitudes. Envisioned as equal partners in a conversation, the participants responded to fictionalized accounts of experiencing racism and anti-Semitism in everyday situations. Weltfish crossed over the boundary between scientists and practitioners when she assumed leadership roles in women's organizations. In 1945, she was elected vice president of the Women's International Democratic Federation (WIDF) at its first meeting in Paris.[22] In 1946, she was elected president of the US affiliate of the WIDF, the Congress of American Women (CAW).[23] Through these platforms, Weltfish urged women to "take office themselves to get federal aid for health, housing, child care, education, equal pay for equal work and the kind of foreign policy that recognizes as long as fascism remains in any country there is danger to peace."[24] As a leader of CAW, Weltfish called for public condemnation of recent lynchings in Georgia, opposed the deportation of Claudia Jones, and executions of women antifascists in Franco's Spain; she urged the United Nations to outlaw all forms of discrimination.[25] In March 1948, Weltfish was elected to the executive board of the Council on African Affairs, serving with W.E.B. Du Bois, Alphaeus Hunton, and Paul Robeson.[26] The essay "Racism, Colonialism, and World Peace" reflects her work with these organizations. Delivered at the 1949 Scientific and Cultural Conference for World Peace, the essay levels substantive charges of racism underlying American governmental policies and corporate activities in the Panama Canal Zone and Africa. In her contributions towards transforming American racial attitudes and practices of discrimination, Weltfish repeatedly challenged artificial boundaries between scholarship and society, and sought to bring knowledge to bear on social injustice.

Excerpt: Weltfish, Gene, "Scientific Paper Number 183: Science and the Race Problem." In *Forty-Third Annual Report of the South Dakota State Horticultural Society* (Sioux Falls, SD: South Dakota State Horticultural Society, 1946) (permission Reverend Neil A. Margetson)

The race problem has many sides to it—social, political, economic and many others. But here I shall limit myself more to the scientific aspects of the problem than to the others.

First, let me take you back to your school days when you were studying geography. Much of what you think about race today dates back to that early experience. The geography book was a big one with many interesting pictures that led the mind toward far-off places. There was a black man leaning against a palm tree and dressed in a loin cloth, doing nothing; and a yellow man pulling a rickshaw like a human horse; and on still another page, a white man dressed in a collar and tie with a lot of smoke stacks behind him. Most of us got the idea that dark skin was somehow connected with doing nothing, and wearing a sarong instead of a business suit; and that yellow skin was connected with pigtails and menial labor.

We were not yet mature enough to untangle these things and to realize that clothing and occupations are not hereditary in the same way as blue eyes or red hair.

Very few of us have had the occasion to reexamine these old childhood categories. But today with the race problem one of the most serious issues of our time, it is important for every citizen to consider the problem again. Clear thinking is part of our fight for a better world.

If you were asked to name the races of man, what would you say? Most likely: the white, the black, the yellow—you might add the brown and the red. Your first impulse, in any case, would be to classify people by the color of the skin. Then you might add, that the yellow race has straight black hair and flat faces, the black race kinky hair and broad noses, and the white race all kinds of hair from kinky to straight, and all kinds of noses. And I will grant you that you might observe such broad differences in different parts of the world's population.

But how can these external differences help you to judge a man's moral character, his ability to participate in a democratic society, his ability to think up new and fruitful ideas, and his artistic capacities—or even his ability to be your neighbor, your business partner, or your good friend? A human being is more than skin, hair, and nose.

[...]

Distaste for physical differences is a cultivated thing like a taste for olives. We all know that standards of beauty have changed down through the ages and the Venus de Milo or the rotund beauty of Reubens [sic] would not appeal to us now as would Mary Pickford, Greta Garbo, Mae West, or Lana Turner. We can, through education, broaden our margin of tolerance for the beauty and the ways of many different people and make our living-together a world-wide cooperative effort rather than a disastrous conflict.

Ignorance accounts for much of race prejudice, but besides, there is the factor of fear. Technically, in individuals, unfounded fears and suspicion of others is called paranoia. However, the fear reactions that are manifest in group prejudice have very real historical bases.

It is little realized that in the old South only 16 per cent of the white people were large plantation owners,—while the rest of the Whites were poor farmers and artisans. The prospects for work and for making a success of their farms were seriously threatened by negro slave labor, or by the negro freeman who would feel impelled to work for less returns. And yet if we look at the matter objectively, it was not the negro who was to blame, nor is a paranoid-like hatred of the negro, the solution.

Similarly with the Chinese, the Mexican, and the southeast European, all have at various times in the past been brought here as a cheap and docile labor supply, threatening the interests of the resident workers. The answer does not lie in group hatred, but in group planning—on the part of the workers in their organizations, and of management in the shops—and a general readiness to plan together and to compromise if need be.

Various types of insecurity and fear are important elements in race prejudice, but job insecurity heads the list. Only by a combination of a humane and realistic employment policy and a program of constructive education, can race prejudice—one of the sorest spots of our social life—be eliminated.

Excerpt: Weltfish, Gene, "Racism, Colonialism and World Peace." In *Speaking of Peace: An Edited Report of the Cultural and Scientific Conference for World Peace, New York, March 25, 26 and 27, 1949, under the Auspices of the National Council of the Arts, Sciences and Professions,* **ed. Daniel S. Gillmor (New York: National Council of the Arts, Sciences and Professions, 1949) (permission Reverend Neil A. Margetson)**

I

The road to peace lies along the path of the ever greater improvement in the lot of mankind. The basic idea that production is more important than people which largely underlies our present way of life is antithetical to this objective. Nowhere is this contradiction clearer than in our dealings with colonial peoples. The special and most effective social device for carrying on repressive colonialism is the doctrine of racism. Under its banner a cold war has been carried on for years by the nations of Europe against the peoples of Africa, Asia, the South Seas and Latin America.

[...]

Contrary to the common belief that racism arises from natural antagonism of different peoples for each other, a study by B. Lasker on Race Attitudes in Children shows that the child masters race stereotypes only by about the tenth year, along with geography, history and other abstract concepts.

[...]

Racism is more than a verbal doctrine; it is a non-employer and a killer. A detailed study* of anti-semitism in employment revealed that the main source of the refusal to employ comes from the executive level of large business companies, whose directives are then carried out in various ways, if necessary through subterfuges. Major offenders are banks, insurance companies, brokerage houses, utility companies; professional fields, accounting, advertising, engineering, law, chemical and allied industries, aircraft.

[...]

The United States Government is not blameless in this respect. In the Panama Canal Zone, which is under complete control of the executive branch [...] Negro workers and their families suffer segregation and discrimination under the term "silver workers"—the term "gold" applying to the whites. These Negro workers of Panamanian and West Indian derivation are largely responsible for the building and maintenance of the Panama Canal. For the same work and skills they receive:

Occupation	Silver rate per hr.	Gold rate per hr.
Blacksmith	.62	2.04
Bricklayer	.62	2.19
Cabinet Maker	.74	2.09
Carpenter	.62	2.09
Cable Splicer	.56	2.20
Painter	.56	2.19
Clubhouse Manager	1.28	2.25

*J.A. Cohen, *Who Discriminates and How*, American Jewish Congress, 1944.

[...]

As to educational differentials in the Panama Canal Zone, the government spends $51.59 per year for a Negro child's, and $160.21 for a white child's education.

[...]

These conditions call for bold and clear action! It is not enough to "let your conscience be your guide"; relentless pressure for legislation and its enforcement are mandatory.

II

Now let us turn from the United States to another area, Africa, in which we are becoming very heavily involved—and point to the high cost of racism to the "discriminated" and to the callous withholding of effective human sympathies on the part of the discriminator:

As a result of a terrible drought in Nyasaland, British East Africa, 2,500,000 people face famine and death through the destruction of root and maize crops which constitute their meager subsistence. In some districts the people were making a meal out of grass seeds and the bulbs of water lilies.

[...]

Meanwhile "New Rhodesia" (September 12, 1947) a weekly journal published in Southern Rhodesia by Europeans, publishes extracts from "a plan for an African Development Company" that had been discussed in various influential quarters in Great Britain, America and France and other countries of Western Europe:

"The whole Anglo-Saxon bloc must go into profit-making development; something which is going to develop entirely new sources of wealth, provide new markets, and smash right through the whole idea of reduction and restraint."

[...]

Meanwhile, the European powers, looking to the colonies for their own recovery, must squeeze a considerable surplus over and above what is drained off to the US out of the colonies.

[...]

With a territory that promises to save two continents, what is the dividend of the African worker? The Trusteeship Council's Visiting Mission to East Africa reports: that a recruiting system very much like slave trading is practiced in Tanganyka; wages for unskilled farm labor at a dollar a month; British laws in the territory allow extraction of forced labor from "able-bodied males between the ages of 18 and 45" for a 60 day period in any one year.

These laws permit flogging of any worker over 16 years of age who uses abusive or insulting language to his employer "calculated to provoke a breach of peace", with an additional penalty of a fine "not exceeding the amount of half a month's wages or a month's imprisonment."

[...]

For criticism of inaction regarding labor and political grievances newspaper editors are fined, jailed or deported. From Uganda in a petition to the U. N. General Assembly December 7, 1948, Mr. Mulumba, head of the Bataka (Elders of the People) organization: "Most of the African news editors (in Uganda) are flung into jail for publishing anything that protests against or criticizes the British Uganda Government." He named 5 editors sentenced to imprisonment for periods of from 3 months to 18 months.

The President of Liberia, it is reported, has asked the Legislature for power to deport Mr. C. Frederick Taylor, a naturalized Liberian citizen and owner and editor of "The African Nationalist" published in Monrovia. This newspaper in several issues has carried criticism of US plans for the establishment of a military base at the port of Monrovia and also of the terms under which the Liberia Company, organized by Edward R. Stettinius Jr., has acquired authority over virtually the whole economy of Liberia. During construction of the port, the workers struck twice for an increase in their wage of 25 cents a day. The strikers were put down when US naval officers with drawn pistols ordered the men back to work.

In all this is the underlying viewpoint that production is an end in itself and that raw materials are the means to its achievement, but the most essential part of the equation is left out: the people who work the raw materials, their wants, their rights, their needs and their power. If the racist-tainted mind in the US, and in the colonial countries, believes that the colonial peoples do not see this error, he is mistaken.

[...]

It is clear that the Americans bear an enormous responsibility to preserve world peace. We must use the gifts of science, telegraph, telephone, and postal, train, jeep and aeroplane, and turn this country into a vast town hall to tell our representatives in the Nation, the State and in the City, that as our employees, we want the job done our way—not the Pentagon, Stettinius, Westinghouse way.

We want peace and trade on a fair basis with all countries,—with sincere and genuine negotiations through the United Nations.

[...]

For a new humanism is arising, and we are throwing off the shackles of racism and colonialism. We want production for the needs of human beings, not human beings broken on the wheel of production. In this, the twentieth century, the world is going to belong to the people who inhabit it, for through peace or through war, they will claim it as their own.

Notes

1 Stanley Diamond, "Preface," in *Theory and Practice: Essays Presented to Gene Weltfish*, ed. Stanley Diamond (New York and London: Mouton Publishers, 1980), vii, x; Gene Weltfish, quoted in Ann L. Margetson, "Some Salient Events in the Professional Life of Gene Weltfish," in *Theory and Practice*, ed. Diamond, 356.

2 Juliet Niehaus, "Education and Democracy in the Anthropology of Gene Weltfish," in *Visionary Observers: Anthropological Inquiry and Education*, ed. Jill B.R. Cherneff and Eve Hochwald (Lincoln, NE: University of Nebraska Press, 2006), 105-108.

3 Douglas Parks and Ruth Pathé, "Gene Weltfish: 1902-1980," *Plains Anthropologist* 30, no. 107 (February 1985): 59; United States Census Bureau, *14th Census of Population* (Washington, D.C.: National Archives and Records Administration, 1920).

4 Margetson, "Some Salient Events in the Professional Life of Gene Weltfish," 356; "Department of Education," *The City Record*, July 31, 1922, 53; "Department of Education," *The City Record*, December 30, 1926, 60.

5 Gene Weltfish, "The Interrelation of Technique and Design in North American Basketry" (PhD diss., Columbia University, 1950); Niehaus, "Education and Democracy," 94. Weltfish could not afford to fulfill the university's publishing requirement and did not receive her degree until 1950. David H. Price, *Threatening Anthropology: McCarthyism and the FBI's Surveillance of Activist Anthropologists* (Durham, NC: Duke University Press, 2004), 110.

6 Price, *Threatening Anthropology*, 111.

7 Ibid., 122-131.

8 Ibid., 131-132. See Price, *Threatening Anthropology*, 122-125, for a discussion of the controversy surrounding Weltfish and the allegation of germ warfare in Korea.

9 Ruth E. Pathé, "Gene Weltfish," in *Women Anthropologists: Selected Biographies*, ed. Ute Gacs, Aisha Khan, Jerrie McIntyre, and Ruth Weinberg (Urbana and Chicago, IL: University of Illinois Press, 1989), 377-378.

10 Gene Weltfish quoted in Alexander Lesser, "Franz Boas," in *Totems and Teachers: Perspectives on the History of Anthropology*, ed. Sydel Silverman (New York, NY: Columbia University Press, 1981), 30; Leonard Lieberman, "Gender and the Deconstruction of the Race Concept," *American Anthropologist* 99, no. 3 (September 1997): 553; Boas' efforts are discussed in Elazar Barkan, *The Retreat of Scientific Racism* (Cambridge, MA: Cambridge University Press, 1992), 332-340.

11 "Scientific Events: Intellectual Freedom," *Science* 88, no. 2294 (December 16, 1938): 562.

12 American Committee for Democracy and Intellectual Freedom, *Can You Name Them?* (New York, NY: ACDIF, 1939), 5; Zoe Burkholder, *Color in the Classroom: How American Schools Taught Race, 1900-1954* (Oxford: Oxford University Press, 2011), 57-64; Peter J. Kuznick, *Beyond the Laboratory: Scientists as Activists in 1930s America* (Chicago, IL: University of Chicago Press, 1987), 196-199.

13 Violet Edwards, "Note on *The Races of Mankind*," in Ruth Benedict, *Race: Science and Politics* (Athens, GA: The University of Georgia Press, 1940), 167-168.

14 Marianne Kinkel, *Races of Mankind: The Sculptures of Malvina Hoffman* (Champaign, IL: University of Illinois Press, 2011), 168–176. For more about the pamphlet, see Tracy Teslow, *Constructing Race: The Science of Bodies and Cultures in American Anthropology* (Cambridge: Cambridge University Press, 2014); Burkholder, *Color in the Classroom*; and Mark Anderson, "Ruth Benedict, Boasian Anthropology, and the Problem of the Color Line," *History and Anthropology* 25, no. 3 (2014): 395–414.

15 Ruth Benedict and Gene Weltfish, *The Races of Mankind* (New York, NY: Public Affairs Committee, 1943), 10.

16 Marianne Kinkel, "Critical Humor in Ad Reinhardt's Races of Mankind Cartoons," *The Brooklyn Rail: Critical Perspectives on Arts, Politics, and Culture*, 2013, https://brooklynrail.org/special/AD_REINHARDT/ads-thoughts-and-practices/critical-humor-in-ad-reinhardts-races-of-mankind-cartoons, accessed April 11, 2022.

17 Teslow, *Constructing Race*, 253–262; Anthony Q. Hazard, Jr., *Boasians at War: Anthropology, Race, and World War II* (Cham, Switzerland: Palgrave Macmillan, 2020), 202–211.

18 Burkholder, *Color in the Classroom*, 122.

19 Goodwin Watson, *A Critical Analysis of the Pictures in 'There Are No Master Races': A Study* (New York, NY: Bureau of Applied Social Research, 1945); Elena D. Hristova, "Imagining Brotherhood: The Comics of the American Jewish Committee, 1941–1948" (MPhil thesis, University of Sussex, 2013).

20 Pathé, "Gene Weltfish," 376.

21 Gene Weltfish, "Science and Prejudice," *The Scientific Monthly* 61, no. 3 (September 1945): 211.

22 Fédération Democratique Internationale des Femmes, *Congrès International des Femmes* (Paris: Fédération Democratique Internationale des Femmes, 1946), 411.

23 Long overlooked in scholarship, these organizations are receiving attention in feminist research; see especially Jacqueline Castledine, *Cold War Progressives: Women's Interracial Organizing for Peace and Freedom* (Champaign, IL: University of Illinois Press, 2012); Francisca de Haan, "Continuing Cold War Paradigms in Western Historiography of Transnational Women's Organisations: The Case of the Women's International Democratic Federation (WIDF)," *Women's History Review* 19, no. 4 (2010): 547–573; Amy Swerdlow, "The Congress of American Women: Left-Feminist Peace Politics in the Cold War," in *U.S. History as Women's History: New Feminist Essays*, ed. Linda K. Kerber, Alice Kessler-Harris, and Kathryn Kish Sklar, 296–312 (Chapel Hill, NC: University of North Carolina Press, 1995).

24 Susan Alexander, "Postwar Living: Congress of American Women," *Federated Press*, May 14, 1946, n.p.

25 "International Women's Group Asks UN to Take Steps to Outlaw Discrimination," *The Afro-American*, August 3, 1946, 20; Olive Sutton, "Women's Meeting Hits Deportations," *Daily Worker*, March 10, 1948, 5.

26 Abner W. Berry, "Council on African Affairs Criticizes Max Yergan," *Daily Worker*, March 29, 1948, 7.

Bibliography

Alexander, Susan. "Postwar Living: Congress of American Women." *Federated Press*, May 14, 1946, n.p.

American Anthropological Association. "AAA Statement on Race." 1998. www.americananthro.org/ConnectWithAAA/Content.aspx?ItemNumber=2583, accessed April 11, 2022.

American Association of Biological Anthropologists. "The AAPA Statement on Race and Racism." 2019. https://physanth.org/about/position-statements/aapa-statement-race-and-racism-2019/, accessed April 11, 2022.

American Association of University Professors, et al. "Joint Statement on Legislative Efforts to Restrict Education about Racism in American History (June 2021)." www.historians.org/divisive-concepts-statement, accessed April 11, 2022.

American Committee for Democracy and Intellectual Freedom. *Can You Name Them?* New York, NY: ACDIF, 1939.

Anderson, Mark. "Ruth Benedict, Boasian Anthropology, and the Problem of the Color Line." *History and Anthropology* 25, no. 3 (2014): 395–414.

Barkan, Elazar. *The Retreat of Scientific Racism.* Cambridge, MA: Cambridge University Press, 1992.

Benedict, Ruth. *Race: Science and Politics.* New York, NY: Modern Age Books, 1940.

_____. *Race: Science and Politics.* Rev. ed. New York, NY: Viking Press, 1947.

Benedict, Ruth, and Gene Weltfish. "The Future of Race Prejudice." *ALA Bulletin* 38, no. 5 (May 1944): 186.

_____. *In Henry's Backyard.* New York, NY: Henry Schuman, Inc., 1948.

_____. *The Races of Mankind.* New York, NY: Public Affairs Committee, 1943.

Berry, Abner W. "Council on African Affairs Criticizes Max Yergan." *Daily Worker*, March 29, 1948, 7.

Boring, Edwin, et al. 1945. "On the Weltfishian Oath." *The Scientific Monthly* 61, no. 6 (December): 497–502.

Burkholder, Zoe. *Color in the Classroom: How American Schools Taught Race, 1900–1954.* Oxford: Oxford University Press, 2011.

Castledine, Jacqueline. *Cold War Progressives: Women's Interracial Organizing for Peace and Freedom.* Champaign, IL: University of Illinois Press, 2012.

Conrad, Earl. "American Viewpoint: A Big 'A' in Anthropology." *Chicago Defender*, April 28, 1945, 11.

de Haan, Francisca. "Continuing Cold War Paradigms in Western Historiography of Transnational Women's Organisations: The Case of the Women's International Democratic Federation (WIDF)." *Women's History Review* 19, no. 4 (2010): 547–573.

"Department of Education." *The City Record*, December 30, 1926.

"Department of Education." *The City Record,* July 31, 1922.

Dewey, John and John Childs. "The Underlying Philosophy of Education." In *The Educational Frontier*, ed. William H. Kilpatrick, 287–319. New York, NY: D. Appleton Century Company, 1933.

Diamond, Stanley. "Preface." In *Theory and Practice: Essays Presented to Gene Weltfish*, ed. Stanley Diamond. New York and London: Mouton Publishers, 1980.

Du Bois, W.E.B. *In Battle for Peace: The Story of My 83rd Birthday*. New York, NY: Masses and Mainstream, 1952.

Edwards, Violet. "Note on *The Races of Mankind*." In *Race: Science and Politics*, ed. Ruth Benedict. Athens, GA: The University of Georgia Press, 1940.

Edwards, Violet and Gene Weltfish. *We Are All Brothers*. New York: Public Affairs Committee. Script for a filmstrip based on the *Races of Mankind* pamphlet. 2nd ed. 1946.

Fédération Democratique Internationale des Femmes. *Congrès International des Femmes*. Paris: Fédération Democratique Internationale des Femmes, 1946.

Flannery, Regina. "Report: Proceedings of the American Anthropological Association for the Year Ending December, 1938." *American Anthropologist* 41, no. 2 (April-June, 1939): 295–308.

Harvey, Joy Dorothy. "Weltfish, Gene." In *The Biographical Dictionary of Women in Science*, volume 2, L–Z, ed. Marilyn Bailey Ogilvie and Joy Dorothy Harvey, 1364–1366. New York, NY: Routledge, 2000.

Hazard, Anthony Q., Jr. *Boasians at War: Anthropology, Race, and World War II*. Cham, Switzerland: Palgrave Macmillan, 2020.

Hristova, Elena D. "Imagining Brotherhood: The Comics of the American Jewish Committee, 1941–1948." MPhil thesis, University of Sussex, 2013.

Huxley, Aldous. *Science, Liberty and Peace*. London: Chatto & Windus, 1947.

"International Women's Group Asks UN to Take Steps to Outlaw Discrimination." *The Afro-American*, August 3, 1946.

Jones, Claudia. "Controversy or Prejudice." *Spotlight* 2, no. 3 (March 1944): 26–27.

Kinkel, Marianne. "Critical Humor in Ad Reinhardt's Races of Mankind Cartoons." *The Brooklyn Rail: Critical Perspectives on Arts, Politics, and Culture*, 2013. https://brooklynrail. org/special/AD_REINHARDT/ads-thoughts-and-practices/critical-humor-in-ad-reinhardts-races-of-mankind-cartoons, accessed April 11, 2022.

_____. *Races of Mankind: The Sculptures of Malvina Hoffman*. Champaign, IL: University of Illinois Press, 2011.

Kuznick, Peter J. *Beyond the Laboratory: Scientists as Activists in 1930s America*. Chicago, IL: University of Chicago Press, 1987.

LaFollette, Marcel C. "A Survey of Science Content in U.S. Radio Broadcasting, 1920 through 1940s." *Science Communication* 24, no. 1 (September 2002): 4–33.

Laton, Anita D. and Edna W. Bailey. *Suggestions for Teaching Selected Material from the Field of Genetics*. New York, NY: Teachers College, Columbia University, 1939.

Lesser, Alexander. "Franz Boas." In *Totems and Teachers: Perspectives on the History of Anthropology*, ed. Sydel Silverman, 1–33. New York, NY: Columbia University Press, 1981.

Lieberman, Leonard. "Gender and the Deconstruction of the Race Concept." *American Anthropologist* 99, no. 3 (September 1997): 545–558.

Lynch, Hollis. *Black American Radicals and the Liberation of Africa: The Council on African Affairs, 1937-1955.* Ithaca, NY: Africana Studies and Research Center, Cornell University, 1978.

Margetson, Ann L. "Some Salient Events in the Professional Life of Gene Weltfish." In *Theory and Practice: Essays Presented to Gene Weltfish*, ed. Stanley Diamond. New York and London: Mouton Publishers, 1980.

"Nazi's Conception of Science Scored." *New York Times*, December 11, 1938, 50.

Niehaus, Juliet. "Education and Democracy in the Anthropology of Gene Weltfish." In *Visionary Observers: Anthropological Inquiry and Education*, ed. Jill B.R. Cherneff and Eve Hochwald, 87–117. Lincoln, NE: University of Nebraska Press, 2006.

Nirenberg, Alice B. "Meet Your Relatives." *American Unity* 2, no. 4 (January 1944): 17–23. Text by Gene Weltfish and dramatization by Alice B. Nirenberg.

Parks, Douglas and Ruth Pathé. "Gene Weltfish: 1902-1980." *Plains Anthropologist* 30, no. 107 (February 1985): 59–64.

Pathé, Ruth E. "Gene Weltfish." In *Women Anthropologists: Selected Biographies*, ed. Ute Gacs, Aisha Khan, Jerrie McIntyre, and Ruth Weinberg. Urbana and Chicago, IL: University of Illinois Press, 1989.

Price, David H. *Threatening Anthropology: McCarthyism and the FBI's Surveillance of Activist Anthropologists.* Durham, NC: Duke University Press, 2004.

Rosenberg, Rosalind. *Changing the Subject: How the Women of Columbia Shaped the Way We Think about Sex and Politics.* New York, NY: Columbia University Press, 2004.

Schachter, Judith. "Foreword to the 2019 Georgia Edition." In *Race: Science and Politics* by Ruth Benedict, including *The Races of Mankind* by Ruth Benedict and Gene Weltfish, foreword by Margaret Mead. Athens, GA: The University of Georgia Press, 2019.

"Scientific Events: Intellectual Freedom." *Science* 88, no. 2294 (December 16, 1938): 562.

Sutton, Olive. "Women's Meeting Hits Deportations." *Daily Worker*, March 10, 1948, 5.

Swerdlow, Amy. "The Congress of American Women: Left-Feminist Peace Politics in the Cold War." In *U.S. History as Women's History: New Feminist Essays*, ed. Linda K. Kerber, Alice Kessler-Harris, and Kathryn Kish Sklar, 296–312. Chapel Hill, NC: University of North Carolina Press, 1995.

Teslow, Tracy. *Constructing Race: The Science of Bodies and Cultures in American Anthropology.* Cambridge: Cambridge University Press, 2014.

Torres Colón, Gabriel Alejandro, and Charles A. Hobbs. "The Intertwining of Culture and Nature: Franz Boas, John Dewey, and Deweyan Strands of American Anthropology." *Journal of the History of Ideas* 76, no. 1 (January 2015): 139–62.

United States Census Bureau. *14th Census of Population*. Washington, D.C.: National Archives and Records Administration, 1920.

Watson, Goodwin. *A Critical Analysis of the Pictures in "There Are No Master Races": A Study*. New York, NY: Bureau of Applied Social Research, 1945.

_____. *The Effect of "There Are No Master Races" upon Knowledge and Attitudes of Readers: A Study*. New York, NY: Bureau of Applied Social Research, 1945.

Weltfish, Gene. "American Racism: Japan's Secret Weapon." *Far Eastern Survey* 14, no. 17 (August 29, 1945): 233–237.

_____. "The Blindness of Prejudice and Its Meaning for the Guidance Worker." In *Proceedings of the Eleventh Annual Guidance Conference Held at Purdue University, November 16–17, 1945*, ed. H.H. Remmers, 36–40. Lafayette, IN: Purdue University, 1945.

_____. "Comments on Miss Abe's Remarks about Mary's Problem of Possible Mixed Marriage," *Journal of Social Issues* 1, no. 2 (May 1945): 33–34.

_____. "The Ethnic Dimension of Human History: Pattern or Patterns of Culture." In *Men and Cultures: Selected Papers of the Fifth International Congress of Anthropological and Ethnological Sciences, Philadelphia, September 1–9, 1956*, ed. Anthony Wallace, 207-218. Philadelphia, PA: University of Pennsylvania Press, 1956.

_____. "Franz Boas: The Academic Response." In *Anthropology: Ancestors and Heirs*, ed. Stanley Diamond, 123–148. The Hague: Mouton Publishers, 1980.

_____. "An Historical Note." *Journal of Social Issues* 1, no. 2 (May 1945): 19–21.

_____. "The Interrelation of Technique and Design in North American Basketry." PhD diss., Columbia University, 1950.

_____. "Introduction." In *Haiti Faces Tomorrow's Peace*, ed. Max L. Hudicourt, trans. Anita Dylan Weinstein, 3–5. New York: L'Association Democratique Haitienne, 1945. https://digital.library.pitt.edu/islandora/object/pitt:31735061539973, accessed April 11, 2022.

_____. "Introduction." *Journal of Social Issues* 1, no. 1 (February 1945): 2–4.

_____. "The Last Word." *The Scientific Monthly* 61, no. 6 (December 1945): 500–502.

_____. *The Lost Universe: Pawnee Life and Culture*. New York: Basic Books, 1965.

_____. "May 4th Is the Day." *Daily Worker*, April 7, 1946.

_____. "Meet Your Relatives." *PM*, November 21, 1943.

_____. *The Origins of Art*. Indianapolis, IN: Bobbs-Merrill, 1953. https://catalog.hathitrust.org/Record/000292113, accessed April 11, 2022.

_____. "The Question of Ethnic Identity, an Ethnohistorical Approach." *Ethnohistory* 6, no. 4 (Autumn 1959): 321–346.

_____. "Racism, Colonialism and World Peace." In *Speaking of Peace: An Edited Report of the Cultural and Scientific Conference for World Peace, New York, March 25, 26 and 27, 1949, under the Auspices of the National Council of the Arts, Sciences and Professions*, ed. Daniel S. Gillmor, 72–76. New York, NY: National Council of the Arts, Sciences and Professions, 1949. https://credo.library.umass.edu/view/full/mums312-b283-i002, accessed April 11, 2022.

_____. "Science and Prejudice." *The Scientific Monthly* 61, no. 3 (September 1945): 210–212.

_____. "Scientific Paper Number 183: Science and the Race Problem." In *Forty-Third Annual Report of the South Dakota State Horticultural Society*, 109–111. Sioux Falls, SD: South Dakota State Horticultural Society, 1946.

_____. "The Scientist Is a Citizen." *The Christian Register* (September 1944): 325–327.

_____. "Some Problems on Which We Need More Facts—and Some Implications for Action." *Journal of Social Issues* 1, no. 1 (February 1945): 47–54.

_____. "Some Roots of Racial and Religious Prejudice in the Individual Personality." *Journal of Social Issues* 1, no. 2 (May 1945): 3–9.

_____. "What the Teacher Should Know and Teach about Races." *Pi Lambda Theta Journal* 22, no. 3 (March 1944): 106–107.

Weltfish, Gene and Dina M. Bleich. "We Are All Brothers." *See and Hear: The Journal on Audio-Visual Learning* 1, no. 6 (February 1946): 30–37. https://archive.org/details/see194546hearjournaloneaucrich/page/n517/mode/1up, accessed April 11, 2022.

Weltfish, Gene and Ronald Lippitt. "Further Remarks on the Re-education of Racial and Religious Prejudice." *Journal of Social Issues* 1, no. 2 (May 1945): 49–53.

Westerman, George W. *A Study of Socio-economic Conflicts on the Panama Canal Zone.* Panamá: Liga Civica Nacional, 1948. Text in Spanish is available at https://es.slideshare.net/The_Afrolatino_Project/foster-pag20-1-estudios-de-los-conflictos-en-la-zona-del-canal-1948, accessed April 9, 2023.

Contributor Biographies

Hadil Abuhmaid

Hadil Abuhmaid is a doctoral candidate in Media Studies with a certificate in New Media and Culture at the University of Oregon. She earned a BS in Journalism and Political Science from Bir-Zeit University in Palestine and an MA in Non-Profit Management from the University of Oregon, with a focus on Arts Administration. She is the co-founder of Filmlab: Palestine, a nonprofit company based in Ramallah that aims at developing the cinema industry in Palestine. Through her research, Hadil aims at examining the effects of soft and hard borders constructed by the Israeli occupation on the formation and self-representation of national identity in Palestinian feature films produced within the historical map of Palestine.

Aimee-Marie Dorsten

Aimee-Marie Dorsten is an associate professor who teaches Media Ethics, Communication Law and Policy, and Media Studies at Point Park University in Pittsburgh, Pennsylvania. Her current research in the feminist political economy of communication critiques the received historiography of the field of communication. Her future political economy of communication research examines representation of the US foster care system and implications for policy. Her work has appeared in *Communication Theory* and *The International Encyclopedia of Communication Theory and Philosophy*.

Miche Dreiling

Miche Dreiling is a doctoral candidate in Media Studies with a certificate in Women, Gender, and Sexuality Studies at the University of Oregon. They have taught at both public and private colleges and universities, as well as served as Design & Web Editor for the journal *Women & Language*. Their research focuses on social constructions of identity, collaborative research methodologies, and critical analysis of representations of gender and sexuality in media. Miche's current work focuses on nonbinary gender as a medium of communication using documentary filmmaking and collaborative ethnographic methods.

Elena D. Hristova

Elena Hristova is a lecturer in Film and Media at Bangor University, Wales, UK. She is a historian of US media and culture and researches the intersection of social movements, media research, visual culture, gender, race, and class. Elena has published in the *International Journal of Communication* and has edited several issues of *Teaching Media Quarterly*. Elena lives in London, England with her husband, and their daughter Daria Rosa who was born during the creation of *The Ghost Reader*.

Diana Kamin

Diana Kamin is lecturer in Communication and Media Studies at Fordham University. Her research interests include the intersections of art, culture, and media history. She has published in *Journal of Visual Culture, Media-N*, and *Art in America*. Her current book project explores the history of circulating image collections in American museums, libraries, and stock photography agencies, and how they anticipate today's image flows. She received her PhD in Media, Culture and Communication from New York University.

Marianne Kinkel

Marianne Kinkel is an associate professor of Art History at Washington State University. She is currently exploring how anti-prejudice cartoons, comic books, and animated films participated in WWII and post-war educational campaigns against racism and anti-Semitism. This research stems from her prior publication, *Races of Mankind: The Sculptures of Malvina Hoffman* (University of Illinois Press, 2011).

Tiffany Kinney

Tiffany Kinney, PhD is an assistant professor of English at Colorado Mesa University, where she teaches courses on rhetorical theory, composition pedagogy, and technical writing. Her research is typically located at the intersection of feminism, historiography, and writing studies.

Elana Levine

Elana Levine is professor of Media, Cinema, and Digital Studies in the Department of English at the University of Wisconsin-Milwaukee. She is the author of *Her Stories: Daytime Soap Opera and US Television History* (Duke, 2020), co-author of *Legitimating Television: Media Convergence and Cultural Status* (Routledge, 2012), author of *Wallowing in Sex: The New Sexual*

Culture of 1970s American Television (Duke, 2007), and editor of *Cupcakes, Pinterest, and Ladyporn: Feminized Popular Culture in the Early 21st Century* (Illinois, 2015).

Malia Mulligan

Malia Mulligan earned a BA in spatial data science and global studies from the University of Oregon. She is passionate about a variety of topics, including GIS, cartography, remote sensing, and environmental issues.

Morning Glory Ritchie

Morning Glory Ritchie graduated from the Clark Honors College at the University of Oregon, with double majors in art history and art and double minors in classical civilization and Italian. Ritchie is primarily interested in misattributions of the women painters in seventeenth-century Europe. In 2020, Ritchie won University of Oregon's Gloria Tovar Lee Scholarship for the Most Promising Student in Art History.

Gretchen Soderlund

Gretchen Soderlund is associate professor of Media History in the University of Oregon's School of Journalism and Communication. She is an expert on the history of media coverage of sex trafficking. Her research examines the relationships among anti-vice movements and the press in the late nineteenth and early twentieth centuries, the transformation of media sensationalism and the rise of journalistic objectivity, and the intertwined histories of scandal and investigative reporting. She is the author of *Sex Trafficking, Scandal, and the Transformation of Journalism, 1885-1917* (2013). Her articles have appeared in such journals as *American Quarterly, Feminist Formations, The Communication Review, Humanity,* and *Critical Studies in Media Communication.*

Carol A. Stabile

Carol Stabile researches and teaches about the history of gender, race, and class in media institutions at the University of Oregon. She is the award-winning author of five books, including *Feminism and the Technological Fix, White Victims, Black Villains: Gender, Race, and Crime News in US Culture,* and *The Broadcast 41: Women and the Anti-Communist Blacklist.* She is the co-editor of *Fredi Washington: A Reader in Black Feminist Media Criticism.* A co-founder of the Fembot Collective, she is currently co-directing Reanimate, a feminist publishing collective, with Roopika Risam.

Shelley Stamp

Shelley Stamp is the award-winning author of *Lois Weber in Early Hollywood* and *Movie-Struck Girls: Women and Motion Picture Culture after the Nickelodeon*, and curator of the award-winning disc set *Pioneers: First Women Filmmakers*. She is professor of Film & Digital Media at the University of California, Santa Cruz, where she currently holds the Presidential Chair.

Laura Strait

Laura Strait earned her PhD in Media Studies from the University of Oregon in 2020. Her interests include feminist media studies and new media, and she currently works in research for a tech company in Boston.

Rafiza Varão

Rafiza Varão is assistant professor in the Department of Journalism at the Faculty of Communication at the University of Brasília, where she teaches Ethics. She holds a PhD in Communication from the University of Brasília (2012), in the area of Theories and Technologies of Communication. She also has a degree in Journalism (1999) from the Federal University of Maranhão (UFMA). She coordinates the SOS Imprensa Project (the first Press Observatory at University of Brasília) and is Editorial Coordinator of FAC Livros. She is a columnist for the Portal Imprensa and vice-coordinator of the National Network of Press Observatories (RENOI).

Acknowledgments

How can collaborators thank each other? Across continents, time zones, a global pandemic, and uncooperative copyright holders, our shared commitment to seeing the work of these women in print kept this project alive. Our contributors were brilliant. Responsive and open to feedback, passionate about the entries they were authoring, their work writing the biographical entries, transcribing excerpts, tracking down copyrights (and in many cases, paying for them out of pocket or out of their own research funds) made this book a joyous reality. The women whose work is included in this volume inspired us at every stage of this project.

As Diana Kamin's entry on librarian Romana Javitz reminds us, without the curatorial and preservation efforts of librarians, the work of recovering, remembering, reviewing, and restoring would be difficult indeed. We are grateful for the commitment and determination of generations of those who have done that work. Stabile thanks Lisa C. Moore, Phillip Cunningham, Amanda Lima, and Amber Kinui of the Amistad Research Center at Tulane University for their help accessing the Fredi Washington Papers, Scott S. Taylor for his support researching Lisa Sergio's papers in the Booth Family Collection at Georgetown University, and Sarah Hutcheon at the Schlesinger for some last-minute help with citations. Hristova is grateful to Charlotte Bonelli, Director of the Archives of the American Jewish Committee, whose unparalleled knowledge of the collection guided Hristova in tracing the life and uses of the anti-prejudice Mr. Biggott cartoons. Dorsten would like to acknowledge the Lissance family for their efforts to collect and share the personal papers of Marjorie Fiske; the Smith family for their enthusiasm in sharing their stories about—and the unpublished works of—their mother, Jeanette Sayre Smith; the Schneewind family for their dedication to keeping the legacy of Helen MacGill Hughes alive and well; and Wyatt D. Phillips at Texas Tech University along with the Churchill family for helping piece together the fascinating career of Mae D. Huettig.

Archivist and librarians who recognized the value of preserving materials by and about women made our work possible in the first place. If it was not for feminist scholar and director of Goldsmiths Press Sarah Kember, you would not be viewing *The Ghost Reader* in a book or on whatever device you are accessing it today. Kember's support for feminist research and scholarship and her efforts to publish the results of these will influence the field for many years to come, ensuring that future generations of readers will have access to materials that might otherwise have remained spectral. We are also grateful to Susan Kelly, Ellen Parnevalas, and Angela Thompson of Goldsmiths for their commitment to this project.

The Ghost Reader had its origins in a course Stabile taught at the University of Oregon in 2019. Hadil Abuhmaid, who contributed an entry on Claudia Jones to this volume, came up with the idea of a ghost reader, and then generously allowed us to use it as the title for this book. Thanks also to all the participants in the seminar: Grace Baker, Anna Caldron, Campbell Condon, Lacey Curran, Miche Dreiling, Mandy Gettler, Madison Heath, Sophia Lindsay, Oshrit Livne, Stephanie Mastrostefano, Caitlin Moffett, Blaine Pennock, Chris St. Louis, Kristinah Session, Elliot Slate, Kacie Van Stiphout, and Olivia Wright.

Hristova received support from a Rockefeller Archive Centre Research Stipend. She would like to extend her deepest gratitude to Carol A. Stabile and Aimee-Marie Dorsten for their tireless work, expertise, and belief in the project, as well as for their personal mentorship and support. A warm thank you to all the contributors who responded to the CFP and developed their contributions into what appears in the collection. Her mother, Liudmila Khristova provided childcare and cooked meals, her father Dimitre Hristov provided an endless supply of Bulgarian treats, and her husband Joe Benge—as always—was there from the beginning with his unfailing support. Hristova carried, gave birth to, and cared for her daughter Daria Rosa while working on *The Ghost Reader*.

Dorsten received support from Point Park University, Campus Academic Resources Committee. Thank you to Carol A. Stabile, Elena Hristova, and all of the contributors who put so much thought, care, and effort into spotlighting the careers of the women featured in *The Ghost Reader*—a true victory! A debt of gratitude is owed to Carol A. Stabile and Angharad N. Valdivia for supporting her early work in revisionist feminist historiography (and Mae D. Huettig for inspiring it). A special thanks to Kathryn Jones and Anunnaqi Withrow-Davis for their transcription and administrative assistance. Her husband, Donald Parks, also deserves many thanks for shouldering more than his share of childcare and home duties to help carve out time to work on this project while her son Gavin was home from school during the pandemic. And special recognition to Gavin, who imbued this project with meaning beyond the printed page.

Stabile received support for this project from the Mt. Holyoke College 1905 Fellowship, the University of Oregon College of Arts and Sciences, and the Robert D. Clark Honors College. Stabile would additionally like to thank

Roopika Risam, Sarah Kember, and Jonathan Sterne, all of whom saw merit in this volume and encouraged it. Laura Strait and Bethan Tyler provided research support during the early stages of this project. The amazing team of Malia Mulligan and Morning Glory Ritchie saw it over the finish line, with Lauren Tokos joining us for the finale. Mrak and Tony were staunch supporters during some of the bleakest days of 2020 and 2021. They make every day a wonder.

We are grateful to the family members and publishers who gave us permission to excerpt the work of these eighteen women, especially those who waived fees, recognizing that university presses and professors do not have resources to pay fees to reprint material.

Thank you finally to Jonathan Sterne and to the anonymous reviewers at Goldsmiths Press for their excellent feedback and encouragement, as well as copyeditor Linda Fisher and the entire production team at Goldsmiths for helping us navigate this complicated project. With their help and yours, readers, we hope that *The Ghost Reader* will take on a life that extends beyond the boundaries of the paper and the binding that holds it together. It is our fervent wish that this project inspires work beyond this modest contribution.

Index

Middletown studies (with Robert
    Staughton Lynd) 161, 162–163
"Realism and the Intellectual in Time of
    Crisis" 163, 167–169
Shame and the Search for Identity 163
Lynd, Robert Staughton 2, 161, 162, 163, 186
    Middletown studies (with Helen Merrell
        Lynd) 161, 162–163
Lynd, Staughton 164
Lysistrata 208

MacGill Hughes, Helen 2, 5
Machiavelli, Niccolò 168
Maiuri, Amedeo 198
"Male-Female-Negro-White American
    Youth Orchestra" 208
Malinowski, Bronislaw 174
Mallard, Amy 113
Mamba's Daughters 207–208
Manifold 10
Marconi, Guglielmo 198
Margetson, Ann Lesser 221
Martin, Kingsley 169
Marxism-Leninism 7
    Fiske 40
    Huettig 76
    Jahoda 88, 90
    Jones, Claudia 110, 111, 112, 116–117
    Karplus 17
    Leacock 147, 149
    Lynd 162
    see also communism
Massachusetts Library Association 103
Maxwell, Clerk 104
McBride, Mary Margaret 199, 200
McCann Erikson 40, 67
McCarthyism 6
    Edwards Lavine 28
    Huettig 75
    Jahoda 89
    Leacock 148
    Lynd 163, 168–169
    "Red Scare" 148, 163

Stewart 28
    Weltfish 148, 221
McDaniel, Hattie 215–217
Mead, Margaret 148, 149
"Mercury Theatre of the Air" 203
methods
    audience research
        Fiske 39–47
        Herzog 65–72
        Kendall 134–141
        Powdermaker 176–178
        Sayre 185–187, 190–193
    content analysis 122, 123, 124
    economics 75–77
    ethnography
        Jahoda 89–90
        Leacock 148
        Lynd 162–163
        Powdermaker 173–180
    focus group 65, 66
    focused interview 40, 41, 136
    interviews 135, 136, 138–141
    participant observation 173–175
    political economy of communication
        76, 186
    social psychology
        Fiske 39, 41
        Jahoda 88
        Lynd 162
        Sayre 186
    uses and gratifications studies 65, 66
    visual theory 99–100, 104–105, 135
Merton, Robert K. 2, 66, 89, 136
    The Focused Interview (with Marjorie
        Fiske and Patricia L. Kendall) 40
    Mass Persuasion (with Marjorie Fiske and
        Alberta Curtis) 39–40
Metraux, Rhoda 147
Metro-Goldwyn-Mayer 178
Miller, Clyde 25, 35n15
Miller, William 47
Mills, Mike 122
Mindszenty, József 113